ANIMAL

SUFFOLK COUNTY
H. OF C.
BOSTON-MASS.
36 620
1 14 66

CASEY SHERMAN

ANIMAL

The Bloody
Rise and Fall
of the Mob's
Most Feared
Assassin

NORTHEASTERN UNIVERSITY PRESS
BOSTON

Northeastern University Press

An imprint of University Press of New England

www.upne.com

© 2013 Northeastern University

All rights reserved

Manufactured in the United States of America

Designed by Eric M. Brooks

Typeset in Calluna by Passumpsic Publishing

University Press of New England is a member of the
Green Press Initiative. The paper used in this book meets
their minimum requirement for recycled paper.

For permission to reproduce any of the material in this
book, contact Permissions, University Press of New England,
One Court Street, Suite 250, Lebanon NH 03766; or visit
www.upne.com

Library of Congress Cataloging-in-Publication Data
Sherman, Casey, 1969–
Animal: the bloody rise and fall of the mob's most
feared assassin / Casey Sherman.
     pages cm
Includes bibliographical references.
ISBN 978-1-55553-822-4 (hbk.: alk. paper)—
ISBN 978-1-55553-821-7 (ebk.)
I. Barboza, Joseph, 1932–1976. 2. Assassins—United States—
Biography. 3. Organized crime—United States—History.
I. Title.
HV6248.B293S54   2013
364.152'4092—dc23
[B]   2012049987

5 4 3 2

For
Bella & Mia,
as always

CONTENTS

CASUALTIES OF THE BOSTON MOB WAR 1961–1967

BERNIE MCLAUGHLIN Charlestown, MA (October 31, 1961)

GEORGE JOINT Medford, MA (July 7, 1962)

WILLIAM SHERIDAN Roxbury, MA (March 15, 1964)

FRANCIS BENJAMIN South Boston, MA (May 4, 1964)

RUSSELL C. NICHOLSON Wilmington, MA (May 12, 1964)

PAUL COLLICI Quincy, MA (July 23, 1964)

VINCENT A. BISESI Quincy, MA (July 23, 1964)

WILFRED DELANEY Boston Harbor (August 20, 1964)

HAROLD R. HANSON Boston Harbor (August 20, 1964)

LEO J. LOWRY Pembroke, MA (September 3, 1964)

RONALD DERMODY Watertown, MA (September 4, 1964)

ROBERT CHARLBOIS Roxbury, MA (October 10, 1964)

ANTHONY SACRAMONE Everett, MA (October 17, 1964)

MRS. MARGARET SYLVESTER Boston, MA (November 10, 1964)

WILLIAM J. TREAMNIE Boston, MA (November 13, 1964)

EDWARD P. HUBER Hingham, MA (November 24, 1964)

GEORGE O'BRIEN South Boston, MA (December 16, 1964)

GEORGE E. ASH South Boston, MA (December 28, 1964)

JOHN F. MURRAY Dorchester, MA (January 10, 1965)

ROBERT J. RASMUSSEN Wilmington, MA (January 15, 1965)

HENRY F. REDDINGTON Weymouth, MA (January 23, 1965)

JOSEPH FRANCIONE Revere, MA (January 26, 1965)

JOHN BARBIERI Rehoboth, MA (March 2, 1965)

EDWARD "TEDDY" DEEGAN Chelsea, MA (March 12, 1965)*

PETER A. CASSETTA Maynard, MA (April 12, 1965)

WILLIAM FERGNANI Tyngsboro, MA (May 20, 1965)

JOSEPH ROMEO MARTIN Revere, MA (July 9, 1965)

EDWARD I. CROWELL Burlington, MA (July 10, 1965)

WADY DAVID Boston, MA (August 21, 1965)

EDWARD J. MCLAUGHLIN West Roxbury, MA (October 20, 1965)

JAMES J. "BUDDY" MCLEAN Somerville, MA (October 29, 1965)

* FBI Memo BS 92–563, filed by SA Dennis Condon in 1967.

RAYMOND DISTASIO Revere, MA (November 15, 1965)

JOHN O'NEIL Revere, MA (November 15, 1965)

ROBERT PALLADINO Boston, MA (November 15, 1965)

DAVID SID LAUSHES Quincy, MA (April 25, 1966)

ANTHONY VERANIS Milton, MA (April 26, 1966)

CORNELIUS HUGHES Revere, MA (May 25, 1966)

ROCCO DISEGLIO Topsfield, MA (June 16, 1966)

STEPHEN HUGHES Middleton, MA (September 23, 1966)

SAMUEL LINDENBAUM Middleton, MA (September 23, 1966)

JOHN W. JACKSON Boston, MA (September 28, 1966)

ARTHUR C. BRATSOS Boston, MA (November 15, 1966)

THOMAS DEPRISCO Boston, MA (November 15, 1966)

JOSEPH "CHICO" AMICO Revere, MA (December 17, 1966)

WILLIAM L. O'BRIEN Stoughton, MA (January 15, 1967)

ANDREW VON ETTER Medford, MA (February 2, 1967)

JOHN LOCKE Revere, MA (March 19, 1967)

JOSEPH LANSI Medford, MA (April 18, 1967)

RICHARD CAMMERATA Charlton, MA (June 26, 1967)

WILLIAM BENNETT Dorchester, MA (December 24, 1967)

J. RICHARD GRASSO Brookline, MA (December 31, 1967)

MISSING (PRESUMED DEAD)

EDWARD "WIMPY" BENNETT

WALTER BENNETT

THOMAS SASSO

RUBEN NEEDEL

PROLOGUE

If Joe Barboza felt out of place, he certainly didn't show it. He was the lone Portuguese mobster swimming with a school of Sicilian sharks in the dark, dangerous water that was the Ebb Tide Lounge. It was their hangout after all—not his. Barboza's dream was to become the first non-Italian inducted into La Cosa Nostra, but to the gathered Mafiosi, Barboza was not one of them and never would be. They called him "the nigger" behind his back, and to them he was nothing more than a blunt instrument used to erase their enemies.

Joe Barboza knew exactly what he was—the meanest, deadliest man in the New England mob. Tonight he'd prove it to these so-called men of respect. Fats Domino had just completed his second set of the night. A waitress was wiping the big man's sweat off the piano as Fats was led upstairs for a rigged game of dice. Poor Fats—he was one hell of an entertainer but he was also a degenerate gambler. He played the Ebb Tide a few times a year, earning twelve grand a week. Most times though, Fats would hit the road owing the house more money than he had earned.

The lounge was relatively quiet now, just a few wiseguys huddled around the bar discussing past and future scores in hushed tones. Joe Barboza sat at a table, with his broad shoulders pressed against a wall and his eyes on the front door. The Ebb Tide was intentionally built with a narrow entrance to block armed men from bursting through the front door all at once. Still, Barboza had plenty of enemies, and the only way to stay alive in this game was to plan for the unexpected. He sipped at his glass of Crown Royale while regaling a buddy with stories from his brief but colorful career as a prize fighter. His deep, baritone voice rose above the other conversations around him, much to the annoyance of one respected Mafiosi.

"Hey, quiet down over there," the gangster shouted in Joe's direction.

Barboza paid little attention and kept talking, so the mobster repeated the order.

Joe raised his thick eyebrows and smiled at his buddy as he slipped out of his chair and made his way toward the man, who was leaning against the bar. Barboza moved through the club slowly, his muscled shoulders carving through the crowd like a sharp blade. All eyes were on him now. He savored the attention. It was the same feeling he got each time he had entered the ring, only the spectators in this crowd were all like him—dangerous men. He approached the Mafiosi and offered a crooked smile followed by an open-handed slap across the face. The sheer sound of the impact—flesh on flesh—echoed through the bar. The Mafiosi staggered back and tried to brace himself for another blow. Barboza kept his own dark eyes on the gangster. "Your move," he muttered.

The problem was—the gangster couldn't move. His hands were trembling, but his arms remained at his sides as if he were paralyzed. Suddenly, a slightly built and bespectacled man made his way to the bar. Wearing a pair of black suspenders and white socks, Henry Tameleo had the meek look of an accountant. In reality, he was the underboss of the New England Mafia, or "The Office," as it was called; he held sway over everything that happened inside the Ebb Tide Lounge. Tameleo was normally an even-tempered mobster. Associates called him the Referee, for his ability to settle disputes calmly. Tameleo's trademark cool exterior was not on display tonight. The outrage over what he had just witnessed was boiling to the surface.

"I don't want you to ever slap that man again!" Tameleo shouted angrily at Barboza. The underboss waved his bony finger around the Ebb Tide. "This is my place. I don't want you to touch anyone here with your hands again. You hear me? Never lay your hands on anybody!"

Barboza did not say a word. Instead, he nodded and lunged toward his victim's face once more—this time with his mouth. Barboza bit off a piece of the gangster's cheek and spat it down on the surface of the bar. A stunned Henry Tameleo looked on in horror as the wounded Mafiosi crumbled to the floor.

Barboza smiled at the underboss as a small stream of blood trickled from his lips. He raised his beefy palms to Tameleo.

"See Henry, I didn't use my hands!"

After this night, Barboza's legend began to grow. He had struck fear in the heart of the Mafia. They no longer called him the nigger. Joe Barboza had a new nickname now — the Animal. This story has become part of New England mob lore, and no doubt it has been embellished over time. Oftentimes, the difference between mythology and reality is difficult to define in the underworld, whose inhabitants are all natural-born killers and liars.

The city of Boston has long been known as Ground Zero for corruption within the ranks of the FBI. The bureau's cozy relationship with Irish mob boss James "Whitey" Bulger has made headlines around the globe. But the story did not begin there. *Animal* is the unbelievable but true tale of the FBI's original deal with the Devil. In 1965, amid the backdrop of one of the deadliest mob wars in American history, two unscrupulous FBI agents forged a Faustian bargain with Joe "The Animal" Barboza. It was a pact that transformed the justice system in America. Here is their story.

ANIMAL

Thacher Island — September 1967

Joe Barboza found it hard to believe that his life might end here — in this place. New England Mafia boss Raymond L. S. Patriarca, known simply as the Man — a moniker that grew out of the respect he had built up among gangsters far and wide — was coming for him, and he would not give up the hunt until Barboza was dead. This Joe knew. Given the life he had led up to this point, Barboza had figured he'd take his last breath sooner or later on the streets of East Boston, seated at the bar at the cavernous Ebb Tide Lounge on nearby Revere Beach, or at any other number of places where mob killers like him plied their trade. But here, on this God-forsaken island? It was nearly impossible to imagine.

Barboza had been holed up for the past month on Thacher Island, an unforgiving fifty-acre pile of jagged rock covered by sea grass and poison ivy about a mile off the coast of Rockport, Massachusetts. The island, under twenty-four-hour protection by the U.S. Marshal Service, was crawling with rats and snakes that had been cultivated to help ward off intruders. The only intruders thus far had been the seagulls that made routine dive-bombing runs to pick off unsuspecting vermin as they scurried out of their island holes. The deep, hollow wail of a foghorn, sounding twice every sixty seconds, rang incessantly in Barboza's head. His enemies had vowed to send Barboza to Hell, but he felt as if he were already there. Joe's only solace came in the companionship of his wife and their young daughter; both had been forced into hiding with him, and the marshals had sworn to give up their own lives to protect them.

Would their protection be enough? It was a question Barboza asked himself again and again. He had never before had to depend on anyone else for his own safety. It was a foreign concept to him. He had always been the predator, an animal stalking its prey. But now he was the quarry — he was the kill. In the eyes of *La Cosa Nostra*, Joe Barboza had become the most wanted man in America. His secrets and, more important, his lies had the potential to destroy the New England Mafia and damage crime families from coast to coast. For this, Joe Barboza had to be killed. The U.S. government had taken extraordinary measures to keep him safe. But the one thing Barboza knew was that if the Mafia wanted you dead — you were dead. The key was to strike first. Joe Barboza had fought his own battles on the streets with pistols, rifles, knives, ice-picks, and bare hands. Not that a weapon would do him any good now. Still, a killing tool in his murderous hands might make him feel more at ease, help to take the edge off. The only thing Joe Barboza could do now was hide. He had never hidden from anything in his life.

Barboza's secret location had been recently revealed in an article printed in a Boston newspaper under the headline "How to Hide a 250-lb Canary." Barboza's protector, U.S. marshal John Partington, had been notified that upon reading the piece, Raymond Patriarca had assembled an assassination squad to silence Joe once and for all. Patriarca had recently summoned mob associate Vincent Teresa to his headquarters inside the Coin-O-Matic Vending Company at 168 Atwell Avenue in the Italian section of Federal Hill in Providence, Rhode Island. The dingy mint-green building was hardly fit for a Mafia king like Patriarca — and that is exactly how he wanted it. Like most successful mob leaders, the Man worked to cultivate a low profile. The only hint of the power within was the fleet of polished Cadillacs parked curbside in front of the Coin-O-Matic's dirty picture windows. When Teresa arrived he was led to a backroom, where the boss dictated his murder decree. "You take (Maurice) Pro Lerner up there and case the island," Patriarca ordered. "See if you can get Barboza!"[1]

Teresa was an unlikely choice for such a mission. Known in mob circles as "Fat Vinnie," Teresa was obese, weighing well over three hundred pounds, with beady eyes and black, slicked-back hair. Teresa was a swindler and a thief. He was a money man, not a button man. Teresa was given the assignment because he had recently purchased a forty-three-foot pleasure cruiser that he named *The Living End*. Built by craftsman at the prestigious Egg Harbor Yachts in southern New Jersey, the vessel had been designed with two large staterooms, a plush living area, and a large galley with a three-burner stove and stainless steel sink. The vessel even had chrome-plated anchors. Teresa had bought the boat to lure suckers with cash-stuffed wallets to crooked card games. Vinnie later claimed that the yacht had made him $150,000 in the first couple of months he owned it.

Now, for the first time, *The Living End* was being used to end a man's life.

Maurice "Pro" Lerner was given the order simply because he lived up to his nickname. Whatever the job, Lerner handled it like a pro. Lerner was also an expert diver. He packed his wetsuit, in the hope of infiltrating the island James Bond style and getting the opportunity to take out Barboza up close and personal.

The assassins boarded *The Living End* armed with high-powered rifles, shotguns, binoculars, and a telescope. Soon the boat's motors roared and the vessel began cutting its way through the rough waters and thick fog toward Thacher Island. The perilous seas surrounding the island are littered with the skeletons of ships that have gone down over the centuries. In fact, that is how the island first got its name. In 1635 the land had been bestowed to Anthony Thacher, an Englishman whose four children were among the twenty-one passengers killed when the vessel *Watch and Wait* was torn apart in a hellacious storm during a sail from Ipswich to Marblehead, where Thacher's cousin, Reverend Joseph Avery, was to be ordained as pastor of the fishing village. The passengers embarked from Ipswich on August 11, 1635, but the first sign of trouble did not appear until three days later, when gale-force winds shattered the evening calm and split the sails of their pinnace — a small vessel with two masts rigged like a schooner. Instead of hoisting new sails, the captain and his crew decided to drop anchor and wait until morning. This would prove to be a deadly mistake.

When dawn broke on August 15, 1635, the crew and their passengers were pummeled by driving rains, howling winds, and gigantic seas. Thacher would later describe it in his journal as "so mighty a storm, as the like was never known in New England since the English came, nor in the memory of any of the Indians." Eventually a monster wave tossed the small vessel against a large rock; it was soon followed by an even greater wave that drowned the victims, including ten children. Somehow, Thacher and his wife survived and washed ashore onto the desolate island, half-naked, freezing, and near death. Stumbling along the rocks half-crazed, Thacher was fortunate to find a drowned goat, flint, and a powder horn. He also found a coat that had belonged to his dead son Peter, with which he and his wife kept themselves warm. The body of his cousin's eldest daughter washed ashore, and Thacher and his wife buried the girl's remains on the island's promontory.

Thacher would long blame himself for the deaths of his children and relatives, and he believed that God had punished him and Elizabeth with their very survival. The General Court offered Thacher the island as compensation for his enormous loss. The shipwrecked Englishman named the island Thacher's Woe. Although Anthony and his wife eventually moved to Cape Cod, the island would stay in the Thacher family for eighty years before it was bought back by the colonial government for the purpose of building a light station. Twin lighthouses, each forty-five feet high and made of stone, were constructed on the island in 1771, providing many European immigrants with their first glimpse of America as they sailed into Massachusetts Bay. The twin lighthouses, some three hundred yards apart, stood sentry over the rough waters off Cape Ann for the next hundred years, eventually earning the nickname "Ann's Eyes." In 1861 the lighthouses were replaced by even taller towers that scraped the sky at 124 feet.

Joe Barboza was now calling one of the twin lighthouses home. Joe and his family shared two small bedrooms and two small bathrooms. Their spartan quarters were weather-beaten and rundown. John Partington's living quarters were equally cramped and bleak. The marshal and his men slept on bunk beds three to a room. Their shower operated from a catch basin that trapped rainwater from the storms that were all too frequent on the island.

The U.S. Coast Guard had taken stewardship of the island in 1948 but had abandoned it a few years before Barboza's arrival. There was no television, no phone, and no link to the outside world. The mobster complained almost nonstop about the isolation, and so did his wife and child. Claire Barboza had no one to talk to, no one to confide in. Little Stacy Barboza had no playmates to go exploring with. Thacher Island had been home to many children over the years: the sons and daughters of light keepers, who lived on the mainland during the week to attend school. Their high-pitched laughter had faded into the seascape long ago, replaced by the unsettling sounds of wave crashing against rock, the whistling wind, and the ever-present fog horn. Joe and his wife always had to keep a close eye on Stacy, out of fear that she could disappear into the fog. The vapors were so thick that the fog horn had once sounded for 211 consecutive hours—the equivalent of 38,145 blasts. Fog was just one of the many concerns for parents raising a young daughter there. The island was also pockmarked with snake holes and surrounded by steep cliffs where a child could get easily hurt or even killed.

John Partington believed that Barboza and his family were well protected, but he also knew that Thacher Island was far from an armed fortress. The marshal had four lookout posts on the island: Partington's deputies were stationed at the boat launch, along the island's perimeter, around the Barboza family quarters, and atop one of lighthouse towers, which provided a view of the entire island and the dangerous white-capped waters beyond.

As *The Living End* entered the waters surrounding the island, Teresa grabbed the binoculars with his pudgy fingers and lifted them to his puffy eyes. He spotted the tip of a lighthouse on Thacher Island. It reminded him of a candle sitting in the middle of a basin. One of Partington's deputies, perched high atop the lighthouse, spotted the boat through a blanket of thick fog about a mile off shore. Partington sensed correctly that the vessel was no simple pleasure boat. No experienced yachtsman would venture out on a day like this. Fortunately, the marshal had a plan. Partington gathered his twelve deputies and lined them up in full view of the approaching vessel. There was no way they could allow the yacht to reach the island. Partington had also received a tip that the assassins were carrying sixteen hundred pounds of dynamite on board, with the intention of blowing up everything on the island. Each of Partington's deputies was armed with a carbine and bad intentions of his own for any possible intruder. Partington had also made Barboza wear a U.S. marshal's uniform, in an effort to confuse the killers.

Seeing the small army standing at attention on the island's edge gave Vincent Teresa and Pro Lerner second thoughts. The choppy waters also made it virtually impossible to get off a proper shot. The chances of getting to Barboza were a million to one. After cruising back and forth several times, *The Living End* turned around and headed back to Boston.

Looking out at the boat, Barboza must have wondered if any of his erstwhile friends were on board — friends he had extorted money with — friends he had killed with. Barboza had painted a target on the backs of both friends and foes alike. Now he was the target, and all he could think about was exacting revenge.

2

Pleased to meet you.

Hope you guessed my name.

○ THE ROLLING STONES

Deviltry, Dirt, and Degradation

The second son of first-generation Portuguese-American parents, Joseph Barboza, Jr., was born on September 20, 1932, in New Bedford, Massachusetts, the historic whaling city made familiar to readers around the world by Herman Melville in his epic novel *Moby-Dick*. Portuguese fishermen, mostly from the Azores, had been immigrating to New Bedford en masse since the early part of the nineteenth century, when the harbor was home to 120 square-rigged ships that brought in more than forty thousand barrels of whale oil each year. Thousands of Azorean harpooners signed on with American whaling crews at busy ports such as Cais do Pico, known for its bountiful whaling grounds, and sailed on to the southern coast of Massachusetts for the prospect of better wages and a better life. By 1857, New Bedford was home to as many as 326 whaling ships, making it the unrivaled whaling capital of the world.

At the time, the city accounted for more than half of the whale oil brought into American ports. Sperm oil was even more valuable than oil derived from other whales, because it burned more cleanly, illuminating the night in millions of homes around the globe. Whalers also harvested baleen, a substance taken from the mouths of the giant mammals; it was used for any number of things, from buggy whips and fishing rods to corset stays and hoops for women's skirts. The whaling industry in North America saw profits of more than $9 million per year, and much of that bounty was generated from schooners sailing out of New Bedford. But with the growth of commerce came an increase in crime. Sections of the city, especially the area around Howland Street near the docks, were rife with hooliganism. As one writer colorfully described it, "Rookeries and gin shops were in full blast and the streets thronged with tipsy sailors and bold women, when the air was filled with the sounds of ribald jest and profanity—deviltry, dirt and degradation reigning supreme."[2]

The mid-1800s saw a steady decline of the whaling industry in New Bedford. The outbreak of the Civil War had lured most sailors away, as had the California Gold Rush and the discovery of oil in Pennsylvania. Furthermore, in 1849, Abraham Gesner, a Canadian geologist, created a method of distilling kerosene from petroleum. This innovation would trigger the end of the whaling industry in America. There were 726 ships in the U.S. whaling fleet in 1846. That number would shrink to 39 just three decades later. The virtual death blow to the whaling industry, however, came in 1871, when 33 whaling ships in the Arctic fleet were lost after becoming trapped by ice before they could return home at end of the summer season. Some 22 of those ships had set sail from New Bedford. By the end of the nineteenth century, many of those who had amassed fortunes from whaling in New Bedford had begun shifting their profits to build the next great industry—textiles.

Once again, an influx of Portuguese immigrants heeded the call to fill jobs at massive brick mills built along the waterfront. Thanks to the textile boom, New Bedford was growing faster than any other city along the East Coast. This growth forced mill owners and city planners to build new tenements to house the workers and their families. The conditions were far from sanitary. As many as twelve families were crammed together in poorly constructed two- and three-story wood-frame buildings with no bath and only one toilet, curtained off in the corner of the room. The families were predominantly Portuguese, although there were also immigrants from Greece, Syria, and Poland. It was not only the men who were put to work for long, grueling hours in the mills; women and children also were forced to sweat eleven hours a day and six days a week for meager wages. There was little opportunity for advancement for Portuguese immigrants who had arrived in America with limited skills and virtually no grasp of the English language. The tenements they lived in were a breeding ground for deadly diseases such as cholera and smallpox. Nearly half of all pregnant Portuguese women continued working in the mills, and their infant mortality rate was twice the national average.[3] Portuguese men often sought refuge from family pressures at any one of a dozen saloons, such as Denny Shay's Barroom at the corners of Elm Street and Acushnet Avenue, where the barkeep served anyone regardless of color, creed, or race, and oftentimes served their horses as well.

Conditions for workers did improve for a short time in the early 1920s, when seventy mills operated across the city employing more than 41,000 of New Bedford's 120,000 residents. Immigrants held nine out of every ten jobs at the mill. Many even saw their wages triple at the height of the boom. The prosperity was short-lived, however. High salaries for mill executives and overproduction combined to create a major drop in revenue. But mill officials never considered tightening their own belts; instead, the losses were handed down to the workers, who were ordered to take a 10 percent cut in pay. Outraged textile workers took to the streets upon hearing the decision, and soon thereafter a labor strike was born. Some 20,000 textile workers, many of them Portuguese, walked out of the mills and off the job for six months. New Bedford police made more than two thousand arrests during the strike. One strike captain, Augusto Pinto, was arrested twenty-two times on the picket lines and was later deported back to Portugal. The fascist government there shipped Pinto to a prison in Cape Verde, and he died en route under mysterious circumstances. New Bedford textile workers eventually returned to the mills under an agreement stating that they would receive a 5 percent wage cut, not the original 10 percent reduction. The agreement had the effect of placing a Band-Aid over a gunshot wound. The damage had been done and was irreversible. Several business owners moved their textile companies out of New Bedford and headed south; those who stayed would not be around for much longer.

In late October 1929, a year after the New Bedford textile strike, the American stock market suffered catastrophic losses, plunging the United States and the rest of the world into the Great Depression. Industrial cities like New Bedford were decimated. Two-thirds of the city's remaining mills shut down completely. The head of one textile union summed up the economic despair this way: "Lowell, Lawrence, New Bedford, Maynard and Fall River . . . and most of the mill towns of the Blackstone Valley . . . are sad places."[4] One unemployed mill worker described eating dandelion greens and raiding garbage barrels to fill his stomach. His story was no different from those of millions around the country whose everyday battles to stave off hunger and disease were life and death struggles. This is the world that Joe Barboza was born into.

His father, Joseph Sr., was a milkman and part-time boxer who fought under the name of Jackie Wolgast. His mother, Palmeda Camille Barboza, worked in a hospital cafeteria and occasionally found work as a seamstress. Together they lived in a dilapidated three-decker on Short Street, which was between Allen and Grape streets and directly across from the hospital where Palmeda worked.

Joe had a brother, Donald, who was four years older. Younger brother Anthony and a sister, Anne, would arrive nearly twenty years later. Grim economic realities and Joseph Sr.'s wandering eye made the air in the Barboza household thick with tension from the very beginning. Joe Barboza's parents had married in 1927, and the relationship appeared doomed from the start. Barboza Sr. was a handsome, strapping man with a hair-trigger temper and a penchant for violence that he displayed both inside the ring and out. Weighing 180 pounds, Joe Sr. carved out a name for himself fighting as a light heavyweight in saloons and fair grounds in southeastern Massachusetts, Martha's Vineyard, and Providence. He also handed out regular beatings to his wife and children and would disappear for weeks at a time, bedding down with mistresses scattered about the city. Joe Sr. had two children out of wedlock. He offered virtually no financial support for his family, and on the rare occasion that Joe Sr. found himself at home, he hovered over his wife and children with an air of sadism and brutality. During one fit of rage, Joe Sr. knocked his wife's front teeth out while she was lying in bed with the infant Joe in her arms. Palmeda had been hugging the baby and weeping softly when Joe Sr. stormed into the room.

"Why the hell are you crying?" he asked with venom in his voice.[5]

Palmeda did not answer.

"I'll give you something to cry about," Joe Sr. shouted as he lunged forward and struck his wife, her head snapping back against the backboard of the bed. Palmeda clutched her baby as her teeth went flying to opposite sides of the small bedroom and her mouth filled with blood.

The next morning, young Donald crept into his mother's bedroom, saw her battered face, and began to cry.

"What happened to you?" he asked, as tears flowed down his cheeks.

"Your father was chopping wood down in the cellar and one of the logs popped loose and hit me by accident," she lied.

It was difficult enough to lie to her child, but Palmeda knew that it was impossible to deceive herself. Constant pressure and sadness surrounding the relationship led Palmeda Barboza to attempt suicide. Joe and Donald came home from playing in the neighborhood one day and were met by the pungent smell of gas as they entered the apartment. They found their mother passed out on the floor and the gas jet open. "The house we lived in was more of sorrow than of happiness,"[6] Joe later wrote in his autobiography, *Barboza*, published in 1975. "We were constantly on welfare. My mother was very much in love with my father regardless of his infidelities, and took out her loneliness by constantly keeping my brother and [me] around her. But both of us were wild."

Like his father, young Joe had shown an affinity for sex and violence at a young age. His family had moved to First Street, on the south side of New Bedford, where he frequently found himself in scrapes with other boys. Young Joe was not a normal looking child. With a large head, long arms, and stubby legs, he was taunted constantly for his "apelike" appearance. However, he was always quick with a comeback and even quicker with his fists. Matching his father's fighting style, Joe would tuck his thick chin to his chest and let his long, powerful arms do most of the work. Young Joe soon built a reputation as a boy who shouldn't be trifled with. He also understood the attractions of the opposite sex early on. During a Halloween dance he attended as a child, Joe approached an attractive girl from the neighborhood who had dressed as a Polynesian princess complete with grass skirt and coconut bra. Instead of asking the girl to dance, Joe grabbed the coconut shells and flipped them over, exposing the poor girl to the public. Hearing her screams, the girl's brothers chased Joe from the dance. Soon others joined in the pursuit as young Joe fled across town toward the waterfront, where he somehow managed to escape the angry mob. Joe later joked that he had felt like Quasimodo fleeing Louis XI's blood-hungry soldiers in Victor Hugo's *Hunchback of Notre Dame*.

Such moments of excitement offered a brief but welcome escape from Joe's home life, where he felt that he was the bait his mother Palmeda would throw out every so often to lure her wayward husband home. Once Palmeda sent the boy to the home of his father's mistress while she waited down the street. Young Joe found his father lounging in the yard with his girlfriend, a Portuguese woman named Cecilia. "I told him (Joe Sr.) that I wanted to see him,"[7] Barboza recalled in his memoir. "He looked at me with anger in his eyes and said: Get outta here you little bastard. I turned around blindly and ran down the street. I couldn't stop crying."

Later feeling a tinge of remorse, Joe Sr. bought his son a pigeon to make amends. The offering did not extinguish the burning rage building up inside the son against the father. "The punk broke my heart," Joe would say years later.

To avoid becoming embroiled in the daily drama of his parent's turbulent marriage, young Joe began to spend less time at home and more time on the streets. His small group of friends was made up mostly of the sons of Portuguese fishermen whose clothes and skin bore the stains and smells of days and weeks spent at sea. The life of a Portuguese fisherman in New Bedford in the 1930s was little better than it had been in the mid-1800s. Fishing was a job for hard men with few prospects, and Joe understood early on that he wanted no part of it. The rugged lifestyle of a fisherman had little appeal for Joe Barboza. Instead, he was drawn to the world of the gangster. As a child of the Great Depression, young Joe grew up in an era in which the American gangster was often cheered rather than loathed. This was the time of John Dillinger, Pretty Boy Floyd, and Al Capone. Their fame, or more accurately, their infamy, rivaled that of the biggest sports and entertainment stars. One can imagine Joe and his group of young friends sneaking into the State Theater on Purchase Street to take in a matinee of gangster dramas like Humphrey Bogart's *High Sierra* or James Cagney's *Each Dawn I Die*. Young Joe was fascinated by the way these big screen hoodlums handled themselves.

However, Barboza did not need to sit in a darkened movie house to be exposed to the gangster lifestyle. For that, all he had to do was take a stroll through his struggling city. The whaling ships might have been long gone, but one could still find plenty of deviltry, dirt, and degradation in New Bedford. The city certainly had its share of hardened criminals, the most notorious being members of the Morelli Gang. Led by Frank "Butsey" Morelli, the gang included his four brothers. Natives of Brooklyn, New York, the Morelli brothers had moved to New England during World War I. With members carrying colorful nicknames like Gyp the Blood and Steve the Pole, the Morelli Gang roamed New Bedford, Providence, Rhode Island, and parts of Connecticut robbing railroad freight cars of textiles and shoes. The gang would eventually be suspected in the Sacco and Vanzetti case, one of the most notorious cases in American history. Ferdinando Nicola Sacco and Bartolomeo Vanzetti had been accused in the robbery and murder of a payroll master and his guard on April 15, 1920, in South Braintree, Massachusetts. The robbers ambushed the pair in broad daylight as they strolled up Pearl Street toward the Slater and Morrill Shoe Company with two metal boxes containing $15,776.73. The paymaster, Frank Parmenter, was shot several times. His guard, Alessandro Berardelli, was cut down by gunfire while trying to flee the scene. The killers sped away in a Buick touring car firing pot shots into neighboring buildings in an effort to keep potential witnesses inside.

Three weeks later, Sacco and Vanzetti, both Italian immigrants and avowed anarchists, were arrested after appearing at a garage in Brockton, Massachusetts, to retrieve the car investigators believed had been used in the holdup. Despite the fact that neither man had a criminal record and that prosecutors had virtually no evidence against them, the men were quickly indicted and put on trial for the murders. Their arrests sparked a fuse that would ignite a conflagration of violent protest around the world. Anarchists sent bombs to U.S. embassies across the globe. Most were diffused, but one bomb sent to the American ambassador in Paris did explode, injuring the ambassador's valet. As the trial got under way at the Norfolk County Courthouse in Dedham, Massachusetts, authorities fortified the courtroom with sliding steel doors and cast-iron shutters to prevent damage from a possible bomb attack. Sacco and Vanzetti were found guilty of murder and sentenced to die in the electric chair.

After the trial, a Portuguese immigrant named Celestino Madeiros made a startling confession while locked up alongside Nicola Sacco in Dedham. Madeiros, a convicted killer and member of the Morelli Gang, slipped Sacco a note stating that he had been involved in the deadly holdup. Police in New Bedford, who had had a long history with the Morelli Gang, suspected them in the murders fifty miles to the north. More than two dozen witnesses had also come forward, many of them offering descriptions of the assailants that generally fit members of the Morelli Gang. Despite the confession of Madeiros, and despite ardent support from notables including Albert Einstein, George Bernard Shaw, and Dorothy Parker, Nicola Sacco and Bartolomeo Vanzetti were sent to their death on August 23, 1927. Nicola Sacco was defiant to the end. As he was being strapped down in the electric chair, he shouted, *Vive l'anarchia!* More subdued, Bartolomeo Vanzetti whispered under his thick mustache that he forgave those who were about to put him to death. Morelli Gang member Celestino Madeiros was sent to the electric chair that same day for an unrelated murder. His execution had been delayed in case his testimony had been required in a retrial of Sacco and Vanzetti. In his 1973 memoir *My Life in the Mafia*, Vincent Teresa claimed that he once had discussed the case with Butsey Morelli decades after the crime. Morelli told Teresa, "We whacked them out. We killed those two guys (Parmenter and Berardelli). These two greaseballs (Sacco & Vanzetti) took it on the chin. They got in our way so we just ran over them."[8] Decades later, a similar case would play out in a Massachusetts courtroom with Joseph Barboza playing the leading role.

The foundation for Barboza's criminal career was set on the streets of New Bedford where Joe, just entering his teenage years, gathered together a small band of roaming bandits and in the spirit of *Oliver Twist* ran about the city stealing from local department stores to fence for cash. In the beginning, Barboza and his young crew would simply gather up the courage to walk into a store and target something small and valuable, such as a watch or piece of jewelry. They would then slide the item into a coat pocket, slip out of the store, and run. Eventually, however, the gang learned how to pick locks and operate like more seasoned criminals — at night. Joe believed that these nighttime raids cut the risk of getting caught. He was wrong. At the tender age of thirteen, Joe Barboza found himself behind bars for the first time. The charge was breaking and entering. Soon after, he was shipped off to the Lyman School for Boys, a notorious reform school located nearly one hundred miles northwest of New Bedford in the small farming town of Westborough, Massachusetts. Established in 1886, the Lyman School was built on the grounds of the State Reform School, the oldest reformatory in the United States. The Lyman School was spread over a thousand acres, half of which was rich farmland maintained by the young inmates, or students, as they were called. The school had its share of notorious graduates, including Albert DeSalvo, who would eventually confess to and later recant his claim of being the Boston Strangler.

For Barboza, this was the first time he had traveled more than ten miles from his home. Gone were the familiar sights and sounds of his New Bedford neighborhood. Gone was the familiar aroma of Palmeda's ethnic Portuguese dishes wafting through their apartment from her tiny kitchen. The choked streets and exotic smells he was accustomed to were now replaced by acre after acre of rolling farmland. It was as much like home to Barboza as the craters of the moon. Many of the students were just like him, kids who had committed petty crimes, rather than violent offenses. Some had been sent to Lyman for being truant from school, or even for the sheer audacity of being a "stubborn child."

Young Joe and the other boys were housed in cottages with pleasant names such as Sunset, Hillside, Wachusett, Elms, and Oak. From the outside, Lyman appeared no different from a prep school that might cater to the sons of blue-blooded masters of industry. The inside told a different story, however. The children were given a strict religious education and taught a trade, such as carpentry, masonry, or plumbing. These so-called benefits were overshadowed by the harsh disciplinary doctrine of the institution. With extreme prejudice, beatings were handed out daily by cottage masters wielding a variety of weapons, including belts and even pick handles. Children who committed even minor infractions were marched down to Oak Cottage (the disciplinary cottage) and given brutal "attitude adjustments." Barboza received countless beatings, including one particularly savage punishment called "the hot foot," whereby a cottage master would strike repeated blows to the arch of a child's naked foot.

There were no walls or wired fences to keep the inmates on the grounds. Instead, fear of reprisal gave potential runaways enough of an incentive to stay put. Those students who did manage to escape were never talked about or heard from again. Rumors were spread among the children, and perhaps even encouraged by the adults, that runaways were killed and their bodies buried in the black waters of a nearby swamp. As frightening as those rumors were, they were not bad enough to dissuade Barboza from running away. He simply walked away from the facility one day and spent two weeks on the run. His parents were harassed daily by New Bedford police officers, all of whom believed they were withholding information on the boy's whereabouts. In reality, Joe's brief stint as a teenage fugitive was as much a mystery to his family as it was to the cops.

One night young Joe turned up at his parent's apartment wearing a big smile and an engineer's hat with the visor turned up. When asked by his mother where he had been for the last two weeks, Joe explained that he had found work selling vegetables from a cart on the street. His parents did not immediately call police as they had been instructed to do; instead they drove Joe back to the Lyman School themselves the next day. Joe Sr. and Palmeda handed Joe back over to school administrators with the promise that he would never escape again. As his parents got into their car for the long journey home, Joe was marched down to Oak Cottage for another "attitude adjustment."

Hating—yet also wanting to emulate—his father, young Joe picked up the sport of boxing while a student at Lyman. Joe's prowess in the ring both astonished and annoyed his schoolmasters, who had not forgiven him for his escape. The school's boxing coach put Joe in the ring with an older student with the aim of teaching the young punk from New Bedford a painful lesson. Joe mauled his opponent from the opening bell, hitting him with a series of savage shots. The boy crumbled to the gym floor wincing in pain and admitting defeat. Joe unlaced his gloves and strode by the boxing coach with a toothy grin plastered on his long face. The frustrated coach followed Barboza into the locker room and attacked him while he was untying his shoes. The coach threw a powerful uppercut that connected with the boy's jaw. Young Joe took a serious beating that day and later somehow managed to get word to his family. An enraged Joe Sr. drove up to the Lyman School and challenged the coach and other school administrators to a fight. It was the one time that young Joe was proud to be his father's son.

Not only was Barboza forced to fend off sadistic school masters, he also had to defend himself against other young inmates. Young Joe was constantly mocked by older boys for his large head, long arms, and stubby legs. Word of Joe's fighting prowess on the streets of New Bedford had not traveled with him to the Lyman School. Instead, his young tormentors would have to learn the hard way, both in the ring and in the dormitory. When out from under the watchful eyes of the cottage masters, the children meted out their own justices and injustices against each other in a struggle for power reminiscent of *Lord of the Flies*. At the Lyman School, a boy was either predator or prey. Weaker children were beaten and molested by stronger students who, growing into their sexuality, looked upon everything with carnal intent and seething anger. Young Joe took to the role of predator early on. Despite his incarceration, he had been granted a freedom that he had never experienced before. No longer tethered to his mother and manipulated by her to keep the elder Barboza in line, Joe's only responsibility now was to himself. Once again, Joe tucked his chin to his chest and came out swinging. The only way to become king of this violent teenage jungle was to fight for it—and fight he did. He would later claim to have been involved in more than three hundred brawls during his three terms at Lyman, and bragged to have won them all.

The goal of the school may have been to reform misguided children, but it sadly had the opposite effect on most. Kids left Lyman with a harder edge, more dangerous than when they had gone in. A classic example was the case of Jesse Pomeroy, who would become the youngest person ever convicted of first-degree murder in the history of the Commonwealth of Massachusetts. Jesse had been sent to the state reform school in Westborough in the late 1800s after he had been arrested and found guilty of torturing young boys in his South Boston neighborhood. Pomeroy would strip his young victims, tie them to a post, and lash them with a thick rope while ordering them to recite an obscene version of the Lord's Prayer. He would then mutilate the faces of his victims with a pocket knife. Like Joe Barboza, Jesse Pomeroy looked different from other boys his age. He had a large head, lumbering frame, and a milky right eye. Pomeroy had gone partially blind after receiving a smallpox vaccination as an infant. Jesse was known to stick needles in the eyes of his victims as retribution against the God who had plagued him with this striking deformity.

Jesse Pomeroy's first reign of terror was brief, as his milky, or "marble," eye, as it was described, was an easily identifiable mark used by police to track him down. Like Barboza, Pomeroy was also sent to reform school at the age of thirteen. But unlike young Joe, Jesse proved to be a good student and a model inmate. Pomeroy himself never broke school rules or acted out in a way to warrant a beating by institution superiors. Most children stayed far away from the disciplinary rooms while their classmates were being punished, but not Jesse. He was drawn to the screams of beating victims and would later ask them to describe to him in vivid detail how they had been flogged. Jesse had always been fascinated by the torture of innocents. He had twisted the heads off birds as a child and later graduated to assaulting young boys. Through his conversations with those young beating victims at the reform school in Westborough, Jesse had learned new methods with which to apply his fiendish trade.

Jesse Pomeroy had served sixteen months and still had two years remaining on his sentence when he was discharged from the state reform school for good behavior. Less than two months after his release, the boy (now fourteen) was back in South Boston working at his mother's shop when a ten-year-old girl wearing a plaid skirt walked in and asked him if she could buy a notebook for school. The milky eyed boy invited the girl to the basement of the shop, where he told her that he had one notebook left but that the cover had been stained with ink. The girl offered to buy it for two cents less than the retail price and was shown the cellar door. Jesse opened the door and followed her down the steps. Moments later, he put his arm around her neck, pulled out a knife, and cut her throat. He then dragged the body of ten-year-old Katie Curran behind a water closet and stuffed it in a trash heap. A few weeks later, Jesse lured four-year-old Horace Millen to the edge of Boston Harbor to see a new steamship. With the same knife he had used to murder Katie Curran, Pomeroy slashed the boy's throat and then tried to castrate him. The young boy's body was discovered a short time later by two boys who were playing on the beach. In addition to stabbing Horace Millen nearly two dozen times, the killer had also punctured the boy's eyeball.

Jesse Pomeroy was the lead suspect from the early stages of the investigation and later admitted to the boy's murder along with the killing of Katie Curran. Dubbed the "Boy Fiend" by the press, he was charged and convicted of first-degree murder and sentenced to death. But because he was only fourteen years old, his sentence was commuted to life behind bars in solitary confinement. The violent culture of the state reform school is certainly not to blame for Jesse Pomeroy's murder spree, but it may have accelerated his homicidal behavior. The same can be said about Joe Barboza. He arrived at the Lyman School a troubled kid and left with a new hunger for violence and eventually murder.

Young Joe was walking the razor's edge when he was discharged from the Lyman School and sent back to the streets of New Bedford. He was looking for new scores with which to put money in his empty pockets. He still had little support at home despite his mother's best efforts. She fed Joe and his brother, Donald, scraps that she brought home from the hospital cafeteria. The bleak financial situation forced Donald to quit school at the age of sixteen in an attempt to help his family out. He got a job as a welder's apprentice at a shipyard in Providence. Donald would hand over a portion of his paycheck to his father every week in the belief that the elder Barboza would use the money to support his family. Years later, Donald Barboza found out that Joe Sr. had pocketed the money.

Young Joe would not make his older brother's mistake. He had no interest in spending long hours leaning over a hot blowtorch at some shipyard — whatever money he made he was going to keep. According to the *Boston Herald Traveler*, Barboza and his gang robbed sixteen houses in the New Bedford area over the span of just a couple of days, stealing money, watches, liquor, and guns. Easy money was not Joe's only motivation. Sometimes he was inspired by the simple act of revenge. When a shop teacher insulted him for his lack of woodworking skills at the vocational school he was attending, Joe broke into the man's house and went on a rampage. Lamps were toppled, photographs were smashed, and that wasn't all. When police spoke to reporters about the incident, they said that the robbers had left a cream pie dripping from the wall. Of course, the press seized on this unique news nugget and dubbed the gang the "Cream Pie Bandits." The real version of the robbery was too vile for even hardened investigators to reveal. What was dripping from the wall wasn't pastry cream at all. Barboza had defecated on the floor and smeared some along every wall in the house.

So this is where it happens.
The power games and bribes
◦ THE DEAD KENNEDYS

3

That Pig on the Hill

Raymond L. S. Patriarca balled his hands into tight fists as he stared across the committee room into the hard-bitten eyes of the bootlegger's son. The air was thick with the acrid stench of cigarette and pipe smoke, and the blood pumping through the mob boss's veins was fueled by a seething hatred for his inquisitor. It was a bitterly cold day in February 1959, and Patriarca had been summoned to Washington, D.C., to testify before the U.S. Senate Select Committee on Improper Activities in Labor Management — or the McClellan Hearings as they were called, after Senator John L. McClellan, the bespectacled Arkansas Democrat and World War I veteran who chaired the committee. McClellan's attack dog was a young attorney from Massachusetts named Robert F. Kennedy. McClellan had hired the thirty-three-year-old brother of U.S. senator John F. Kennedy (also a committee member) as lead investigator and chief counsel for the Permanent Subcommittee on Investigations. It was Kennedy's job to investigate and expose the mob's violent infiltration of labor unions from coast to coast.

This was a plum assignment for Kennedy, who hoped his racket-busting crusade would one day overshadow the high profile Kefauver Hearings, which had been broadcast nationwide in 1952. Under the alias Mr. Rogers, RFK traveled far and wide documenting horrific tales of mob-labor abuse, including the story of a union organizer in San Diego who had received the ultimate indignity of having a cucumber shoved up his ass as a painful and humiliating warning to stay away. If the organizer did not heed the warning, mobsters had vowed to split his rectum with a watermelon on the next go-round.

Accounts like this outraged Kennedy, who went after the mob with unfettered zeal. During the committee's 270 days of testimony, RFK went toe to toe with Teamsters Union president Jimmy Hoffa, and had even accused Chicago mob boss Sam Giancana of "giggling like a little girl" while

Kennedy tried to question him about mob activities. Giancana had invoked his Fifth Amendment right during the hearing, as did all the Mafia bosses — except Raymond Patriarca.

When grilled about allegations of beatings and threats dished out by his employees at the National Cigarette Service vending machine company in Providence, Patriarca insisted that the stories were pure fantasy. The mob boss painted himself as an honest businessman unfairly targeted and harassed by police. "I've been a goat around Rhode Island for twenty years,"[9] Patriarca said, in a deep, booming voice. When grilled by Kennedy about the origin of the $80,000 to $90,000 used by Patriarca to start his vending machine business, the mob boss claimed that the cash had been a gift from his dying mother. According to Patriarca, the small fortune had been left for him in a box in the family basement. Kennedy took another hard look at the witness's lengthy rap sheet and shook his head.

"Why, if you had $80,000 or so sitting in the basement, did you become involved in burglaries?" Kennedy asked.

"Why do a lot of young fellows do a lot of things when they haven't a father?" Patriarca replied incredulously.

The mob boss also pointed out the sheer hypocrisy of the proceedings, knowing how the father of his main inquisitor had amassed his fortune. "The only mob I know of are the Irish hoodlums," Patriarca announced in a veiled reference to Joseph P. Kennedy, who had acquired much of his wealth as a bootlegger. No doubt this comment angered and embarrassed RFK. But Patriarca didn't want only to embarrass young Kennedy; he wanted to hurt him deeply. At the close of testimony, a confident Patriarca strolled by the committee table where Kennedy was still seated. With his ever-present cigarette dangling from his lips, he leaned close to RFK and said sotto voce, "Your [retarded] sister has more brains than the two of you [RFK and JFK] together."

Raymond Patriarca was referring to Rosemary Kennedy, the third child of Joseph and Rose Kennedy, who had undergone a prefrontal lobotomy at age twenty-three and was kept far out of the public eye in a mental institution in Wisconsin. For years to come, Robert Kennedy would call Patriarca "that pig on the hill" in reference to the gangster's headquarters on Federal Hill in Providence. Kennedy also vowed to his closest confidantes that one day he would bring Raymond Patriarca down.

At the time, there was no way for Patriarca to forecast the impending storm that would build between Bobby Kennedy's Justice Department and the mob. Until now, Patriarca had been both lucky and smart.

Raymond Salvatore Loredo Patriarca was a first-generation Italian-American born on March 17, 1908, on Shrewsbury Street in Worcester, Massachusetts, about forty miles west of Boston. He did not stay in the City of Seven Hills (as Worcester was known) for long. As a toddler, young Raymond moved with his family to Providence, Rhode Island, where his father, Eleuterio, ran a liquor store. Unlike Barboza, Patriarca grew up in a loving family, and his early childhood offered no indication of his future life of crime. The family lived on Atwells Avenue, where his mother, Mary Jane (DeNubile) Patriarca, kept a tidy home. Although considered a bright student, Patriarca left school at the age of eight to help support his family as a bellhop and shoeshine boy.

Raymond Patriarca stayed out of trouble until the earth crumbled under his feet with the death of his father in 1925. Raymond was just seventeen years old at the time. Without his father's moral compass to guide him, Raymond's focus shifted quickly to the dark side. Shortly after Eleuterio's death, his son was arrested for the first time for bootlegging. Raymond had talked his way into the mob as an associate and was given a low-level job as a guard for liquor shipments. What his bosses did not know, however, was that the enterprising and fearless Patriarca had often arranged for the hijacking of liquor shipments that he had been hired to guard. The bosses never questioned the coincidence, or at least had never raised their suspicions directly to Patriarca. Eventually, Raymond was picked up by police in Connecticut for violating the state's prohibition laws. He offered investigators a phony address—Bonodow Street in Worcester—but other than that, he didn't say a word. The teenager proved to be a devout follower of the mob's cardinal rule—Omerta— "Keep your mouth shut." Four years later in 1929, at the age of twenty-two, Patriarca would find himself in jail again, this time on a litany of charges including conspiracy to commit murder, armed robbery, auto theft, violating the White Slave Act (prostitution), breaking and entering in the night time, and even adultery.

During that same year, Raymond L. S. Patriarca would also be formally inducted into the Mafia. It was the era of Prohibition, and the mob had no shortage of young soldiers ready to cheat, rob, and kill their way up *La Cosa Nostra*'s corporate ladder. Raymond Patriarca proved to be an adept pupil and an eventual master of the mob's criminal techniques. He was a methodical, strategic chess player who could also jam a rook in a man's eye if the situation called for it.

In 1932, Patriarca and two others were charged with robbing the Webster National Bank in central Massachusetts. Raymond and his men held the manager, tellers, and customers at gunpoint while they coolly robbed the safe of $10,000. Patriarca was later identified as the culprit by scores of eyewitnesses. But by the time he went on trial, those witnesses had suddenly been overcome by a case of mass amnesia. They recanted their testimony, and the young gangster walked.

Patriarca's luck continued until 1938, when he walked into a factory in Brookline, Massachusetts, brandishing a pistol and pressed it against the owner's head. Raymond ordered the man, Clarence A. Wallbank, to open the company safe, which was believed to hold a small fortune in jewelry. Patriarca and his men ordered the owner and two employees to strip naked while they looted the safe of $12,000 in necklaces, rings, and at least one oddly shaped gold pin. Patriarca and his crew then stole the factory owner's car and, for good measure, dumped the men's clothes. This was a particularly brazen robbery, as it occurred only a few blocks from a police precinct.

The heist had investigators stumped until just a few days later, when they learned of a similar crime in Webster, Massachusetts, the same town that Patriarca had targeted years earlier. Thanks to a barking dog, police were alerted to a burglary at the United Optical Plant. The plant stored an estimated $8,000 in gold, which was used to manufacture gold eyeglass frames. While the robbers were still inside, six local police officers surrounded the factory and ordered the men out with their hands up. The robbers complied, walking out into the frigid February night with their arms raised toward the stars above. Patriarca gave police a fake name: John Roma. The police discovered his true identity, however, when they searched his car. They also discovered what was then described as "one of the most complete set of burglary tools ever seen in this part of New England."[10] A suitcase found in Patriarca's automobile held a drill, hammer, pinch bar, sets of gloves, and other assorted burglary tools. Also in the suitcase was that oddly shaped gold pin stolen in the Brookline heist earlier in the week. Clarence A. Wallbank, the factory owner who had been left naked and humiliated by Patriarca and his gang, was all too ready to get even. He identified several of the stolen items found in Patriarca's car and fingered the gangster as one of the men who had robbed him.

Wallbank was the type of witness prosecutors had longed for. He was a credible business leader who proved completely resistant to Patriarca's strong-arm intimidation tactics — or so they thought. In December 1938, at the urging of a corrupt Irish politician and a member of the Governor's Council named Daniel H. Coakley, Raymond's brother Joseph visited Clarence Wallbank on two occasions. Joseph Patriarca offered the factory owner $7,000 in cash and his life if he would recant his testimony. Wallbank responded by writing a letter to the Governor's Council urging the panel to pardon Raymond Patriarca. When the letter landed on Daniel Coakley's desk, the former defense attorney argued that it wasn't powerful enough to sway then Massachusetts governor Charles Francis Hurley. Coakley tossed the letter away and wrote his own version, which Wallbank signed. Coakley delivered the new letter to Governor Hurley, who signed it without any fuss. Coakley's fellow Governor's Council members did the same. With a pardon in hand, Raymond Patriarca was a free man once again, after having served less than three months behind bars. Soon thereafter, Daniel Coakley deposited $28,995 into his bank account. Both Coakley and Wallbank proved that their integrity could be bought for the right price. Fortunately, the same could not be said for local reporters, who blasted the pardon on the front pages of newspapers across the region. The Patriarca pardon stirred one of the largest political corruption cases in New England history. Pressure from the fourth estate and the public at large triggered a lengthy investigation that resulted in Coakley's impeachment.

The pardon petition, as revealed by the fourteen articles of impeachment, displayed several irregularities, including the fact that Coakley's document contained the support of three priests, two of whom insisted that their signatures had been obtained by fraud. The third priest named in the petition did not exist. Coakley also wrote that Patriarca, as admitted by all, was "wholly guiltless" of armed robbery. Coakley had failed to disclose the fact that the gangster had actually pleaded guilty to the crime.

The rogue politician also called Raymond "a virtuous young man eager to be released from prison so that he might go home to his mother."[11] Investigators later found out that upon his release Patriarca did go home, but only for a change of clothing. The mobster then took off for Miami Beach with a beautiful blonde in tow.

The Massachusetts state senate voted to remove Coakley from the Governor's Council in October 1941. He was the first state official have been impeached in more than a century.

By this time Patriarca was newly married to Helen G. Mandella, a nurse whose sister worked for Leverett Saltonstall, the successor to Massachusetts governor Hurley and a future U.S. senator. Helen would give birth to the couple's first and only child, Raymond J. Patriarca, a few years later. The baby's father would soon gain a growing reputation as a man to be feared and respected. He had shown that he had the requisite political skills to corrupt susceptible lawmakers and had also proved willing to remove his rivals with brutal efficiency.

In 1952, Patriarca took out his last remaining rival in Providence. Forty-nine-year-old Carlton O'Brien was a former bootlegger and armed robber turned racketeer who competed directly with the Mafia for the city's lucrative race wire services rackets, which gathered horse racing results from tracks around the country and transmitted them to bookmakers for a price. At first O'Brien worked hand in hand with the Italians. He bought into the Ferrara-Rossetti wire service, which operated in East Boston. But the Ferrara-Rossetti operation was constantly on the move in order to elude the watchful eyes of law enforcement. New locations meant new telephone equipment, which drove up the fee for the service. Carlton O'Brien refused to pay higher prices, so he started his own race wire service, a move that did not sit well with the Mafia. But O'Brien was not about to hand over his golden goose without a fight. He was a tough Irish gangster who had once been given the dubious distinction of "Public Enemy Number One" by Rhode Island law enforcement officials. There was no way for the two wire services to coexist. Two is always a crowd in the underworld, especially in a small city like Providence, Rhode Island, located in the heart of the smallest state in the union. Raymond Patriarca was given the order to bust up O'Brien's operation. Patriarca trashed O'Brien's betting parlors, robbed his bookies, and savagely beat his runners. Still, the stubborn Irishman would not budge. At this time, O'Brien was fighting a war on two fronts. A jailhouse informant had recently fingered him as the "mastermind" behind the infamous 1950 Brink's Job in Boston. The story made sense, as O'Brien was a close friend and associate of Joseph "Specs" O'Keefe, a former Lyman School delinquent who was now a key suspect in the $2,775,395 heist, at that point the largest in U.S. history. It would only be a matter of time before his Brink's cohorts turned up to ensure his silence.

Raymond Patriarca would get to him first. His men delivered their death notice to O'Brien with murderous zeal as the Irish gangster returned to his Cranston, Rhode Island, home one night after spending several hours at a local roadhouse he owned. Patriarca's gunmen welcomed O'Brien home with two shotgun blasts to the chest. The hoodlum was dead before he hit the ground. When his body was discovered, O'Brien was lying on his back with both arms stretched wide. His legs were also positioned outward in an unnatural state. The gangster's blood was everywhere. Police believed O'Brien had been murdered in connection with the Brink's robbery. No one suspected Patriarca. Carlton O'Brien's killers were never found. Raymond L. S. Patriarca was now the undisputed king of Providence, and soon the other New England states would fall like dominoes under his control in a seismic shift of power radiating from the tight, crowded streets of Boston's North End to Federal Hill in Providence.

From the early 1930s through the late 1950s, the rackets in New England were controlled by two men, Felippo "Phil" Buccola and his second in command, Joe Lombardo. The pair had killed their way to the top on a brisk December day in 1931 when Lombardo lured the boss of the powerful Gustin Gang to the third floor office of his importing business on Hanover Street in Boston's North End. The Gustin Gang, which took its name from a street just a block long in the heart of their own territory in South Boston, was led by the Wallace brothers — Steve, Jimmy, and Frank. The mob had formed just before World War I and, like any gang, its members started small, targeting delivery trucks at city intersections. By handing down a serious beating to the driver, or simply by the mere threat of one, the Wallace brothers had terrorized South Boston and then spread fear to other city neighborhoods. Known originally to police as the

Tailboard Thieves, the Gustin Gang grew and diversified during Prohibition to the point that they controlled much of the illegal booze coming into New England. What shipments they didn't control became theirs through other means. Armed with fake badges of the kind used by government agents, the Gustin Gang confiscated cases of liquor from rival bootleggers and then sold them through their distribution network in Southie.

The Wallace brothers had far-reaching political influence in the city, making the Gustin Gang the most powerful in all of Boston, which is why they were shocked and angry to learn that the Italian upstarts wanted in on their business. The Gustin Gang owned and operated more rum running boats than most of their rivals combined. Their vessels would steam out of Boston Harbor several times a week to rendezvous with liquor ships stationed three miles offshore in international waters. The bootleggers would stock up along "Rum Row" and head back to Boston, where eager patrons were happy to plunk down twenty-five cents for a watered-down beer that would have cost only a nickel before Prohibition.

At first, Joe Lombardo offered a compromise. He sent word that the Mafia was willing to divide territories along Boston's waterfront with the Gustin Gang. This was a bold request, since the Italians had no real power to leverage in the city. The Wallace brothers thought so, too. Negotiations got heated and threats were exchanged until, finally, Frankie Wallace was invited to a meeting in an effort to clear the air. Wallace quickly accepted the offer and planned to tell the Italians exactly where they could stick their deal. The first tactical error made by the Irish mob boss was to agree to a meeting at his enemy's headquarters. Wallace arrogantly thought that his political power would protect him against assassination in his own backyard. Who would dare make a run at the Gustin Gang, knowing all the cops they had in their back pocket? To attempt such a move would be to write your own death warrant.

Still, Wallace traveled to the meeting with two bodyguards, fellow Gustin members Barney Walsh and Timothy Coffey. The second tactical error was made when Wallace failed to position a lookout outside the meeting place. Had he done so, the lookout might have noticed seven rough looking Mafiosi entering the building in the hour or so leading up to the sit-down. Instead, Wallace and his bodyguards marched confidently into the Testa Building on Hanover Street and quickly climbed three flights of stairs to the office of C and F Importing, which was owned by Lombardo. With Christmas just three days away, the mood inside the building had been festive up to that point. On the floor above C and F, a group of veterans of the Great War were busy stocking Christmas baskets for neighborhood children. The holiday cheer was interrupted by loud pounding on Lombardo's office door. His men responded by unleashing a barrage of gunfire in the direction of the sound. Wallace was struck once in the heart, causing him to stagger into a nearby law office where he collapsed on a chair and died. Lombardo's men chased Barney Walsh down to the second floor landing while shooting in midstride. Their bullets hit their mark, and Walsh crumbled to the floor, his lifeless face pressed against the worn tile. Timothy Coffey, the third member of the Gustin Gang, escaped to an office down the hall, where he hid quivering until police arrived.

Joe Lombardo went on the lam for over a week before turning himself in at Boston police headquarters on New Year's Eve. He respectfully declined to discuss his whereabouts on the day of the shootings and was held on probable cause along with two other men, Salvatore Congemi and Frank Cucchiara, both of the North End. The charges were quickly dropped, however, after Timothy Coffey refused to testify before a grand jury.

The explosively bold ambush elevated Lombardo's reputation in the Boston underworld, which was largely fractionalized at the time. The Gustins had been top dog up until that point, but their position had been precarious at best. The Mafia had accumulated power in the North End, and that power began slowly to grow. Lombardo may have been second in command to the older Buccola in the eyes of local cops and the public, but he was certainly the power behind the throne. Lombardo was the fist inside Buccola's velvet glove.

Felippo "Phil" Buccola had immigrated to the United States from Palermo, Sicily, in 1920. He was an unlikely Mafia don from the very beginning. Born into a respected, wealthy family, Buccola was a highly educated world traveler. He attended school in Switzerland and the Universita degli Studi in his home city of Palermo before he was ordered by the Sicilian Mafia to Boston to organize underworld activities in the North End.

Buccola was no Edward G. Robinson, and he certainly did not look the part of mob boss. With his bow ties and rimless glasses, Buccola dressed and carried himself like something of a college professor. He was a self-described "sportsman" who managed a stable of hungry prize fighters in and around the city. Buccola had also been anointed as leader of the New England Mafia in 1932 by Charles "Lucky" Luciano's mob commission in New York.

With the Gustin Gang no longer a threat, Buccola and Lombardo set their sights on another local mob rival, Charles "King" Solomon, a Jewish gangster, bootlegger, and narcotics trafficker who, like Buccola, also managed local boxers. Solomon was the Boston equivalent to Dutch Schultz. Like the Dutchman, "King" Solomon was brash and flashy. He was one of the most powerful Jewish mobsters in the country and arguably the most important bootlegger in Boston. Solomon was also an original member of the Seven Group, a precursor to Luciano's Commission. The Seven Group, which included Luciano, Meyer Lansky, and Frank Costello, gathered in Atlantic City in May of 1929 to add organizational structure to crime syndicates around the U.S. "King" Solomon literally helped organize organized crime. He was head of the dope racket and also ruled the Boston nightclub scene, where he operated several of his own including the Coconut Grove, scene of one of the deadliest fires in American history where, in 1942, 492 people were killed and hundreds more were injured. Solomon's own demise had come nine years earlier inside another one of his nightclubs, the Cotton Club in the South End. The year was 1933 and Solomon had recently been indicted with three others on bootlegging charges. Running dope and pimping girls turned a nice profit, but booze smuggling was far and away the biggest cash cow during Prohibition. Authorities estimated that at least five thousand bootleggers operated in the Boston area alone, servicing about four thousand speakeasies. The annual spend for bootleg booze in Massachusetts was said to be a whopping $60 million per year.

The impending bootlegging trial was a major cause for concern for Solomon's gangland associates, including Buccola and Lombardo, as well as for Joseph P. Kennedy; all wondered whether the King would give up his partners in hope of striking a deal with the feds. On January 24, 1933, four Irish hoods followed Solomon from his table into the washroom at the Cotton Club and opened fire. Solomon was shot three times and stumbled out of the bathroom clutching his bleeding gut. He was rushed to City Hospital where, on his death bed, Solomon performed a final soliloquy straight out of a gangster movie. When questioned by detectives, the King wouldn't give any up any names. Instead, with his final breaths, he damned "the dirty rats" who had shot him.

Those "rats" included James "Skeets" Coyne and John Burke, a couple of Irish "pug uglies" with no direct gang affiliation. Coyne was captured in Indiana one year later. He and his accomplices claimed they had targeted Solomon because he was known to carry a fat bank roll. "Skeets" Coyne was sent to prison for manslaughter, while the other gunmen were all acquitted on murder and robbery charges.

Virtually no one believed Coyne's account of the shooting, and over the decades there has been widespread speculation about who directly ordered the hit on Solomon. Buccola and Lombardo are as likely as anyone to have orchestrated the murder. Both had much to lose and so much to gain with their Jewish rival out of the picture.

With Buccola's status as Godfather of Boston, the Sicilian native gained the attention of the federal authorities despite his attempts to stay above the criminal fray. The boss was rarely seen in the North End, choosing instead to live in nearby Newton, a predominantly Jewish suburb that was a short distance but a world away from Hanover Street. Buccola lived in an apartment with his Irish wife, Rose Hogan, and their live-in maid. Joe Lombardo also chose to live outside of Boston's gangster hemisphere. Although he spent much of his time at his North End importing company headquarters, Lombardo lived twenty miles away in the leafy town of Framingham, where he ran a horse stable and was considered a pillar of the community. He was known to dress in understated light gray suits, and his neighbors had little or no idea of the power Lombardo wielded in the back rooms, smoky bars, and dark alleys of Boston. The only hint of his membership in the mob was the pearl gray sapphire ring he flashed on his finger.

"Lombardo was the Mr. Big of the mob,"[12] recalled criminal associate Vincent Teresa. "There was no doubt of what he was when you saw him with others. Everyone bowed down to him—treated him with respect. Whether you were a boss in Rhode Island or in Springfield or in a section of Boston, you went to Mr. Lombardo for a decision. If he said no, that was it—there were no further arguments." In contemporary parlance, Lombardo was to Buccola what Dick Cheney was to George W. Bush. Lombardo was happy to stay in the background, where the heat brought by law enforcement was less intense. His official title was *Consigliere*, but it was Buccola who followed Lombardo's orders, even when it meant taking control over the rackets in Providence where Frank "Butsey" Morelli had recently announced his "retirement."

Buccola wasn't cut out for the expanded role. Running gambling operations and resolving territory disputes in two states proved too much for the patrician from Palermo. With investigators from the Kefauver Committee hot on his trail, Buccola fled with his wife to his native Sicily, where he had built a six-room villa just after World War II. Buccola lived there in semiretirement, conferring every so often with Lucky Luciano about mob related matters back in the United States. For the most part, though, Buccola lived out his remaining years in complete content, working as a chicken farmer with birds he had imported from New Hampshire.

Buccola's graceful exit was not seen as an affront to the Mafia, either in New England or in New York. Instead they welcomed it. New England's Mafia was in dire need of strong leadership. Joe Lombardo's strength had come in his ability to remain in the shadows. Thus there was no real structure to organized crime in New England. It was every gang or organization for itself, with the Italians exerting the most influence. What the mob needed was a hammer. That hammer would be swung when, in 1954, Lombardo and other high-ranking Mafia leaders chose Raymond L. S. Patriarca as Phil Buccola's successor.

Tonight there's gonna be a jailbreak
somewhere in this town.
○ THIN LIZZY

Wild Thing

On New Year's Eve, 1949, Joe Barboza was arrested for the break-ins he had committed in New Bedford as leader of the Cream Pie Bandits. He was now seventeen and considered too old for the Lyman School, and too young for state prison, so the judge sentenced him to five years and one day at the Massachusetts Reformatory in Concord. Opened in 1884, the institution had been established as a school where males under the age of thirty could learn a trade that would be useful upon their re-entry into the community. The jail had seen its share of tough and crafty prisoners, including a red-haired African American drug dealer who would later change his name from Malcolm Little to Malcolm X. Barboza entered the prison on February 9, 1950, the same day that Wisconsin senator Joe McCarthy made headlines around the world, in a speech given to a women's club in West Virginia, by claiming that the U.S. State Department was infiltrated with communists.

At this stage in his life, Barboza was no doubt more comfortable under guard than he was on the streets. Prison was home to him. He understood the culture, and he understood what it took to survive. He was first put to work in the weaving mill but asked to be transferred to the cafeteria, where he wanted to learn to be a cook. Barboza's new assignment did not last long. He quickly picked a fight with an older inmate, one with a fearsome reputation, and laid the guy out with a ferocious punch, breaking the man's jaw in two places. Barboza was immediately tossed into solitary confinement for nine days. Once he was let out, the guards ordered him down to the boiler room, where he was assigned to shovel coal. The punishment was worth it. He had accomplished his first goal. Barboza was now the alpha dog. He knew that if he took down the toughest guy in jail, the others would fear him. He was right. Shoveling coal might have sounded like back-breaking work to some prisoners, but

Barboza welcomed it. He treated the penalty like a reward, using the work to build up his muscular arms and thick, sturdy legs.

Eventually, his jailers believed that there was more than just a sliver of hope that the young tough from New Bedford could be rehabilitated. A year after his incarceration at Concord, he was shipped off to the Norfolk Prison Colony, considered at the time to be a "model prison community." Once again, Barboza was following in the steps of the future Malcolm X, who had served as a member of the Norfolk Debating Society while incarcerated there. Joe, now eighteen, had no interest in joining the debate team, glee club, or any other jailhouse extracurricular activity. The prison did, however, have a boxing ring where he could continue his training. Joe wanted to best his father in every way—from the amount of money he earned to the number of wins in the ring. Joe's hatred of his father continued to fuel his fire behind bars. He trained as a middleweight, routinely thumping fellow prisoners who were oftentimes older and heavier than he. Sparring sessions and ring work kept him in superior physical condition and kept his brain sharp. Yet once he stepped foot outside the gym, the monotony of prison life weighed heavily.

To escape boredom, Barboza spent his days looking for new ways to get high. Normally a buzz would mellow out a prisoner, which is why guards often turned a blind eye to the use of drugs. But chemicals had the opposite effect on Barboza. When he got high—he got even meaner. Not only did Barboza set out to dominate his fellow prisoners, he sought to dominate his jailers as well. One night after sniffing paint thinner, Joe led a prison revolt and challenged the guards to a brawl. Joe waited in his cell with pupils dilated, throwing lightning quick combinations and howling at the moon. He challenged the guards to come in after him. One, two, three at a time—Barboza called on all the guards as he spewed obscenity-laced insults about their mothers, wives, and girlfriends. The guards had seen the kind of violence Barboza was capable of inside the ring, and no guard was crazy enough to go near him. Instead, the warden negotiated peace terms during a tense two-hour stalemate. Once his buzz wore off, Joe gave himself up without a struggle, smiling at his jailers as they handcuffed him and led him off to solitary. The stunt proved one thing to prison administrators—Joe Barboza was "beyond rehabilitation." He was transferred back to Concord to serve out the remainder of his sentence.

Joe continued boxing upon his return to Concord Reformatory. He also began lifting weights and adding muscle to his stocky frame. His arms grew wider and his neck got thicker. Eventually he climbed weight classes from middleweight to light heavyweight. Barboza did not surrender any of this explosive power with the extra weight. He proved this by claiming the prison boxing championship with a win over a tough thug named Walter "Rocky" Stone. Unlike his constant taunting of guards at the Norfolk Prison Colony, Joe got along well with his jailers at Concord — so well that he convinced one guard to sneak in drugs, booze, food, and even knives that Joe would sell to his fellow inmates.

Still, Barboza was far from a model prisoner. He was all too happy to join in on a prison riot despite promises from the warden for preferential treatment if he wouldn't act out. Once again Barboza was tossed into solitary confinement, this time for thirty days. He was given only bread and water, and Joe feared the dietary restriction would shrink his growing muscles. Once out of solitary, Barboza was sent to work on the prison farm, where he would be isolated from the rest of the prison population. For Joe, it was a vacation. He would peel off his prison clothes and swim naked in an adjacent water reservoir and would steal chickens from the henhouse to fry up in the prison kitchen. Like his counterpart at Norfolk, the Concord warden was constantly playing a game of "Let's make a deal" with Joe. The warden promised that he would shave time off Barboza's sentence if he would cause no further trouble. But Joe did not follow through. One night, while he and a few inmates were drinking smuggled booze in the boiler room, Barboza convinced some fellow prisoners to escape. They easily overpowered the guards, tied them up, and stole a car. A drunken Barboza howled and growled as the escapees laughingly made their getaway down Route 2 West, headed for Boston. The frivolity ended a short time later when the car they had stolen broke down. The prisoners abandoned the vehicle and stole another after Joe slugged its driver. The brazen jailbreak lasted only one day, and Barboza was picked up by police in Revere — the mob-controlled city where he would later earn his reputation as a stone-cold killer. While he was getting processed, Joe punched out a photographer who tried to take his picture. This would eventually become a normal occurrence; he routinely threatened to kill anyone who tried to snap a Polaroid of him, whether in court or on the street.

Barboza was brought back to Concord and placed into solitary confinement once more. A guard whom Joe had tied up during his escape paid him a visit in solitary. The guard, clearly embarrassed by the episode, cussed Barboza for making him look like a fool. It was a fool's move. Barboza was unshackled. He grabbed the leg of a wooden table, lifted it high over his head, and brought it crashing down on the jailer's skull. Barboza continued to beat him with the table until six guards rushed into the cell and hogtied the prisoner.

The warden now realized that his prison was too small and his men too inexperienced to control such a madman. Joe Barboza was sent immediately to the Charlestown State Prison just outside Boston and given a new sentence of ten to twelve years. Called the Old Gray Monster, the Charlestown State Prison was considered escape proof. Inmates ate their meals in damp, dark cells with no plumbing. Coal dust blowing in from a nearby railroad yard made breathing nearly impossible for prisoners and guards alike. Built in 1805 on the grounds that now house Bunker Hill Community College, the Charlestown State Prison was once called "a verminous pesthole unfit for human habitation" by *Time* magazine.

It was the worst possible place for Joe Barboza, yet it was the best possible place. Joe was no longer surrounded by petty criminals and hoods; Charlestown State Prison was the home away from home for many of the area's most notorious mobsters. Throughout his young life, Barboza had idolized these gangsters much as a kid would look up to his favorite baseball player. Joe's ultimate goal was to be the first Portuguese inducted in the Mafia.

And Barboza could be as cunning as he was vicious. According to a prison psychiatrist, he had a higher than average IQ and could persuade people to do just about anything. "His features make him look less bright than he actually is," the psychiatrist wrote. "His IQ is of the order of 90–100 and he has the intellectual ability to do well in a moderately skilled profession." The psychiatrist also wrote that Barboza had a "sociopathic personality disturbance and there is a great possibility for further antisocial behavior in the future."

Barboza's incarceration at Charlestown was short lived, however, thanks to an audacious prisoner revolt that would lead to an eighty-two-hour stand-off with authorities (the second-longest prison siege in U.S.

history at the time). This time, Joe Barboza was merely a spectator. Just a few months after Barboza's arrival, four armed prisoners held six fellow inmates and five guards hostage in the segregated section of the prison known as Cherry Hill (where the worst criminals were housed). Using smuggled hacksaw blades, the inmates sawed their way through the one-inch bars of their solitary cells and captured their guards. They then used blocks of wood, rope, and other items to construct a makeshift ladder that proved too short and too weak to support their weight. These were desperate men making a desperate attempt at freedom. All were serving life sentences, or close to it. There was a former paratrooper in the group, as well as a cop killer and a violent rapist. The would-be escapees began digging a tunnel through the prison's concrete floor but were turned back when water came rushing through the hole. They quickly demanded a getaway car and delivered an ominous threat to the warden.

"One shot, one gas bomb, and all five of your screws [guards] die!" shouted hostage taker Teddy Green, who was serving a forty-five- to fifty-two-year sentence for bank robbery and was also considered a major suspect in the Great Brink's Robbery.[13]

"If one of those guards dies, you'll all die in the electric chair!" promised Massachusetts attorney general George Fingold over the prison's public-address system.

The siege was eventually put down with the help of an army of state troopers and an armored tank. The stand-off dominated the news, and the publicity surrounding it led many critics to call for widespread reform. The old prison was finally shuttered, and all inmates were transported to the state's newest prison, in the town of Walpole.

Once there Joe concentrated on winning his own freedom — the right way. During an inmate evaluation prior to Joe's appearance before the parole board, a psychiatrist described Barboza this way: "He is a 26 year-old man serving a 10 to 12 year sentence for a series of offenses occurring on and after an escape from Concord in 1954. A review of his record reveals that he has had a difficulty with the law since the age of 10 and has been either at Lyman School or in correctional institutions since then. His behavior has been poor. He (Barboza) has a 6th grade education . . . however he has conformed better since 1956. During the present interview he is pleasant, answers questions relevantly and coherently, is in good contact and shows no evidence of mental disease. He states that he has learned a few things; that he is grown up and realizes that his previous behavior was childish."

The days and hours ticked away, and Barboza was finally paroled from prison in June of 1958. He was met at the prison gates by his brother, Donald, who drove him back to their New Bedford home. But this time Joe would not be returning home alone. He had a girlfriend that he was intent on marrying. The woman's name was Philomena "Fay" Termini, and she was sixteen years older than Joe. Barboza never explained how they had met, only that she had been writing him in prison. Termini, a divorcee with four children, owned property in East Boston, but, more important in Joe's eyes, she was Sicilian.

Barboza had done his research behind bars. He knew the Mafia inducted new members only if they were of Sicilian heritage and if they were willing to kill. Joe would have no problem accomplishing the latter, and he felt that he had found a loophole in the former requirement. If he married a Sicilian woman, Barboza believed the Mafia just might be willing to overlook the fact that he was not Italian himself.

Upon his release from prison, Joe worked briefly on the docks in New Bedford, where he unloaded fishing boats of their daily catch. The menial labor and the overpowering stench of the wharf quickly reminded him why he had sworn off such work. He immediately quit his job, packed his suitcase, and headed north to reunite with his soon-to-be bride Fay in East Boston. Barboza was hell-bent on making a go of it as a prize fighter. He had dominated his foes in prison, and he believed strongly that his jailhouse opponents were much tougher than anyone he would face on the outside. In August 1958, Joe walked into a sweaty gym on Hawthorne Street in Chelsea and urged boxing manager Johnny Dunn to take him on. The veteran manager sized up the young tough from New Bedford and decided to give him a shot. Barboza fought four times during the months of August and September 1958. He won three out of four fights, all by knockout. Barboza was paid $30 for each match but needed extra money to support his training, along with his new wife and her four kids. He couldn't find a decent job, as no respectable businessman would take a shot on a former convict like him. Barboza voiced his frustration and his intentions to his older brother, Donald.

"No one's gonna hire me because of my past," Joe confided. "It means I gotta do the only thing I know how to do."

Joe did not tell his brother what that was. He didn't have to. In September 1958, just three months after getting paroled from prison, Barboza was arrested while trying to break into a house. Joe pleaded his innocence to the arresting cops, but the burglary tools in his possession told them all they needed to know. He was given a three- to five-year sentence and sent back to Walpole State Prison. Joe had recently applied for a boxing license through the Massachusetts State Boxing Commission but was shipped off to jail before he could obtain it.

Once back in prison, the Walpole warden again offered Barboza a deal of easy work outside the prison walls if he behaved himself. Joe accepted the offer but because of his violent nature could not deliver. A few weeks into his sentence he attacked a fellow inmate while both were working in the prison cafeteria. The prisoner, a guy named Eddie Kilrow, had made the grave mistake of giving Barboza lip. Joe returned Kilrow's wise-ass comments with a knockout punch. Another inmate tried to revive Kilrow with a bucket of water poured over his face, but the man did not move.

"He looks dead," the inmate whispered to Barboza.[14]

Guards loaded the unconscious Kilrow onto a stretcher and brought him to a hospital where he was given a spinal tap. The man could not move his arms or legs. Kilrow remained paralyzed for two days before he snapped out of it. However, the effects of the severe concussion he was given at the hands of Joe Barboza would last much longer.

Barboza was never fingered for the beating, but everyone, inmates and jailers alike, knew exactly what he had done. Although the warden fully suspected that Barboza had turned his back on their deal, he still followed through on his side of the bargain and allowed Joe to work outside the prison walls. No doubt he felt that Barboza would do less damage if he were given some semblance of freedom. And freedom he got. While working outside the walls at Walpole, Joe would sneak into the woods and drive off for hours at a time with friends. They'd give Joe a sports coat to wear over his prison uniform and then whisk him away to local restaurants or to go fishing or swimming. The Animal was caged, but that cage had been left open by cooperative guards who were willing to look the other way if the price were right. Barboza always promised to come back, and surprisingly he always did. He was paroled again in 1960. By that time he had built up a lucrative business inside prison walls through bookmaking and loansharking. He had also allied himself with another equally ferocious prisoner: a cherubic psychopath named Vincent "Jimmy the Bear" Flemmi.

Like a blind man's first see,
This conspiracy cuts deep
○ SOULFLY

5

Top Echelon

It had now been two full years since Bobby Kennedy was verbally skewered by Raymond Patriarca during the McClellan Hearings, but the newly appointed attorney general of the United States treated the insult like a festering wound and deemed that the only remedy was amputation. Kennedy had already issued a letter to Internal Revenue commissioner Mortimer M. Caplan targeting the New England Mafia boss for investigation and prosecution by adding his name to a list of thirty-nine top-echelon racketeers in the nation. Much had happened to Kennedy since he had first tangled with Patriarca in the winter of 1958. He was no longer the bootlegger's son; now Kennedy was America's top law enforcement official and brother to the sitting president of the United States.

Kennedy had the power he needed, at least in his mind, to take the Mafia down once and for all. FBI director J. Edgar Hoover had been reluctantly dragged into the fight by Kennedy, and by the mere fact that Hoover could no longer sell his idea that the Mafia did not exist. "No single individual or coalition of racketeers dominates organized crime across the country," Hoover had long claimed. But while the director had his agents searching for communist sympathizers under the beds of virtually every home in America, Mafia leaders were tightening their grip on labor unions, the construction and garment industries, and of course gambling, prostitution, and racketeering. Hoover could deny reality no longer, thanks to the sharp eye of New York State Police sergeant Edgar L. Croswell, who, on November 14, 1957, noticed a fleet of black cars driving in a convoy through the small town of Appalachin. Croswell had a good idea where the convoy was headed. Joseph Barbara, a shadowy figure who had been arrested twice for murder, had purchased a fifty-three-acre estate in the small village cradling the Susquehanna River. Croswell decided to set up a roadblock and called for three local deputies for backup. When word traveled to Joseph Barbara's home, the gathered Mafiosi scrambled to escape, fleeing through the woods or in their cars. Edgar Croswell and his men were able to identify sixty-three men with ties to organized crime, including heavy hitters like Vito Genovese, Carlo Gambino, and Joseph Profaci. Despite hard evidence of the existence of organized crime, it would take J. Edgar Hoover another four years to face this major problem head on.

In a memo sent out to all special agents in charge of field offices around the country on March 1, 1961, the FBI dictated that,

> through well-placed informants we must infiltrate organized crime groups to the same degree that we have been able to penetrate the Communist Party and other subversive organizations. Today the press, television and radio along with the express interests of the Administration keep this phase of criminal activity in a position of prominence in the public eye. Certainly we cannot relax even momentarily our efforts in combating the criminal underworld including the prosecution of Top Hoodlums. The foundation from which we forge our attack must be kept strong and fresh with a full flow of information from well placed informants. All agents in conducting investigations of criminal matters should be constantly alert for the development of new informants and new potential informants who may be in a position to assist us.[15]

J. Edgar Hoover supplied words, but what Bobby Kennedy wanted was action. A month after the memo was issued, the attorney general called a meeting in his office with his deputies, along with his friend and longtime mob investigator Walter Sheridan, and Edward Silberling, head of the Justice Department's Organized Crime and Racketeering Section. Kennedy paced back and forth across the room angrily demanding that more needed to be done to put mob leaders like Raymond Patriarca and others behind bars. Kennedy's deputy attorney general, Byron White, a future justice on the U.S. Supreme Court, pleaded with his boss for a more methodical approach and warned against acting too quickly without enough information. Upon hearing this Kennedy hit the roof. He blasted his team and demanded that they be more aggressive on organized crime. The attorney general threatened his staffers that they had one month to produce results or else he would take other action to get the job done.

Bobby Kennedy's staff no doubt leaned heavily on the FBI, which finally inaugurated its Top Echelon Criminal Informant Program on June 21, 1961. The Federal Bureau of Investigation outlined the program as follows: "Criminal Informants — Criminal Intelligence Program: It is now urgently necessary to develop particularly qualified, live sources within the upper echelon of the organized Hoodlum element who will be capable of furnishing the quality information required."

FBI director J. Edgar Hoover also pointed out that the "most significant information developed to date indicates organization among the nation's hoodlum leaders." Hoover claimed that this information had been obtained from highly confidential sources in Chicago, New York, Philadelphia, and Newark, New Jersey. The intelligence also suggested that a nine- or twelve-member commission controlled all major criminal activities in the United States. The memo listed several alleged Mafia bosses, including Vito Genovese, Thomas Luchese, Carlo Gambino, Joseph Bonnano, Joseph Profaci, and Sam Giancana. In addition, the memo named Raymond Patriarca as "Top Boston Hoodlum," and identified Joseph Zerilli, John LaRocca, Steve Magaddino, Joseph Ida, and Angelo Bruno as the bosses of Detroit, Pittsburgh, Buffalo, Newark, and Philadelphia, respectively. The feds had also determined (according to a New York source) that Carlo Gambino was the current head of the commission, a position he occupied while Vito Genovese remained in prison. Sources called commission members *avugat*, which is short for the Italian word *avvocato*, which means "lawyer."

The FBI memo broke down the Mafia hierarchy identifying the boss and underbosses of small cities, while large cities like New York had as many as six *Caporegimes*, or lieutenants. The Top Echelon Criminal Informant Program stressed quality criminal informants above all else, and that the program be implemented immediately and greatly expanded. The program also outlined likely personal reasons for informants to turn against the mob, which included concern over possible prosecution of children, wives, or girlfriends, or relief from pressure being exerted by associates or rivals. The feds wanted their agents to identify a gangster's pain points and do their best to exploit them. The program also stressed the need to protect those who did come forward. "You should ensure that no dissemination is made of information obtained from such sources unless informant is fully protected," the FBI memo urged agents.

With more than a subtle nudge from Bobby Kennedy's Justice Department, the FBI finally appeared ready to take a "gloves off" approach to organized crime. The memo went on to read: This program presents a definite new challenge to the field which to be met calls for new and untried methods and situations may arise which will be evaluated by the Bureau based upon the realization of the need for unusual and extreme methods.

The bureau instructed all offices to designate a squad of special agents to participate in the program. According to the memo, those agents must have demonstrated ability in the field, be mature, aggressive, and resourceful, and possess a keen knowledge of criminal activities in their area. How should a special agent approach a possible mob informant? The bureau suggested that its men conduct background checks of known mob associates that included marital and sexual status, hobbies, and financial affairs. The bureau also would authorize substantial remuneration for informants who provided information on hoodlums of national stature. Another lever worth pulling, according to the memo, was identifying and cultivating compromising positions. "Threats of prosecution and deportation could be one of the most effective methods used against older top echelon hoodlums," the directive stated. In the nine-page FBI memo outlining its Top Echelon Criminal Informant Program, the words "quality criminal intelligence informants" were underlined six times to stress their significance. The battle had now been joined, and the FBI was willing to match methods used by an enemy that did not play by the rules.

With the FBI's new program came new power. Later in 1961, and at the urging of U.S. attorney general Kennedy, Congress passed the Interstate Travel in Aid of Racketeering Statute (ITAR), which shifted many of the mob's criminal enterprises, such as gambling and extortion, under the jurisdiction of the FBI.

While efforts to develop Mafia turncoats were ongoing, the FBI hit pay dirt in March of 1962, when agents first installed electronic microphone surveillance inside Raymond Patriarca's office at the Coin-O-Matic Distributing Company at 168 Atwells Avenue in Providence. The operation was conducted under the supervision of FBI special agent John Kehoe, Jr., out of the bureau's Boston office. Logs and tape recordings of conversations inside Patriarca's office were hand delivered each day to Kehoe, who would dissect and break down the information. Kehoe was employing a practice that had first been used by the FBI's Intelligence Division to hunt communists in the late 1950s. Under the cover of national security, Hoover's men broke into the homes and businesses of suspected Soviet sympathizers to tap telephones and plant listening devices, which they monitored from safe houses nearby. Electronic surveillance — or ELSUR — could very well have been deemed illegal by civil libertarians. The feds called the practice "extralegal." Still, agents deployed on the bugging jobs were ordered to leave their FBI badges and other identification at home. If they happened to get picked up by local police, the FBI would invoke plausible deniability of the agents' activities.

Questions of law were of little concern for J. Edgar Hoover. Despite his initial reluctance to take on the mob, or even confirm its very existence, Hoover was downright giddy over the prospect of destroying the New England Mafia through Raymond Patriarca's own words. Hoover quickly shot off a memo to the special agent in charge (SAC) of the Boston office, praising him for "the wealth of worthwhile information" obtained through the use of the hidden microphone and authorizing the Boston SAC "to give immediate consideration to submitting recommendations for incentive awards and commendations for the (FBI) personnel responsible for the success of this matter." The FBI director sent another memo just two months later, authorizing that the wiretapping of Patriarca's office be extended for another four months, because it "has shown that Patriarca exerts real control over the racketeers and racketeering activities in Rhode Island and Massachusetts." Hoover went on to state that the FBI's gypsy wire provided further evidence to strongly suggest that Patriarca was a member of the commission, the Mafia's governing body. All memos were kept confidential, as Hoover and the FBI made a concerted effort, at least publicly, to ascribe the successful collection of information about Patriarca to a human source. The feds had even given the Patriarca wiretap its own informant identification number — BS 837C*.

Because of his distrust of Director J. Edgar Hoover, Bobby Kennedy made sure the FBI was not the only law enforcement agency targeting Patriarca. The IRS and U.S. marshals were also keeping a close eye on the

Man. The marshals had set up shop in a two-story apartment building across the street from Patriarca's office. They took countless rolls of film of the comings and goings of various Mafia soldiers and mob associates. Most of the gangsters drove cars with borrowed license plates. Marshals would then track down the real owners of the plates and lean on them for information regarding their underworld friends. The operation worked for a while, until one of Patriarca's spotters looked up at the building and noticed the sun reflecting from a camera lens. The gangsters charged into the building, only to be met by the shiny badges of the U.S. Marshals Service. A young marshal named John Partington got the opportunity to meet Raymond Patriarca face to face while serving him a subpoena. Partington, who would later play a major role in Joe Barboza's life, was at that time an army veteran and former police patrolman in his hometown of Cumberland, Rhode Island, who had been working for the U.S. Marshals Service for only a short time. In his 2010 memoir, *The Mob and Me*, Partington described the 1962 meeting with Patriarca: "No sooner had I crossed the doorstep than two "made men" intercepted me," he wrote. "Raymond Patriarca was eating a slice of pizza and peered around the corner to see who the intruder was. As I reached for my badge inside my coat pocket, Patriarca dove back into his office, dropping the pizza on the floor. His bodyguards pinned me against the wall. They thought I was going to assassinate him."[16]

Partington quickly identified himself as one of the bodyguards checked his identification. The Mafia boss then emerged from the back room and accepted the subpoena with great disdain.

"Anytime you want me, kid, I'm here," Patriarca told Partington. "Don't ever go to my house on Lancaster Street since I don't want my wife upset, *capise?*"[17]

At this point, Partington had no idea that the FBI had bugged Patriarca's office. After Partington's visit, Patriarca was captured on tape complaining to his attorney. "A goddamned boy scout just left after serving me papers," he shouted into the telephone.

Patriarca had always been conscious of the overwhelming burden his reputation had brought on his family. He had once sued the *Providence Journal-Bulletin* for libel, and had even gone to the lengths of paying for a large advertisement to criticize the newspaper's coverage of him.

Since my release from prison in 1944 after completion of a sentence for a crime committed in 1938 when I was thirty years of age, my time has been continuously and assiduously employed in honest endeavors. The tranquility of my family has many times and oft been rudely disturbed by the rehashing of my criminal record in your news columns. I, more than you, deplore that record. How bitterly I realize the truth of a great poet's words: "The evil that men do lives after them; the good is often interred in their bones." Your newspapers seem to take a fiendish delight in their unwarranted and unjustifiable characterizations of me . . . what can I, with my criminal record expect from a newspaper which often has paraded in its obituary columns the peccadilloes of many former decent Rhode Island citizens.[18]

The FBI quickly expanded its investigation of Patriarca to include other members of his inner circle, including his underboss Henry Tameleo, and the man who had bought his way into the Mafia—Gennaro "Jerry" Angiulo.

Jerry Angiulo was born on March 20, 1919, on Prince Street in Boston's North End, just three months after a freak disaster that nearly destroyed the entire neighborhood when a massive fifty-foot-tall tank, holding 2.5 million gallons of molasses (to be distilled into rum or industrial alcohol), exploded on nearby Commercial Street. Stunned witnesses were first alerted by the sound of steel bolts firing off the tank like machine gun bullets. Large sections of the tank's thick metal siding came flying off next, the shrapnel raining down on a nearby elevated train track, buckling its steel supports just seconds after a car packed with passengers had passed by. A short time later, an enormous wall of molasses poured into the streets. Moving at a speed of thirty-five miles per hour and two stories high, the syrupy tsunami oozed its way through the neighborhood, devouring everything in its path. Twenty-one people were killed, including two children—a boy and a girl. The boy, ten-year-old Pasquale Iantosca, was swallowed up by the sticky flood while gathering firewood for his family around the base of the tank. Some 150 people were injured in the spill, which many believe was caused by a spike in temperature. Somehow, Caeser and Giovannina Angiulo and their three-year-old son, Nicolo, survived the disaster unscathed. A second son, Gennaro, would be born as winter changed slowly to spring, with the nauseatingly sweet smell of molasses still overpowering the ravaged neighborhood.

Caeser and Giovannina "Jennie" Angiulo ran a grocery on Prince Street. The place was a neighborhood hotspot, serving up steamed hot dogs, candy, and soda to neighborhood kids and adults alike. But despite the grocery's popularity, money was tight in the Angiulo household. Jerry's mother padded the family finances with her amazing skills as a card player, gin rummy being her game of choice. Angry at first at his mother, young Jerry soon changed his view when it came to gambling. Like Jennie, Jerry Angiulo saw gambling, just short of robbery, as the easiest way to separate suckers from their cash. Jerry had an affinity for numbers, which gave him an inner strength and confidence that belied his short and scrawny appearance. He knew that he would not make a name for himself with his fists, like many of his rugged neighborhood pals. After all, a powerful left hook could take you only so far. Instead Angiulo exercised his mind, scoring high marks in grade school and then at Boston English High School. He also had a quick wit and would undress any potential tormenter with a few biting remarks. Angiulo was a natural born debater and always appeared eager to engage both students and teachers alike. When it came time to write his life's ambition in his high school yearbook, Angiulo announced that he intended one day to become a criminal lawyer. He would eventually become well versed in criminal law, but not the way he had intended.

Following his high school graduation in 1936, Angiulo toiled around the North End, working in his family's grocery store until the outbreak of World War II, when he and millions of America's young men enlisted to fight for their country and take revenge on the Japanese following the attack on Pearl Harbor. Flat footed, Angiulo was originally rejected by the U.S. military, but the crafty son of the North End enlisted again using a different middle name. This minor switcheroo was enough to do the trick, and he was allowed to join the U.S. Navy, where he served four years, eventually achieving the rank of chief boatswain's mate. Angiulo found himself in the heat of battle on several occasions as he steered landing craft packed with brave yet terrified troops during the bloody island-hopping campaign in the Pacific.

The horrors of war tested Angiulo's mettle and no doubt gave him a steely eyed reserve that would serve him later in life. Nothing he would ever see on the streets could compare to what he had witnessed in battle. After receiving an honorable discharge in 1946, Jerry Angiulo returned home to Boston, where he drove a fruit truck and spent late nights talking with his three brothers, Donato, Frank, and Michele, about ways to get their hands on some big money.

The rackets were the key. This Jerry knew all too well. He approached Nicola Giso, one of Joe Lombardo's racket operators, and asked for a job. Giso cut the kid a break and gave him a job taking bets in Joe Lombardo's "horse room." Soon Angiulo was making big money and bigger plans. Eventually he approached Lombardo himself with an attractive proposition. Lombardo had been feeling the heat from Senator Estes Kefauver's dogged federal investigators. The glare was so bright that Lombardo was forced to shutter all mob-controlled gambling operations in Boston. Angiulo convinced Lombardo to allow him to resurrect the gambling parlors while offering him a slice of the pie. It was a low-risk, high-reward proposition for the Boston boss. Angiulo would divert the attention of Kefauver's federal investigation away from Lombardo, while still providing him a seat on the money train that continued to roll and rumble through virtually every street and back alley of the city.

Angiulo soon realized that despite Joe Lombardo's business acumen, the boss had run what was really just a small-time numbers racket, one that his protege would soon expand to include dog and horse racing. Eventually, Jerry and his brothers would employee about fifty office workers to handle the exploding growth of their gambling enterprise.

Despite his new-found wealth, Jerry Angiulo still had one major problem. He was an independent operator — not a made member of the Mafia. Thus his gambling joints were often targeted for mob shakedowns. Mobsters would walk into Angiulo owned clubs like the Monte Cristo and demand that Jerry hand over a couple grand as a "tribute." Angiulo would grudgingly pay, only to entice the gangsters to come back for more. When Angiulo drew a line in the sand and refused to pay more, he would get slapped around until he came up with the rest of the cash.

This was humiliating for the proud bookie, and it was also cutting into his hard-earned profits. The scrawny Angiulo knew that he was no physical match for the muscle-bound neighborhood mobsters, but what he lacked in size he more than made up for in intellect. Jerry Angiulo was the ultimate criminal tactician. After getting fleeced once again by some North End toughs, Angiulo sat his brothers down at the Monte Cristo and came up with what he thought was a bullet-proof plan.

Armed only with an envelope stuffed with cash, Angiulo drove down to Providence in hopes of making New England's Mafia Godfather an offer he couldn't refuse. The crafty Boston bookmaker arrived at Raymond Patriarca's headquarters unannounced and asked for a meeting with the Man. After presenting his bona fides and being subjected to a serious pat-down, Angiulo was allowed an audience with the most powerful mobster in the region. The two men had never met before, and Angiulo made sure to keep his confidence and cockiness in check. At this point, he needed Raymond Patriarca much more than Patriarca needed him.

Angiulo spent several minutes explaining his situation—the shake-downs and the overall lack of respect he had been subjected to back in his hometown. Patriarca was better versed than Anguilo realized, as he himself was the one who most likely gave mob soldiers like Ilario "Larry Baione" Zannino carte blanche to bust up Jerry's place.

"If you don't like it, why don't you fight them?" Patriarca asked Angiulo.[19]

Angiulo placed the envelope, containing $50,000, in Patriarca's hand. He then promised to pay the Mafia boss at least twice that amount each year. In return, Angiulo asked that he not only be allowed to operate his businesses in peace, but that he be granted the privilege of running the city of Boston on Patriarca's behalf. The Man accepted Angiulo's lucrative offer and ordered the shakedowns to stop. "Angiulo's with me now," Patriarca announced.

At this point Jerry Angiulo had become an anomaly in the annals of organized crime. Patriarca soon brought his junior partner to New York for a lunchtime meeting with national crime boss Vito Genovese, where he was inducted as a fully fledged member of *La Cosa Nostra* without ever having to fire a shot. Jerry Angiulo made his bones not with a gun, a knife, or a garrote; instead he was allowed entry into the Mafia's dark world by simply preying on the insatiable greed of Raymond Patriarca.

With the easy payment of fifty grand and the promise of more, Jerry Angiulo's life changed virtually overnight. No longer would tough guys like Larry Zannino be muscling him for money. Now Zannino and his fellow Boston Mafiosi would be answering to Angiulo. The former bookmaker turned mob underboss was on top of the world — or so he thought.

In August 1962, Angiulo reached the FBI's radar screen in a big way as a result of his newly minted association with Patriarca. The feds were looking for ways to tear down the barriers that Patriarca used to insulate and protect himself from prosecution. This meant going after the boss's lieutenants and associates with both barrels.

Investigators had already discovered one chink in Angiulo's armor. Eavesdropping agents had picked up chatter between the Boston underboss and Raymond Patriarca about the bribery of an Internal Revenue Service agent who had been paid $3,000 to straighten out a tax case involving Angiulo's older brother, Nick. A few months later, in November 1962, J. Edgar Hoover authorized microphone surveillance on Angiulo, whom he called "the overall boss of rackets in the Boston area and chief lieutenant of Raymond L. S. Patriarca." A bug was planted in the basement office of Jays Lounge, Angiulo's club at 255 Tremont Street in Boston, and given the FBI reference code 856-C. This number-letter combination equaled dollar signs for agent, Dennis Condon, who ran the operation and was awarded $150 by the bureau for establishing what the FBI called "a highly confidential source of information."

New England was the most dysfunctional and yet one of the most profitable Mafia territories in the United States. It should not have worked, but it did. Unlike other territories where power was concentrated in big cities, such as New York, Chicago, and Los Angeles, New England's Mafia family took its orders not from Boston but Providence, an "afterthought city." Boss Raymond Patriarca provided the fear and influence, while his Boston underboss, Jerry Angiulo, provided the financial smarts and influx of cash to keep the crime machine going strong. Both men had a small army of about three hundred soldiers and associates out on the streets every day, hustling or "outfiguring the straights." Fencing stolen goods and operating gambling parlors and brothels had supplied the New England Mafia with traditional revenue streams, but gangsters were always encouraged to be creative — to think outside the box. Men like Patriarca and Angiulo did not care where the money came from as long as it came. The scores ranged from rudimentary and violent stickups to sophisticated schemes pulled off with a high degree of ingenuity and smarts.

One particular scam involved a talented printer who could create duplicate checks of originals from insurance companies like John Hancock, and phony driver's licenses. Mobsters would thumb through telephone books from regions across New England and select names of unsuspecting people whose identities they would then use on the checks and the licenses needed for identification to cash them. The names were always chosen from the areas the gangsters were looking to hit. Fate was always on their side, because not once did a bank teller recognize any of the names presented to them, and over time the mobsters walked away with thousands of dollars.

A percentage of the score was always kicked up to Jerry Angiulo and then kicked up further to Raymond Patriarca. Many times mobsters would ask the bosses to invest in a particular score before it went down. That was the case with the Great Plymouth Mail Truck Robbery of 1962. A local bank robber and mob associate, named Billy Aggie, approached Angiulo and asked him to finance an operation he was planning on the South Shore. Aggie told the underboss that he had been tracking a mail truck over the past two months as it collected money from small banks on Cape Cod and delivered it to the Federal Reserve Bank in Boston. Aggie wanted to rob the truck and asked for about $8,000 in up-front money to purchase shotguns, disguises, and other special equipment needed for the heist. If the job was successful, Aggie would hand over all the cash to Angiulo, who would pay him between 60 and 80 cents on the dollar. Anguilo would then clean the money through a multitude of businesses he owned. Angiulo gave the start-up money to Aggie, who then pulled in several other gangsters including John J. "Red" Kelley and Maurice "Pro" Lerner. A week before the heist Aggie suffered a heart attack and was hospitalized, forcing him to postpone. His partners agreed, but then decided to go ahead without him.

Just before dusk on August 14, 1962, two cars blocked the highway on Route 3 in Plymouth, forcing the mail truck to stop. A robber wearing a police uniform and brandishing a shotgun demanded that the driver and his partner open the back of the truck. The two men were tied up by other members of the gang and told to lie face-down in the back of the truck. The robbers then grabbed parcels of cash and transferred them to a waiting car. The score netted the gang $1,551,277, which at that time was the biggest cash robbery in U.S. history. Angiulo paid Kelley 80 cents on the dollar for the loot. Hearing that the heist had taken place without him, Billy Aggie demanded his cut. Angiulo brokered a meeting, and a settlement was presumably reached to prevent the robbers from becoming embroiled in a bloodbath. Kelley and two others were eventually indicted for the heist. Both Kelley and codefendant Patricia Diaferio were acquitted, while the third suspect, Thomas Richards, vanished and was presumably murdered before the trial. His remains were never found, and the loot from the Great Plymouth Mail Truck Robbery was never recovered.

Mob associates often used the Mafia as a central bank where they could secure loans (most at high interest) and launder money that was too hot to circulate themselves. Those who went on ill-conceived spending sprees after a particular score did not last long on the street. But mobsters understood that they had to be really careless and really stupid to get unwanted attention from the cops. Many officers in Boston and Providence were on the mob's payroll, while others in law enforcement looked the other way so as not to spoil a good thing for their comrades. Police always had the most leverage in their unwritten partnership with the Mafia. One high-ranking Boston cop was so bold as to return a Christmas envelope stuffed with $500 to an Angiulo soldier because it simply wasn't enough.[20] Angiulo griped privately but dug deeper in his pocket for an extra $1,000. The cops provided Angiulo and Patriarca with tipoffs and other services when needed. In fact, when Angiulo's mother died, in 1975, a high-ranking Boston police superintendent directed traffic at her funeral, while four motorcycle cops escorted the hearse to the cemetery. It was a send-off fit for a popular mayor, certainly not the mother of a Mafia leader.

In the New England mob respect was earned, and membership in the Mafia was a rare honor. Many Sicilian associates toiled along the periphery of true power for a decade or more before even being considered for initiation. One soldier explained his induction into the New England Mafia to the feds in 1971. Dennis "Fall River Danny" Raimondi had been carrying out various orders for Patriarca and underboss Henry Tameleo for fifteen years before being told in early 1970 that he would be "made" if he continued to keep the respect of his masters. Raimondi did just that and was invited to participate in a Mafia induction ceremony inside a Boston-area home later that year. Raimondi stated that a Godfather had been selected among the high-ranking Mafiosi to sponsor him for the honor, which exposed him to a whole new world. The former mob gofer and bodyguard was now given control over certain areas of Patriarca's criminal empire, while also receiving a greater share of the profits.

This organizational structure made the Mafia more powerful than other ethnic gangs, especially the Irish, who were clannish by nature and fought their battles neighborhood to neighborhood instead of quelching their hatred and bitter rivalries so as to organize themselves more effectively. The Irish gangs had long been the rabid dog tugging on the end of the Mafia's leash. When the Italians needed to turn a threat into reality, they often called on their Hibernian associates to handle the dirty business. The Irish were also the most expendable. Unlike Jewish gangsters, who had won the respect of the Mafia for their business acumen and keen eye for diversification, the Irish were considered infantry—trench fighters with muddy knees and bloody elbows merely looking to fight another day. The Irish gangs did not possess the forethought and strategic planning needed to take on the Mafia. The battle would be left instead to their blood brothers on the opposite side of the law.

Skullduggery

Named after his father, Boston Fire Department captain Dennis M. Condon, the younger Condon was born and raised in Charlestown, Massachusetts, on Bunker Hill Street in the shadow of the famous monument. Condon's parents, most notably his mother, Nora, instilled a sense of duty and the need for education in her nine children from an early age. Condon was an exceptional student who attended Boston English High School a few years after Jerry Angiulo, and then went on to earn a degree in education from Boston College in 1947. As was the case with most young men at that time, Condon's college years were interrupted by the war. He joined the U.S. Navy at the tail end of World War II but missed seeing any real action, as the escort carrier he was assigned to, the USS *Siboney*, arrived at Pearl Harbor the day after hostilities with Japan had ceased. The closest Condon and his shipmates got to any real excitement occurred when the *Siboney* was involved in air search operations to locate Rear Admiral William D. Sample after his plane went missing near Wakayama, Japan. The forty-seven-year-old Sample had been the youngest rear admiral in the Pacific theater. Search crews found no sign of Sample, who was officially declared dead a year later. Following the war, Condon made his way back to Massachusetts, where he finished up his studies at BC and then received a graduate degree from Boston University before joining the FBI in January 1951, just one month before the arrival of his future partner, H. Paul Rico.

Condon and Rico were polar opposites in just about every way. While both were graduates of Boston College, Condon was a street kid with a patrician's demeanor, while Rico, a product of an affluent Boston suburb, cultivated the image of the very gangsters he was looking to put behind bars. Harold Paul Rico was born in Belmont, Massachusetts, in 1926. He had an Irish mother but had inherited his dark, swarthy looks from his

Spanish father, who worked for New England Telephone. Rico graduated from Belmont High School in 1944 and went on to serve in the U.S. Army Air Forces during World War II. Like Condon, after the war he enrolled at Boston College, where he received a degree in history in 1950. In Rico's Boston College yearbook, *Sub Turri* (Latin for under the tower), both faculty and the graduating class stressed "a strength in ideals . . . a purpose in life." No doubt that many of Rico's classmates took this pledge to heart. But Rico himself had different plans. In his senior picture, H. Paul Rico wore a flashy tie to match his crooked grin. His sense of style would serve him well in his future career.

Rico joined the bureau on February 26, 1951, and was immediately dispatched to the FBI's Chicago office, where he spent a year learning the ropes before getting summoned back to Boston when his father became gravely ill. Rico was reassigned to the Boston office, where he would stay for the rest of his FBI career. H. Paul Rico made his way onto J. Edgar Hoover's radar screen early, first by working behind the scenes assisting fellow agent Jack Kehoe's investigation of the infamous Brink's Job. The case had remained unsolved for five years before Kehoe broke it wide open in 1955, when he convinced robber Joseph "Specs" O'Keefe to cooperate with authorities. Kehoe had learned that O'Keefe was outraged that thieves had snatched his cut of the stolen money. To add insult to injury, O'Keefe's former Brink's partner, Tony Pino, had hired a hitman to silence Specs once and for all. The gunman, Elmer "Trigger" Burke, drove up to Boston from New York City and found O'Keefe at a Dorchester housing project. After chasing him around the building for thirty minutes, Burke finally shot Specs in the leg. The wound required hospitalization. Kehoe paid Specs a bedside visit and used O'Keefe's anger to his advantage. O'Keefe eventually cooperated with Kehoe, and soon all the Brink's robbers (including Tony Pino) were behind bars.

Jack Kehoe became a legend within the ranks of the FBI, and H. Paul Rico nibbled around that fame until he landed a major collar himself just a year later in 1956. The feds were on the hunt for a twenty-five-year-old accused bank robber from South Boston named James "Whitey" Bulger. During the previous year, Bulger and his gang had knocked over two banks, one in Pawtucket, Rhode Island, and another in Hammond, Indiana, for a combined take of $54,612.28. During the Indiana job, Bulger served as a cover man, holding two pistols on customers and bank employees while another member of the gang cleaned out the tellers' cages. The witnesses all got a good look at the robbers, as they were not wearing masks. Instead, Bulger and his bandits sported Elmer Fudd–like hunting caps with flaps covering their ears.

An arrest warrant was issued for Whitey Bulger on January 4, 1956. Bulger knew enough to steer clear of his old haunts, at least for a while. His one reported visit back to Boston occurred during the Christmas holiday. Whitey Bulger kept moving; he'd be in California one week, New Mexico the next. He traveled with a girlfriend under several aliases, including Leo McLaughlin, Martin Kelley, and Paul John Rose. Not only had Bulger changed his name, but he also changed his appearance. He dyed his soft blond hair jet black and began to sport horn-rimmed glasses. The FBI had also learned that Bulger (a nonsmoker) had taken to walking around with a cigar stuffed in his mouth in an attempt to distort his facial features.

H. Paul Rico had known Bulger for a couple of years. The two ran into each other often in Boston's gay nightclub district, where Bulger worked as a hustler and where Rico cultivated informants. There has been much speculation over the years, however, that their interests in Boston's homosexual scene had more to do with pleasure than it did with business. In March 1956, Rico and another fellow FBI agent, Herbert F. Briick, received a tip that Bulger had returned to Boston and was spending time at a nightclub in Revere, just a few miles north of the city. Rico and Briick staked out the place for a couple of nights until they spotted a disguised Bulger walking out of the joint with another local thug named John DeFeo. Rico and his men swooped in and captured the fugitive Bulger, who was unarmed. During his arraignment the next day, the prosecutor called Bulger "a vicious person, known to carry guns, and [who] by his own admittance has an intense dislike for police and law enforcement officers."[21]

A few months later, Bulger was sentenced to twenty years in prison. He was shipped off to federal lockups in Atlanta, Georgia, Lewisburg, Pennsylvania, and then the "Rock" itself—Alcatraz. Meanwhile, H. Paul Rico stayed in Boston and reaped the rewards connected with the high-profile capture. Rico's boss in the Boston office sent a personal and confidential memo to J. Edgar Hoover praising the young agent for taking Whitey Bulger off the street. The special agent in charge described the South Boston hoodlum as "extremely dangerous," a person with remarkable agility and reckless daring in driving vehicles and overall unstable and vicious characteristics.

Upon receiving the memo, J. Edgar Hoover swiftly promoted Rico to special agent and wrote him a letter in which he stated, "It is a pleasure to approve this promotion in view of your superior accomplishments in connection with the Bank Robbery case involving James J. Bulger Jr. and others." The FBI director went on to praise Rico for his ability to develop valuable and confidential sources of information. Rico's new special agent status also came with a cash bonus and a trip to Washington, DC, for a celebratory photo with Hoover himself. Rico boasted to colleague and criminal alike that he had a close relationship with the nation's top cop. Given the rumors about each man's sexual orientation, Rico's braggadocio no doubt triggered snickers behind his back.

The FBI's use of electronic surveillance (ELSUR) had been paying dividends in the bureau's fight against the mob, but Hoover continued to stress the need for his agents to cultivate informants in the hope of gathering solid human intelligence (HUMINT). One confidential source developed by the Boston office provided agents with significant information about disharmony at the highest levels in the New England Mafia. The story began to unfold when underboss Jerry Angiulo awoke to find his car riddled with bullets outside his apartment in Boston's North End. Was it merely a warning? Or had the gunman believed Angiulo to be in the car at the time? The informant had no way of knowing. What he did tell the FBI was that a gangster named Salvatore Iacone had gone to Raymond Patriarca the day before the shooting to complain about Angiulo. Iacone and Angiulo had recently gone in on the Indian Meadow Country Club in Worcester, Massachusetts. The two men had been arguing about proprietorship of the club when the short-tempered Angiulo launched into an obscenity-laced tirade against his business partner. Iacone wanted to kill Angiulo on the spot, but chose not to act out of respect for Patriarca. When Iacone described the incident to the Man, Patriarca just scoffed.

"You shoulda killed him," Patriarca told Iacone. He also gave Iacone the green light to whack Angiulo on the spot with no questions asked if the underboss disrespected him in the future. As stated by the Boston office in a confidential memo to a top FBI official in Washington, "We have had recent indications of a growing coolness in attitude by Patriarca toward Angiulo." These "indications" were exactly what the bureau had been waiting for. It suggested a soft spot in Patriarca's impenetrable armor and gave agents hope that the growing divide between the boss and underboss would spread to the rest of the New England mob family.

In the early 1960s, the nation's most infamous gangster was not Raymond Patriarca, Sam Giancana, or any of their counterparts. Instead, America's most celebrated mobster was a low-level, square-headed drug smuggler named Joseph Valachi. Valachi had been in prison since his conviction on federal narcotics charges in 1959. Agents from the U.S. Treasury Department's Federal Bureau of Narcotics (FBN) approached Valachi while he was behind bars at the federal penitentiary in Atlanta, Georgia. The drug smuggler had just killed a man in the prison yard he believed had been sent by New York Mafia boss Vito Genovese to assassinate him. Valachi crushed the man's skull with a two-foot section of iron pipe. It had been the desperate act of a desperate man. Valachi had already survived three attempts on his life. He believed that he had been marked for death after another mobster began spreading erroneous rumors that Valachi had turned informer. Valachi told authorities that Genovese had planted his lips on Valachi's cheeks, giving him the "kiss of death" while the two shared a cell shortly before the deadly jail-yard confrontation. By the time Valachi smashed the pipe against his victim's head, he was weak and delusional, having been on a self-imposed hunger strike for several days out of fear that his prison food was poisoned. The sad truth was that Valachi's "assassin" had not been trying to kill him at all. The victim, John Joseph Saupp, was serving time for mail robbery and forgery and had no mob ties. Valachi had mistaken Saupp for a dangerous mobster named Joseph "Joe Beck" DiPalermo. FBN agents informed the paranoid Valachi that he had in fact killed the wrong man and then threatened to return him to the prison's general population unless he cooperated.

Valachi made up his mind quickly. In an attempt to save his own neck, he agreed to flip on old friends as well as total strangers, and in doing so broke the Mafia's cardinal rule of *Omerta* (Silence). Valachi was transferred to New York's Westchester County Jail in late June 1962 under the alias Joseph DeMarco. Initial questioning had been done by the FBN, but once Attorney General Bobby Kennedy learned about the underworld defection, he pressed J. Edgar Hoover to insert one of his own agents into the interrogation.

Despite Valachi's low-level status within the mob, he was able to provide a wealth of information both real and imagined about the syndicate's organizational structure and its most influential and ruthless members. This information was not gleaned easily, however. At first, Valachi tried to say as little as possible. The FBI assigned Special Agent James Flynn to the case with an order to break down the mobster's stone wall of silence. "I could see there was a definite hatred on Joe's part against anybody in law enforcement at that point," Flynn recalled years later in a documentary for A&E television.[22] "He would talk and not talk. He would recognize the fact that you were in the room and stop talking altogether." Flynn worked on Valachi for two months, plying the overweight prisoner with Italian specialties including Genoa sausage, pasta, and cheese. But the key to Valachi's heart turned out not to be his stomach after all. It was information. Special Agent Flynn sat Valachi down for a talk that would either make or break his case.

"Joe, I'm gonna tell you one word and I want you to give me the other. If you don't give it to me, we're finished," Flynn told Valachi. "*Cosa*," the special agent whispered.[23]

"*Cosa Nostra*," Valachi replied, nodding his head. "You know about it?"

Flynn nodded back. He had heard the words *Cosa Nostra* mentioned several times on wiretaps but was not fully aware of its meaning. Valachi would have to fill in the rest. Valachi informed Flynn that those inside the mob never referred to themselves as members of the Mafia. "That's the expression the outside uses," Valachi told him. The mobster explained that *Cosa Nostra* was a Sicilian phrase that meant Our Thing. *La Cosa Nostra* (the FBI added the *La*) quickly replaced words like "syndicate" and "hoodlum" in the bureau's lexicon. Valachi then broke down LCN's business model, which was a combination of best practices from both the corporate world and the military. Valachi described himself and others as soldiers, criminal infantry working in tightly knit crews called *regimas* who were led by *capo regimes* (lieutenants) that reported to twelve *capos* (heads) in select geographical areas.

Contrary to popular belief, Valachi had not been the first man to expose the inner workings of the mob. That information had been provided decades before, in 1940, by a Jewish contract killer named Abe "Kid Twist" Reles. Kid Twist, a vicious killer for the notorious hit squad Murder Inc., came under indictment for a string of gangland slayings in which he had applied a number of different killing methods from pistols to his personal favorite — the ice pick. With threats of the electric chair, prosecutors realized they could twist Kid Twist into giving up his Murder Inc. boss, Louis "Lepke" Buchalter. Abe "Kid Twist" Reles implicated Buchalter in the murder of a Brooklyn candystore owner for which he was later convicted and sent to the electric chair. Reles also turned in five other mobsters who were all found guilty and later executed for their crimes. The Murder Inc. turncoat was not done yet, however. Prosecutors had set their sights on Albert Anastasia, a high-ranking member of *Cosa Nostra*. Reles had given investigators key information to tie Anastasia to the murder of a longshoreman and union activist named Pete Panto, who had led an unsuccessful revolt against International Longshoremen's Association leader Joseph P. Ryan, a close ally of the New York mob. Pete Panto disappeared in July 1939, and his remains were not discovered until nearly three years later, when they turned up in a lime pit in Lyndhurst, New Jersey.

Panto's story was later used as an inspiration for the Oscar-winning 1954 film *On the Waterfront*, starring Marlon Brando. While Panto was still missing and feared dead, Reles told investigators that the union activist had been killed by fellow Murder Inc. hitman Mendy Weiss on orders from Albert Anastasia. Before Reles could testify, however, he took flight from a sixth-floor window at the Half Moon Hotel on New York's Coney Island while guarded by six detectives. Investigators claimed Reles was killed while trying to escape, but popular theory suggests that the guards had been paid $100,000 to push Kid Twist out the window to his death. With his early and mysterious demise, Reles was immortalized by one New York newspaper as "the canary who sang, but couldn't fly."

Abe "Kid Twist" Reles never got the chance to point fingers and tell his story in a public forum. That job would be left for Joseph Valachi. It wasn't enough for Valachi to give up the goods on *La Cosa Nostra* behind closed doors. Attorney General Kennedy and FBI director Hoover both wanted a spectacle. These powerful men wanted the story told, but each through his own prism. J. Edgar Hoover originally tried to break the story in *Reader's Digest*, with the FBI taking full credit for exposing *La Cosa Nostra*, but he was overruled by the attorney general, who leaked his own version of the story to reporter Peter Maas at the *Saturday Evening Post*. Hoover was furious over the slight. "I never saw such skullduggery," he complained in a May 23, 1962, memo. Hoover also added that Bobby Kennedy's aides were "exploiting this whole situation for their own benefit."[24]

Despite much infighting behind the scenes, Kennedy and Hoover presented a united front against the mob when they paraded Joe Valachi before Congress and the world in October 1963. The gangster's highly anticipated testimony before Senator John L. McClellan's committee on organized crime had become the hottest ticket in town. The attorney general's wife, Ethel Kennedy, arrived early for a front-row seat. Caroline Kennedy's White House kindergarten teacher was also there. Curiosity also got the better of Civil Rights pioneer James Meredith and Alice Roosevelt Longworth, who were both in attendance. "I wanted to get the smell of it," the daughter of President Theodore Roosevelt told newspaper reporters.[25]

Once again, Valachi re-created the Mafia's organizational blueprint for lawmakers and reporters in attendance. He also described the history of *La Cosa Nostra* in America as he knew it. The gallery hung on the informant's every word, and as a reporter from *Time* magazine observed, "Valachi seemed to enjoy it thoroughly." Battling a sore throat, the gravelly voiced Valachi sucked from a juice filled plastic lemon as he described his motive for breaking *Omerta*.

"First of all I want revenge," Valachi told the committee. "I want to destroy them, Cosa Nostra, the leaders, the bosses, the whole thing that exists. . . . What did I get out of it? Nothin' but misery."[26]

Valachi's testimony was carried live on national television for two straight weeks. He identified Vito Genovese as his *Cosa Nostra* boss and listed the names of Joseph Bonanno, Gaetano Gagliano, Charles "Lucky" Luciano, Vincent Mangano, and Joseph Profaci as the original bosses of *La Cosa Nostra*'s five families. Valachi also revealed the Mafia's secret initiation ritual for the first time in public. It started with a finger prick and the sharing of blood and culminated with the burning of the image of a saint in the palm of one's hand. Valachi demonstrated the ceremony for the committee and muttered the words he claimed he was once ordered to recite during his own induction. "This is the way I burn if I expose this organization."

America was captivated by Valachi's testimony and overlooked his penchant for mistakes. Despite having what was called a "photographic memory," Valachi stumbled several times during the hearing, mixing up names and places of his alleged underworld exploits. Committee member Edmund Muskie of Maine called the hearings "a waste of time." The true impact of Joe Valachi's testimony would not be felt until years later, when Congress passed the Racketeer Influenced and Corrupt Organization Act of 1970, better known as RICO, which strengthened and extended criminal penalties against the mob. Valachi also paved the way for FBI agents like H. Paul Rico and Dennis Condon to go after other mob associates, hoping to use them as weapons in the ongoing war against *La Cosa Nostra*.

Uncaged

Following his parole in 1960, Joe Barboza carried over his bookmaking business from prison to the street. Starting with a $2,000 loan from his boxing manager, Eddie Fisher, Barboza managed to parlay the money into $25,000 in just one year. Fisher also kept Barboza on the books as an employee at Scooterland, a scooter sales showroom behind the Hotel Statler. He worked there for nine months and was made assistant manager despite the fact that he rarely set foot in the place. Instead, Joe took to running around with like-minded young thugs looking to make a quick score. One of those men was Guy Frizzi, an East Boston tough guy who reminded Barboza of the actor George Raft. Frizzi had a short temper and a long rap sheet. He was known to slap around his girlfriends and anyone else that fell out of his favor. Barboza was drawn to Frizzi partly because of to their similar backgrounds. Both had grown up in reform school and prison and had been behind bars at the same places at different times. Frizzi had also been incarcerated at the Concord Reformatory, where he once had his two front teeth knocked out. The two made a dangerous pair, and even on the nights they weren't looking for trouble, trouble certainly found them.

In May 1962, Barboza and Frizzi walked into Alphonso's Clam House to check out a new lounge act when they encountered a red-headed gangster believed to be a bookie on the rise in the Boston suburb of Malden. Barboza and Frizzi took a table with their friend Skinny Spindale. Guy Frizzi gave the Malden bookie the once over and was not impressed.

"Fuck him," Frizzi said to Barboza.

The red-headed shylock must have overheard the slight, because at that moment one of his companions walked over to Barboza's table and ordered Skinny Spindale to put out his cigarette.

"We don't wanna start no fire," the man said.

The Animal sensed a problem and stepped in to try to defuse the situation. Barboza was on parole, after all.

"Look, we don't want no trouble," Joe told the man. "You want trouble, bother somebody else."[27]

But the guy wanted trouble, and at that point so did Guy Frizzi. The two men began launching haymakers at each other in the middle of the club as patrons began to clear out. Barboza remained close by while the pair continued to slug it out. His eyes narrowed and his anger grew. Ferocity soon replaced his fear of violating parole and going back to prison. The Animal wrapped his thick hand around a beer bottle and smashed it on a table. He then lunged forward with the shank and stabbed the man in the back; the bottle's broken edges lacerated the man's skin under his coat. Much to Barboza's disbelief, the man barely flinched and kept swinging at Frizzi, connecting with his nose and sending Guy's eyeglasses flying through the air. Joe knew that his friend was blind without his glasses, so he decided to end the battle once and for all. The Animal stared over to the red-headed bookie, who seemed to be taking great pleasure in the violence.

"Fuck you and fuck Malden," Barboza shouted.

The Animal then stepped in between Frizzi and the bookie's henchman and knocked the man cold with two crushing blows.

Barboza was arrested and booked for assault and battery with a dangerous weapon. Surprisingly, he was not kept behind bars because of the parole violation. Instead, he was allowed back on the streets while the case against him was pending.

A few months later, one of Barboza's bosses at Scooterland secured him a job at Duffy's Tavern in the shadow of Paragon Park along Nantasket Beach in Hull, Massachusetts. Joe worked part-time as a bouncer during the busy summer season. The area was a breeding ground for fights, especially on those hot summer nights when temperatures rose and tempers flared. Joe kept a close watch on Duffy's and the surrounding businesses. Young men looking to make names for themselves quickly learned to stay clear of Nantasket Beach on the nights Barboza was on duty. One group of young trouble makers did not get the message, however. Barboza spotted the gang huddled near the go-cart track, harassing the ride operator. Joe could have simply told the group to move along, but the Animal was not in a talking mood on that particular evening. Instead, he launched himself at all seven men, knocking down the two biggest guys he could find. A friend of Joe's also joined in the melee. Barboza looked over to his buddy and was caught off guard by the gang's biggest guy, who managed to wrap him in a tight bear hug. Joe's powerful arms were now pinned against his sides as the thug continued to squeeze. What Joe's opponent did not realize, however, was the fact that Barboza had learned during his many years in prison to use every part of his body as a weapon. Joe broke one arm free and grabbed the guy's head and pulled it toward him. The Animal opened his mouth wide and chomped down on his opponent's face, tearing away a part of his cheek. Barboza easily broke free as the young thug covered the gaping wound on the side of his face. Police sirens wailed and the Animal fled into the darkness with the metallic taste of fresh blood on his lips.

Barboza's reputation as a wild thing spread like wildfire across the South Shore. It was the kind of attention that he could ill afford, especially with the assault and battery case still pending against him in Boston. Police in Hull began taking an interest in the fierce young man who had been hired to keep the peace at Duffy's Tavern. Joe did not help his situation when he ran afoul of a high-ranking cop in town. Barboza had broken the jaw of the officer's son during a scuffle outside the bar. When word reached the Hull police station, the officer threatened to send Joe back to prison unless he was paid $2,000. Barboza's boxing manager offered the cop $1,000, and the deal was sealed. The cop would keep quiet if Joe left Nantasket Beach for good.

Barboza moved back to East Boston and back in with his wife, Fay, although their relationship was anything but *Ozzie and Harriet*. The couple barely spent time together, as Joe had no interest in domestication. The relationship was also strained by the fact that Fay had suffered a miscarriage early in the marriage. The news devastated Joe, and he began spending more time alone or on the streets, where the environment heightened his senses as well as his instinct for survival. Fay was looking for a tabby cat that would stay close to her home and her kids, but Joe was a tiger that yearned to be on the prowl both day and night.

Barboza was now working tirelessly on his pursuit of two dreams. He was growing a lucrative shylock business in hopes of building enough underworld equity to get him noticed by local leaders of *La Cosa Nostra*. With his money working for him on the street, Barboza could dedicate the rest of his time to training to become a legitimate light heavyweight contender. The world champion at the time was a Philadelphia slugging machine named Harold "Hercules" Johnson. Johnson, although highly skilled, had weathered a series of grueling bouts against boxing legends Archie Moore and Jersey Joe Walcott. Barboza and many others believed that the champ was on the downside of his career and that the field was open to any man with a concrete chin, thunderous punch, and a willingness to win at any cost.

Barboza had his first big fight and his first major setback at the fabled Boston Garden on September 23, 1961, just three days after his twenty-ninth birthday. The Animal, who had chosen the ring moniker the Baron, was matched against a block of granite from Boise, Idaho, named Don Bale. The two were fighting on the undercard of a televised bout between Paolo Rossi and Jackie Donnelly. Bale had been fighting professionally since 1959 and had collected ten wins against eight losses before facing Barboza. Bale was coming off two straight losses and had something to prove. Barboza hadn't fought competitively in nearly two years, and the rust showed when he stepped into the ring against a much more seasoned opponent. The two men appeared to be evenly matched during the early rounds, as each offered the other a taste of his overwhelming power. At the fight's midway point, however, Barboza's ring rust began to show, and Bale seized upon Joe's flaws to pin him against the ropes. Bale caught Barboza with a vicious shot to his lantern chin, causing Joe's knees to buckle. The Animal hit the canvas, an unfamiliar place for him, and was counted out before he could get back to his feet. The stunning defeat before the hometown crowd could have been a crushing blow to Barboza, but instead he rebounded with six straight wins, four that came by knockout. Don Bale, on the other hand, could not parlay his win over Barboza into much future success. In his next fight, which also took place at the Boston Garden, Bale was cut badly during a loss against another Boston area slugger, Joe DeNucci, who would go on to become the longest serving state auditor in Massachusetts history.

Barboza sparred more than a hundred rounds with DeNucci inside the dilapidated New Gardens Gym on Friend Street. Although the Animal had great affection for DeNucci, the two were rivals in the gym. DeNucci was a more polished boxer than Barboza and toyed with him in the ring. Angry and frustrated, Barboza would curse DeNucci incessantly, which would only open himself up to more punishing blows. But the Animal respected DeNucci and did not let his anger flow outside the ropes. That wasn't the case when he faced off against another rising pugilist named Cardell Farmos. Farmos was taller, stronger, and quicker than Barboza, and it seemed that his gloved right hand was conjoined to Joe's chin over much of their three sparring rounds. Finally, Barboza had had enough. He jumped out of the ring before the final bell sounded and headed for the locker room. Moments later, the Animal returned waving a pistol. Joe chased Farmos around the gym until the boxer sought refuge behind the heavy bag. As other fighters also ducked for cover, Joe DeNucci stepped forward and successfully calmed Barboza down.

Joe Barboza's penchant for violence outside the ring certainly curtailed any possible success inside the ring. While celebrating a recent boxing win with friends at Boston's Peppermint Lounge, pals Guy and Connie Frizzi got into a scuffle with another man that spilled outside onto the curb. One of the Frizzi brothers stabbed the man, who immediately pulled out a gun and began firing. Barboza's crew escaped unscathed but became wanted men the next day when it was learned that the victim was a decorated Boston police officer and war hero. The newspapers milked the story for all it was worth. One reporter wrote that the officer was stabbed while investigating loansharks. The article was accompanied by a photo of the officer's wife waiting bravely by his side at the hospital.

"That isn't the girl he was with at the Peppermint Lounge," Joe muttered to himself as he gazed at the newspaper photo. Barboza could barely get the words out before Boston police officers were blocking his street and storming his front door. They brought him to the District 4 police station, where he was grilled through the night. The investigators told Barboza that several witnesses had placed him at the scene of the crime. Joe claimed that he didn't know what the hell they were talking about. Despite his refusal to offer any information, the cops treated him well. Most of the officers were boxing fans and had seen his name on the fight cards at the Garden. Still, one of their own had been stabbed, and Boston police were going to find the culprit no matter how long it took. They escorted Barboza to a waiting squad car and drove him over to City Hospital, where the officer was recovering from his stab wounds. A handcuffed Barboza was escorted past the officer's scowling wife and into his hospital room. The officer's mouth curled into a slight smile. He recognized the Animal immediately.

"Did you see me in the Peppermint Lounge?" he asked Barboza.[28]

"Yessir, but it wasn't with the girl standing outside this door."

The smile disappeared from the officer's face.

"This isn't one of the men," the officer told investigators. "He's too big."

The cops escorted Barboza out of the hospital room and unlocked the handcuffs. The Animal was free to go.

The freedom and fortune of good luck did not last long, however. Barboza was sent back to prison in September 1962 for numerous parole violations. The Animal had another two years to serve on his original sentence, and serve them he did. He would not be released until April 30, 1964. During that time, the climate of Boston and the underworld began to shift dramatically.

War

It all began with a trickle of blood dripping off a young thug's face inside a quaint little cottage on Salisbury Beach at the northernmost tip of Massachusetts. Once it hit the ground, the trickle of blood formed a small stream that gained strength as it flowed southward, eventually growing into a raging river of red when it finally reached the streets Somerville and Charlestown. The war had been started over a woman. It is a story as old as time, as empires have been won and lost over the pursuit of softer flesh. There is nothing remotely romantic, however, about the incident that triggered the Irish mob war. It came down to two simple yet dangerous things—booze and broads. Amid the colorful backdrop of saltwater taffy shops, penny arcades, and waterfront pizza stands, a group of low-level Irish gangsters gathered to soak up the sun on their pale skin and drink into the wee hours of the morning. It was September 2, 1961, in the throes of the Labor Day weekend celebration, when twenty-two-year-old Georgie McLaughlin of Charlestown demonstrated his liquid courage by reaching out and grabbing the breast of the attractive wife of Bill Hickey, a Somerville Teamster and associate of the local Winter Hill Gang. The wife did not appreciate the unwanted advance, and neither did her husband.

Hickey and his Teamster buddy George "Red" Lloyd pounced on McLaughlin with flying fists, elbows, and knees. McLaughlin suffered a deep cut on his right cheek, but that was an overt sign that only hinted at more serious injuries. By the time the Teamsters were done with him, Georgie had also suffered a busted nose, broken jaw, and fractured elbow. He was unconscious, and neither Hickey nor Lloyd could find a pulse. The attackers feared McLaughlin was dead, and that was not good news. Georgie's older brothers, Bernie and Punchy, ran the rackets in Charlestown and would no doubt seek revenge. Bernie McLaughlin was a loanshark and leg breaker for Jerry Angiulo, while his brother Punchy was a psychotic former boxer who was prone to violence to settle even the most minor dispute.

Hickey and Lloyd had to dispose of the body quickly, so they carried their victim out of the cottage and stuffed him in the backseat of a car. The men drove off in search of a quiet, out of the way spot to dump the body. They were driving along a desolate beach-side road with headlights dimmed when Georgie McLaughlin suddenly came back from the dead and popped his battered head up in the backseat. McLaughlin was dazed, confused, and mumbling to himself as he tried to gain his bearings. Hickey and Lloyd gave each other a concerned look as they jerked the car around and headed south. They drove to nearby Newburyport and pulled up to the entrance of Anna Jacques Hospital, where they spilled McLaughlin out of the backseat and onto the sidewalk near the entrance. The men then took off, hanging on to the faint hope that McLaughlin had been too drunk to remember what had happened and how he had ended up in the emergency room.

When Georgie finally came around, his brothers were at his bedside seething with anger. Bernie and Punchy demanded to know who had not only beaten their brother in savage fashion but who had ultimately disrespected their crew. Georgie pointed the guilty finger at Hickey and Lloyd, who were both known associates of Winter Hill Gang leader James "Buddy" McLean. The McLaughlin brothers combed the streets of Somerville for several days looking for Lloyd and Hickey, who had both gone AWOL from the neighborhood. Finally they approached Buddy McLean, a strapping six footer with an impish grin, and asked him for a favor.

"I want you to help me set up these guys that beat up Georgie," Bernie McLaughlin asked his Somerville counterpart.[29]

"Listen, I'm friends with you and I'm friends with those guys," McLean tried to reason. "I don't set up my friends."

"You're still friends with those motherfuckers after what they did to Georgie?" Bernie asked, getting angrier by the minute.

"From what I hear, Georgie was way outta line," McLean countered. Buddy then told Bernie McLaughlin that he did not want to get involved. The cavalier statement made Buddy the enemy in Bernie McLaughlin's eyes.

Several nights later, Buddy McLean's wife was awakened by the sound of barking dogs out on the street. The wife got out of bed and opened the window and saw three men huddled around her husband's car. She alerted Buddy, who jumped out of bed, grabbed his Luger, and crept out the back door. Still in his boxer shorts, McLean took position behind a large bush adjacent to his house. Buddy raised the Luger and fired in the direction of the intruders, who immediately fired back. McLean chased the three men down the road and caught a glimpse of one intruder under a bright street lamp. Buddy recognized the man immediately — it was Bernie McLaughlin. McLaughlin and his two accomplices jumped into a waiting car and took off. The stench of burned rubber was still fresh in Buddy's nostrils as he made his way back to his house. He approached his automobile with the concerned look of a physician inspecting his patient. McLean immediately spotted the car's malignant tumor, which took the form of five sticks of dynamite wired to the ignition switch. The booby trap had certainly been meant for him, but Buddy could not think of himself at that moment. Instead, he thought of his wife and their children, who most certainly would have been killed when they took the car to school the next morning.

The next day, when the clock struck noon on Halloween, October 31, 1961, Buddy McLean stepped out of a black Oldsmobile in Charlestown's City Square. He caught up with Bernie McLaughlin directly in front of the police station, pulled out a shotgun, and fired a shot into the back of his enemy's head. Dozens of witnesses stood watching as McLean, wearing a Charlestown "Townie" football jacket, fled the scene in the Oldsmobile with its trunk open to conceal the license plate. Buddy McLean was arrested a short time later inside a Somerville donut shop along with his alleged accomplices, an off-duty Metropolitan police officer named Russ Nicholson and a young thug named Alex "Bobo" Petricone.

When it came time to empanel a grand jury to hear the case, no witness would identify McLean, Nicholson, and Petricone as the men who had gunned down Bernie McLaughlin, and the case went away. Nicholson, the former cop, was eventually gunned down himself, while Petricone traveled west to Hollywood and changed his name to Alex Rocco. Under the name Alex Rocco, Petricone would go on to land memorable roles as Las Vegas casino owner Moe Green in *The Godfather* and as Jimmy

Scalise in the 1973 Boston-based gangster film *The Friends of Eddie Coyle*, opposite Robert Mitchum.

Punchy McLaughlin could not exact his pound of flesh from Buddy McLean himself, as Buddy was shipped off to prison for a two-year stint on a weapons charge unrelated to Bernie McLaughlin's murder. Instead, the McLaughlin Gang went after Winter Hill member George "Ox" Joynt, a first-generation Irish-American whose parents had emigrated from Limerick. Ox was a well-known brawler who served as muscle for the Winter Hill crew. Joynt disappeared a short time after Bernie McLaughlin's murder. His remains were discovered nearly a year later on a hot July day in 1962 when a work crew dug up his bones while building a new shopping center in Wellington Circle in Medford, Massachusetts.

The Irish mob war would simmer for another year while McLean was incarcerated. During that time, each gang looked for vulnerabilities in the other. The Wild West show formally opened just two days before St. Patrick's Day in 1964, when Georgie McLaughlin, now fully healed from his beating, attended a party in Boston's Roxbury neighborhood. Georgie was drunk as usual and got into an argument with another man at the party. Georgie left the celebration only to come back a short time later with a gun. He approached twenty-year-old William Sheridan, who bore a resemblance to the guy Georgie had been beefing with. Sheridan told McLaughlin that he was not the man Georgie had argued with, but it was too late. McLaughlin shot Sheridan dead right in the middle of the party.

A month later, on April 30, 1964, Joe Barboza was paroled from Walpole. He had been corresponding with a young blonde named Claire Cohen, whom he had met while working at Scooterland. They were polar opposites in every way. While Joe had spent much of his youth locked up, Claire had been raised outside the realm of violence in the quiet and predominantly Jewish community of Swampscott along Boston's North Shore. Claire was Jewish, the daughter of a local grocer, and the only way for the couple to have a future together was if Joe converted from Catholicism to Judaism. Barboza loved Claire too much to allow any religious barriers to stand in the way of their relationship, so he agreed. He knew that his mother, Palmeda, a devout Catholic, would have concerns, but he had very little faith in the God, who had showed him little mercy over the course of his life. As part of his conversion, Joe changed his last name from Barboza to Baron, the moniker he had used in the ring. He also got circumcised at Beth Israel Hospital; he later said it was the worst pain he had ever experienced in his life.

The couple got married immediately following Joe's release from prison. They had exchanged vows in a small ceremony in Maine and were driving to their honeymoon in Johnston, Rhode Island, when Joe decided to make a pit stop at his friend Guy Frizzi's place in East Boston. Frizzi presented Joe and Claire with a wedding cake and introduced Joe to another guy Frizzi wanted to bring into their gang. The hood's name was Joseph "Chico" Amico, and the three men would go on to form a formidable crew. Barboza promised his new partners that he would be in touch and continued on to his honeymoon.

Two days later, while Joe was relaxing with his bride in a suite at the Colonial Motor Lodge in Johnston, he got a frantic call from Frizzi back in East Boston.

"Did you hear the news?" Guy asked.[30]

Before Joe could respond, Frizzi blurted out the bulletin. "They found a body in the trunk of a car with his head missing."

"His head missing?" Joe replied astonished. "Did they identify the body?"

Frizzi told Barboza that he had no idea who the victim was, but the mystery of the headless gangster would soon be solved. When Barboza returned to East Boston, Frizzi told him that the body belonged to a former convict named Francis "Frank" Benjamin. Joe had known Benjamin since they were kids. Like Barboza, Benjamin was fresh out of prison and, like Barboza, Frank Benjamin had built his reputation with his fists.

"He was a tough southpaw and a right-on mother," Joe told Frizzi.[31]

Frank Benjamin had made countless friends while in prison, including fellow Roxbury native Vincent "Jimmy the Bear" Flemmi. Flemmi was also back on the streets and beginning to make a name for himself when the two men bumped into each other one night at a Dorchester bar. They shared old jailhouse stories, but the more Benjamin drank, the more he talked, and that began to annoy the Bear. Benjamin began spouting off that he was connected to Buddy McLean and that he was going to whack out members of the McLaughlin Gang. This didn't sit well with Flemmi, or with the tavern's owner, Roxbury rackets king Edward "Wimpy" Bennett, who was tied in with the McLaughlins. Finally Flemmi had had enough of Benjamin's big mouth, so he slipped off his bar stool and walked out into the chilly April night. The Bear came back a little while later with a gun, walked up to his old prison pal, and shot him in the head. With the help of Wimpy Bennett, Flemmi dragged Benjamin's body into the storage room while they tried to figure out what to do with the corpse.

A short time later, Wimpy went back into the storage room to check on the body and was shocked to see that Benjamin was alive and crawling around. Blood flowing from a gaping wound in Benjamin's head was virtually everywhere. The scene was like something out of a zombie movie. Bennett pulled out his own gun and shot Benjamin again—killing him. There would be no coming back from the dead this time. Still, Bennett and the Bear had other problems. Wimpy Bennett looked around the bar and realized that there was no way a simple mop job would soak up all the blood, so he decided the best course of action was to torch the place. Flemmi had used a cop's gun in the shooting and he knew that a ballistics test on the bullet would mean big trouble, so he got a saw and severed Benjamin's head. No head, no ballistics test. The Bear stuffed the head in a plastic bag and buried it in the woods while Wimpy Bennett soaked the bar with gasoline and lit a match. Frank Benjamin's headless body was placed in the backseat of a stolen car and later abandoned on a side street in South Boston. The head was never found.

Barboza had known Jimmy "the Bear" Flemmi from their prison days. They had both come from tough backgrounds. The son of a bricklayer and a homemaker, Flemmi had grown up in the Orchard Park housing project on Ambrose Street in Roxbury with his brothers Stephen and Michael. Brother Stephen, or "Stevie" as he was called, was a year older than Jimmy and had served as a paratrooper in Korea, while Michael would later embark on a long dubious career with the Boston Police Department. All three Flemmi brothers had a penchant for crime, including Michael, who used his position as police sergeant and later detective to act as mole, intelligence gatherer, and full-blown accomplice for his siblings.

Older brother Stevie was first arrested at the age of fifteen for "carnal abuse" and had spent time in juvenile detention before enlisting in the U.S. Army two years later. Stevie Flemmi joined the 187 Airborne Regimental Combat Team, serving two tours before receiving an honorable discharge in 1955. Classified as a Rifleman by the military brass, Flemmi carried the nickname back to the streets of Boston, where he soon made a name for himself as a bookie, pimp, and killer. Stevie Flemmi began operating out of the Marconi Club in Roxbury while also nibbling around the edges of Jerry Angiulo's growing kingdom in the North End. The Italian Mafiosi appeared to respect the very businesslike, older Flemmi brother while keeping younger brother Jimmy at a safe distance. The slight did not seem to bother the Bear, who did not create any strong alliances, as he was willing to pull the trigger for the highest bidder. Predators in the truest sense, "the Animal" and "the Bear" should have been natural rivals, but instead they chose to hunt as a pack, each with an insatiable appetite for bigger game. Once Barboza had heard about the early demise of the now headless Frank Benjamin, he decided to pay his old friend a visit on Flemmi's home turf. Barboza and Guy Frizzi hopped into Guy's 1962 gold Cadillac and drove from East Boston through the Sumner Tunnel toward Dearborn Square in Roxbury. They spotted the Bear in the doorway of a restaurant, his eyes darting nervously up and down the street. Barboza waved to his fat friend, who waddled over to the Cadillac and jumped in the backseat.

"Gotta watch it," Flemmi told Barboza. "The area is loaded with law."[32]

Joe needled his old friend about not coming to see him after Barboza had been released from prison.

"Man, I got more heat on me. I did you a favor by not coming by," Flemmi responded.

Barboza pulled the Cadillac off the curb, and the trio began a leisurely drive around the winding streets of Roxbury. Flemmi pulled his ever-present cap down over his bald head just above his eyes. Barboza told him there was plenty of talk on the street that the Bear had been involved in Benjamin's murder. Flemmi shook his head firmly, his puffy cheeks making him look like a basset hound attempting to dry itself after a heavy rain. Flemmi retold the story, but this time inserting Punchy McLaughlin's name in place of his own.

"They drove off with two cars, Wimpy in his own car and Punchy driving his car with the cut-up in it," Flemmi insisted. He then told Barboza and Frizzi that Bennett and McLaughlin dumped the car with the body in it, and drove away together with Benjamin's head in a bag between them. They were looking for a quiet place to bury the skull while eyeing each other as a potential threat. The men had just spilled blood together, and that meant each had enough information to send the other to the electric chair. Like pirates in the centuries before, these mobsters lived by the code, *Dead men tell no tales*. There were two killers in the car and only one gun between them.

"When they got to a wooded area, Punchy asked for Wimpy's gun," Flemmi told them. "When Wimpy asked Punchy, What for? Punchy said he would not dare go in the woods with no gun while Wimpy was armed."

Of course, Bennett refused to hand over his weapon, and each man stared at the other, wondering if they too would survive the night. Finally Wimpy broke the silence. "I'll drive you to your car," he said.

"Where are you going now?" Punchy asked him.

"I'm taking my head and leaving," Bennett replied coldly.

Upon hearing Flemmi's retelling of the incident, Barboza just nodded his head, while Frizzi was truly horrified.

"That's the story," Flemmi said, trying to convince himself of his own words. Barboza knew the real truth but was unwilling to call out his friend, especially with Frizzi in the car.

Jimmy "the Bear" Flemmi's murderous exploits had gained him plenty of attention within the Boston underworld, and his reputation soon reached the local office of the FBI. Special Agent Dennis Condon asked one of his gangland informants to reach out to Flemmi just weeks after the murder of Francis Benjamin for an "off the record" conversation. Condon was startled to see how glib Flemmi, whose only known fear was getting pinched by police, could be when discussing his chosen profession.

"All I wanna do is kill people," Flemmi told the informant without a trace of insincerity in his voice. "It's better than robbing banks."[33] Flemmi went on to say that he had his eye on becoming the number one hitman in New England.

Special Agent Condon immediately typed up a memorandum to FBI director Hoover detailing Flemmi's conversation with the informant. "Flemmi is suspected in a number of gangland murders and has told the informant of his plans to become recognized as the No. One hit man in this area as a contract killer," Condon wrote. He later informed Director

Hoover that Joe Barboza had been telling his closest friends that he believed Flemmi had been involved in the decapitation of Frank Benjamin.

Just eight days later, another mob associate would be taken off the streets for good. Former MDC police officer Russell Nicholson had been looking over his broad shoulder just about every day since getting fingered as the wheelman in Buddy McLean's 1961 assassination of rival Bernie McLaughlin. Like both McLean and fellow alleged conspirator Alex "Bobo" Petricone, Nicholson had been spared jail time because several key witnesses had refused to testify at trial. But Nicholson had spent his last years in his own psychological prison, waiting for his day of reckoning to arrive. That day came on May 12, 1964, when several members of the McLaughlin Gang forced the six-foot, seven-inch Nicholson into a waiting car. The killers drove the thirty-three-year-old Nicholson out to another wooded area, this time in the Boston suburb of Wilmington, and put two bullets into the back of his head.

The month of June 1964 would be relatively bloodless as both warring factions contemplated their next move. Joe Barboza spent this time on the sideline as well, eager but somewhat helpless to join the fight. The Animal was in pain, although he refused to let even his closest friends know. When Barboza had converted to Judaism upon marrying his new wife, Claire, she had insisted that he follow through with the sacred tenet of circumcision. The Animal assented to his wife's demand and prayed the pain would subside quickly. Instead, it lasted several weeks, despite Barboza's cautious attention to protecting and cleaning his wound. While he was stitched up, Joe refused to use most public bathrooms because of their filth. Barboza and his crew had just begun using the corner of Bennington and Brooks streets in East Boston as their operational headquarters. The gang frequented a drugstore located on the corner when they were in need of cigarettes, soda pop, or the daily newspaper. Barboza and his crew were always scouring the late editions of Boston's competing newspapers to see how the mob war was playing out in print. Gangsters referred to the police blotter as the "Irish sports page." While most of Barboza's associates treated the drugstore owner with great disdain, Joe was always polite and soft-spoken in front of the old man. He figured this show of respect would come in handy when he needed something, like a quick escape route through the back of the store. While still recovering from his circumcision, Barboza asked the store owner if he could use the man's private bathroom. The druggist replied with a terse no, which enraged the Animal.

"Because I don't fuck with you and demand respect, you take that for weakness and mouth off to me," Barboza shouted at the man with eyes bulging. "Well, I'm not threatening you; I'm promising you."[34]

Exactly what Barboza had promised, he did not say. The druggist would learn his punishment soon enough, however. That evening, Joe and his crew smashed out all the windows of the store. The next morning, Barboza walked into the drugstore which now had plywood covering the windows.

"Can I use your bathroom?" he asked the druggist. This time, Barboza got the answer he was looking for and whistled his way toward the restroom as if nothing had happened.

The murders continued in the summer months and for crook and cop alike, it appeared that the blood would never stop flowing. In late July, the bullet-riddled bodies of two Providence mobsters, Paul Collicci and Vincent Bisesi, were pulled from the trunk of a car in the parking lot of a Quincy, Massachusetts, motel. This was a hit sanctioned by Raymond Patriarca himself. Collicci had recently done a stretch in jail for a crime that involved the Man. While behind bars, Collicci had sent Patriarca several letters promising trouble if the Mafia boss did not pull strings with the right politicians to win him parole. Patriarca did not respond immediately to the threats. Instead, the boss waited patiently for Collicci to be released from jail and then sent two assassins to Quincy, where Collicci and Vincent Bisesi were running a stolen television and air conditioner scam. Both men were shot inside their motel room and then stuffed in the trunk of their car. Their remains were discovered days later after a motel guest complained about a vile smell emanating from the trunk of the vehicle.

A month later, the bodies of two other men, Harold Hannon and Wilfred "Willy" Delaney, were fished out of Boston Harbor; their bodies had been trussed with baling wire. Hannon had been a marked man for some time. He had been on a lucrative run robbing Mafia protected bookies, and his last score had netted him $80,000. But what had really put a target on Hannon's back was his long friendship with Punchy McLaughlin.

Hannon had long served as the tip to McLaughlin's spear. It was Hannon who had exacted revenge upon a former light heavyweight boxer from South Boston named Tommy Sullivan after Sullivan nearly killed' McLaughlin during a street fight.

The brawl began in a barroom when Punchy clubbed Sullivan over the head with an iron pipe. Sullivan collapsed on the floor but somehow managed to get back to his feet. Both men had spent years in the ring, and they went after each other with all the ferocity of a championship bout. Punches flew and the fight spilled out onto the street. Sullivan was a much better fighter than McLaughlin and had kept himself in excellent shape even after his professional career had ended. The same could not be said for Punchy, whose daily exercise consisted of twisting the cap off a bottle of booze. After taking several unanswered blows to the head and stomach, Punchy tried to escape by rolling under a nearby car. Most witnesses thought the fight was over until a crazed Sullivan lifted up the back end of the car and dropped it on the curb, giving him plenty of access to his enemy hiding underneath. When the brawl finally ended, Punchy McLaughlin limped home with bumps, bruises, and half of his ear torn off. For Punchy, the humiliation would not stand. Days later, he sent Harold Hannon into South Boston to deliver the message. It was Christmas Eve 1957, and Hannon spotted Sullivan outside the East 5th Street home he had shared with his mother. Hannon called Sullivan over to his car and the former prizefighter foolishly obliged. Hannon shot Sullivan five times — three bullets piercing the man's skull. nearly tearing it off his shoulders.

Four years later, in 1961, Hannon would come of the defense of the McLaughlin brothers once again after Buddy McLean shot and killed Bernie McLaughlin. Georgie McLaughlin, who had instigated the Irish mob war that resulted in his brother's murder, scoured the streets of Somerville looking for any sign of his brother's killer. He drove around slowly with Harold Hannon hidden in the trunk of the car, the barrel of his rifle pointing through a makeshift peephole in the back of the vehicle. Hannon and the McLaughlin brothers would have no luck this time, but the attempt had put Harold Hannon directly in Buddy McLean's crosshairs.

Three years passed before McLean would have the opportunity to execute his plan of vengeance. McLean got an attractive woman to lure

Hannon and his friend Willie Delaney to her South Boston apartment for sex. When the two men walked through the front door, the femme fatale was nowhere to be found. Instead, they were met by Buddy McLean and a menacing welcoming party that included Joe Barboza. The crew grabbed Hannon immediately, while Delaney made an attempt to flee. Delaney was rounded up quickly and both men were handcuffed. McLean then brought out a butane blow torch and sparked the flame, signaling to each man that his death would be slow and excruciatingly painful. Hannon struggled against his restraints and his captors as the flame inched closer to his body. McLean lowered the torch to Hannon's crotch and asked the doomed man a series of questions, to which Hannon replied amid loud screams. Delaney watched in horror as the executioners roasted Hannon's genitals. Harold Hannon was then garroted with wire and put out of his misery. The killers then set their eyes on Willie Delaney, who had been warned to steer clear of his friend Hannon. Buddy McLean did not have any personal animosity toward Delaney, so he showed the man a bit of mercy. Delaney was given a fifth of whiskey and ten Seconal capsules, which eventually caused him to pass out. Once Delaney was unconscious, McLean ordered Barboza and his crew to strangle him and bundle his body with Hannon's. Their corpses were then driven to a pier along Boston Harbor and dumped into the cold water.

Although he considered himself an independent operator, Barboza had aligned himself with McLean's Winter Hill Gang in the Boston mob war against the McLaughlin's. Barboza and McLean were drawn together over a shared heritage. James "Buddy" McLean may have been Irish by birth, but he considered himself Portuguese at heart. As a young boy McLean was orphaned by his birth parents and was then adopted by a Portuguese immigrant couple. Buddy had been blessed with Angelic blue eyes and a welcoming smile. He was considered to be a fair young man by all he had met, but he could also hand out a vicious beating to those who crossed him. One companion summed up McLean this way: "He looks like a choir boy, but fights like the devil." Those fights left McLean with visible scars running along his neck and permanent damage to his left eye. Still, he was considered movie star handsome, and when it was time to marry, McLean broke many hearts in Somerville by offering his hand to a Portuguese-American nurse. Barboza often kidded McLean that he would one day steal her away from him. The two gangsters, who referred to each other by the code name Seagull, spent hours together discussing their mothers' favorite Portuguese recipes while planning more nefarious activities. Barboza was a frequent visitor to McLean's operational headquarters inside the Tap Royal Bar on Broadway in Somerville, where Buddy would whisper orders to his men while sitting on a stool against a back wall, so he could keep his good right eye on everyone who entered the bar.

The Irish mob war was not concentrated only in the cities of Somerville, Charlestown, and Boston. The blood also flowed as far south as the sleepy town of Pembroke some thirty miles away. Founded in 1712 and popular with cranberry farmers and horse breeders, Pembroke was virtually the last place one would think of as a burial ground for the mob — and that is what made it so attractive to the killers of Leo "Iggy" Lowry. Iggy Lowry was a bisexual, smalltime crook who had sold his body to the highest bidder while behind bars at the old Charlestown State Prison. Once he was released from jail, he floated back to the softer sex and became embroiled in a love triangle. Lowry was spotted in a local tavern making time with the wife of a known gangster. When confronted by the gangster's brother, Lowry defended himself by claiming that all's fair in love and war, as the gangster had seduced Lowry's wife the night before. The brother stormed out of the bar but remained close by for the rest of the night. When he saw Lowry and the woman leaving the tavern hours later, the brother forced Lowry into his car and drove off. As Lowry tried to fight his way out of the automobile, the brother pulled out a four-shot Derringer and fired once into the back of Iggy's head. The spray of blood along the interior of the car looked like a Jackson Pollock painting, with streaks of red splashed across the car seat and dashboard. To make matters even worse, the brother then pulled out a knife and tried to cut off Iggy's head, causing more blood to flow. The brother then picked up his sibling and together they drove to the leafy town of Pembroke, where the body of Iggy Lowry was dumped in a quiet location.

Barboza was told the story of Iggy's demise by Jimmy "the Bear" Flemmi, who provided great detail. A few weeks later Iggy Lowry's killer was himself shot in the leg, not by a rival mobster but by the wife of the gangster Lowry had tried to make it with that night. Clearly, she did not agree with the way the love triangle was handled.

In September 1964, Bostonians had taken their minds off baseball after an injury had ended the season for Red Sox rookie phenom Tony Conigliaro, who had smashed twenty-one home runs before breaking both his arm and several toes in August. The Red Sox would finish with seventy-two wins, which was not enough to secure a playoff berth. Still, locals were provided with plenty of excitement in the "Irish sports pages." Iggy Lowry's murder was the eighth mob murder in only nine months, and there would be no letup in sight. Investigators and mob insiders had very little time to debate whether Lowry's bloody murder would have any significance on the Northeast version of the Hatfield and McCoy feud. On September 4, 1964, the day after Lowry's body was recovered from the Pembroke woods, another mobster better known among cops and crooks alike would meet his fate at the order of Buddy McLean, and this time McLean would have help from a most unlikely source — the FBI.

Ronald Dermody was a son of Cambridge and a former member of James "Whitey" Bulger's bank robbing gang. Dermody was a hood to the core. In fact, it was in his DNA. His father, Joe, had been murdered in Charlestown State Prison in 1954. Ronnie's brother, Joe Jr., was serving time at Norfolk Prison. Ronnie had just been released after serving a lengthy stretch for helping Bulger pull off a heist in Pawtucket, Rhode Island, in 1955 that had netted the gang $42,000. Since Bulger was still imprisoned at Leavenworth at the time of Dermody's release, the gangster fell in with the McLaughlin Gang for both money and love. Ronnie Dermody was a handsome, muscular guy who, like Iggy Lowry before him, had eyes for a rival gangster's girl. In this case, the rival was a vicious triggerman named James "Spike" O'Toole, who was also a close associate of Buddy McLean. Dermody had fallen hard for O'Toole's girlfriend, Dottie Barchard, the Virginia Hill of the Boston mob. Like Hill, who became famous dating gangsters such as Joe Adonis and most notably Benjamin "Bugsy" Siegel, Barchard was a twenty-nine-year-old German-English beauty who was drawn to the excitement of dangerous men capable of deadly deeds.

When Barchard began her relationship with O'Toole, she was still married to an underworld thug named Richard Barchard. Despite the fact that O'Toole had fathered two of her children, Dottie Barchard had gone prospecting once again and had become captivated by the handsome, muscular Dermody. The feeling was mutual. In fact, Ronnie Dermody would do anything—even kill—to have her all to himself. After he was sprung from jail, Dermody approached Georgie McLaughlin with a unique proposition. Somewhat reminiscent of the diabolical Crisscross method in Alfred Hitchcock's classic 1951 film *Strangers on a Train*, Dermody said he would kill the McLaughlin Gang's main rival, Buddy McLean, if Georgie would whack Spike O'Toole. With O'Toole out of the way, Dermody would then be free to marry his mistress. The proposal was a curious one, and even a drunkard like McLaughlin must have had reservations. To show his good faith, Dermody promised Georgie that he would kill McLean first. The lovelorn gangster hit the streets to take care of his part of the bargain. A few days later, he opened fire on a man he believed was Buddy McLean. It wasn't. A civilian got hit, and word quickly spread that the Winter Hill boss had been the actual target of Dermody's botched assassination attempt. Panicked and now marked for death, Dermody hid out in Cambridge and contemplated his best chances for survival. He decided to reach out to FBI agent H. Paul Rico in an attempt to surrender for the shooting of the bystander.

It had been Rico who had arrested Dermody years before, after the bank heist with Whitey Bulger. What Dermody did not know was that Buddy McLean was now one of Rico's prized informants. McLean was one of the most important mobsters in all of New England, and Rico had him in his back pocket. The information McLean could provide against the Mafia was invaluable to the FBI, and to Rico's blossoming career. These things weighed on the special agent's mind as he decided what to do. The answer was simple, and it signaled Rico's crossover from cop to criminal. He told Ronnie Dermody to meet him on the border of Watertown and Belmont, close to the agent's home. Rico then placed a call to McLean and provided him with the address of the rendezvous spot. Buddy was waiting for Dermody when he arrived and shot him three times in the head, leaving Dermody dead in his car. When Joe Jr., found out about his brother's murder, he didn't blame McLean but instead pointed the guilty finger at Barboza. Joe Jr. promised revenge once he got out of jail. The two had known each other since their days at the Concord Reformatory. Barboza never had anything personal against the Dermody brothers and did not take kindly to the threats. The Animal sent the grieving brother a message through the grapevine. Through a prison intermediary, Barboza told Joe Dermody Jr. that he did not kill Ronnie, but also promised that he would be waiting for Joe Jr. on the streets to settle the dispute once and for all. Joe Jr. never got out of jail, however. He was later found stabbed to death in his prison cell.

God help the beast in me

⊙ JOHNNY CASH

Ruthless Men

Following the murder of Ronald Dermody, there would be seven more mob-related slayings on the streets of Boston and the surrounding suburbs from October through December 1964. The killings were particularly gruesome, and of course most involved alcohol. Gangster William Treannie, a small-time gangster, was shot twice through the back of the head after becoming embroiled in a heated argument with his roommate inside their apartment on Washington Street in Boston. Both men had been out drinking together for much of the day and night. Treannie was then decapitated and dismembered by his roommate and another man, who stuffed his head, torso, and limbs inside three suitcases and a quilt and then dumped the evidence in a vacant lot.

George Ash had been out spreading the yuletide spirit with a friend just a few days after Christmas when he met his untimely demise. The friend was Jimmy "the Bear" Flemmi. Ash had much to celebrate and much to fear on that day. The convicted killer from Somerville had just been assigned his secret identification number as an informant for H. Paul Rico and the FBI. Ash and Flemmi had a few cocktails and found themselves sitting in a Corvair that belonged to Ash's sister-in-law outside a church in Boston's South End. Ash either said or did something to enrage the drunken Bear, who shot him and stabbed him more than fifty times in the back. According to author Howie Carr in his 2011 book *Hitman*, Flemmi stumbled away from the crime scene blissfully unaware that the murder had been witnessed by two uniformed Boston police officers.[35] Fortunately for the Bear, both cops were crooked. They immediately went to his brother, Stevie Flemmi, and demanded and received $1,000 for their silence.

If Jimmy Flemmi was on mission to become the Boston mob's most prolific killing machine, he would face stiff competition in the form of his friend Joe Barboza. The Animal had been told that investigators were still sniffing around the unsolved murders of Harold Hannon and Willie Delaney. Boston police had recently questioned a South Shore bookmaker named Gariton Eaton about the double homicide. Eaton had not been directly involved in the murders, but rumors of McLean's handiwork were hot in the Boston underworld. The Winter Hill Gang chief asked Barboza to handle Eaton and shut his big mouth. The Animal cornered Eaton in his late model Cadillac on Mingo Road in the town of Malden and sent two .38 caliber bullets whistling through his skull. Somehow word quickly got back to the police that Barboza had been the triggerman on the job.

An attorney friend called Joe immediately and warned him that investigators would arrest him soon if he didn't skip town. Barboza took the advice and fled to New Hampshire for a few days. It would give the lawyer enough time to conduct a little investigation of his own as to what evidence the police might have had against his client. When he learned that cops had nothing but speculation to go on, the attorney set up an interview with the Malden police. Joe walked into the station, joked with a few officers, and answered a few questions. Did he shoot Eaton? Barboza shook his head no. Did he know who shot Eaton? Again, Barboza shook his head no. With no end to the stalemate in sight and no evidence to hold him on, Malden detectives were forced to let Joe go. The murder of Gariton Eaton was the first directly tied to the Animal. Barboza might have killed before, but there is no record of it. Now without a doubt, he had crossed the bridge from violent gangster to cold-blooded killer. It was at this moment that he also realized that he had a true aptitude for murder.

° ° ° ° ° ° ° ° ° ° ° ° ° ° ° ° ° ° °

It was around this time that Barboza first met Henry Tameleo, second in command to Raymond Patriarca at "the Office." Technically, Tameleo shared the underboss role with Jerry Angiulo, but everyone knew that Patriarca despised Angiulo and that Tameleo was Patriarca's eyes and ears in Boston. The Animal was introduced to Tameleo at the wake for a gangster friend who had been shot in the back of the head — the result of yet another mob love triangle. Barboza was impressed by Tameleo's subtle power. The understated underboss did not feel the need to project his importance to his fellow gangsters. Instead, Tameleo was quiet, thoughtful, and complimentary to Joe. "I learned to admire and look up to Henry more than any man living,"[36] Barboza wrote later in his memoir. Although Joe admired Tameleo, he certainly did not fear him. Just a few weeks after their introduction, the two men met again at the Ebb Tide Lounge in Revere, and this time the discussion was not as cordial. Barboza had just beaten a Mafia associate named Arthur Ventola with a baseball bat. It was in retaliation for an earlier brawl inside Ventola's club, the Ebb Tide Lounge, where a friend of Joe's had been pummeled for complaining about a watered-down drink. Ventola was a bookmaker who sold sports betting action out of a little shop in Revere called Arthur's Farm. The shop was about as big as a two-car garage and offered a litany of goods at discount prices. The shop was a popular mob hangout and was also frequented by Boston Patriots quarterback Babe Parelli and several teammates who practiced at a field nearby. Barboza was unfazed by Ventola's Mafia ties. He had given Arthur a beating to remember, and now the Animal had one more man on his hit list, Arthur's brother, Junior.

Once Tameleo learned of the situation, he brought Barboza to the nightclub for a talk. With Tameleo's power, he could have sent a gang of men after Joe in order to teach him a lesson, but the underboss was keenly aware of Joe's reputation and knew that such an order would only lead to more bloodshed. Tameleo asked Joe to give up the chase for the other Ventola brother with the promise that he would always be shown respect by Tameleo and the Office. The two men shook hands and the issue was dropped—but for only a short while. A few nights later, Barboza was back at the Ebb Tide having a drink when Junior Ventola walked in and ordered Joe to leave. Barboza could hardly believe his ears.

"Henry said I wouldn't ever be insulted again in here,"[37] Joe reminded the gangster.

"I don't care, I want you out," Ventola replied with confidence.

Barboza did not want to make a scene in the middle of the Ebb Tide.

"Let's go into the kitchen, you motherfucker," he whispered.

Ventola followed Joe into the kitchen and once there, the Animal swung around with his .38 automatic. Barboza stuck the gun under the man's chin.

"Now pull your right hand out of your pocket . . . or I'll blow your tonsils out of the top of your head."

Barboza was about to kill Ventola then and there, but was talked down from his state of fury by others at the club. When Tameleo later found out about the incident, he put his support behind Barboza and bought out the Ventola brothers' interest in the club. This show of trust and friendship was something Joe had always yearned for. It was one thing to have the respect of gangsters like Jimmy Flemmi and Connie Frizzi, but a show of support from Henry Tameleo brought Barboza one step closer to his ultimate goal. He had always been fascinated by *La Cosa Nostra*, but Joe had found himself on the outside looking in. He was Portuguese, after all. He had long been in the frustrating throes of class envy, much like a Catholic or Jewish student at Harvard who was prohibited from joining the best social and academic clubs. Joe had made a promise to himself early on that he would one day be inducted into the Mafia—even if he had to kill his way in.

° ° ° ° ° ° ° ° ° ° ° ° ° ° ° ° ° °

The Animal went to work on his career advancement immediately. Tameleo had sent Barboza on the prowl for a hood named Joe Francione, who was supposed to deliver to him a shipment of stolen furs. Instead, Francione sold the furs down in New York and pocketed the cash, leaving Tameleo embarrassed and seeking revenge. A friend of Barboza's had also been screwed in the deal, so for Joe the contract was also personal. Barboza learned that Francione was staying in an apartment in Revere, Massachusetts. With the nonchalance of a traveling salesman, Joe approached the apartment in broad daylight and knocked on the door. Francione was in the middle of a phone call with his partner when he heard the knocks. He placed the phone receiver down and went to answer the door. Listening intently on the other line, Francione's partner heard him scream: "No, don't do it!" The doomed man turned his back on Barboza in a desperate attempt to flee. The Animal shot Francione once through the back of the head and then two more times for good measure. Francione's partner, who had just heard his friend die, marched right down to the police station and turned himself in on an outstanding warrant. He knew that it was better to be in jail than out on the streets within reach of Joe Barboza.

Barboza's enemies feared him, and police were frustrated over their inability to put him and his fellow mob killers behind bars. In fact, of the fifteen mob murders committed over the previous ten months, authorities had made only one single arrest in one of the crimes. Boston police commissioner Edmund McNamara threw his hands up over the situation.

"In killings of this type, where vengeance may be part of the motive, one usually leads to another. There's no telling how many more there will be or who will be next,"[38] McNamara told a reporter from the Associated Press. "And these are the tough ones to solve. Whenever ruthless men are involved, as in these cases, nobody knows anything. Nobody sees anything. Nobody hears anything."

The past four years had been especially taxing on Boston area police detectives, who were forced to divide their time between investigating the gang war and the sensational strangling murders of eleven women that had left the Greater Boston area in a panic. Authorities had little to show for their efforts in either crime spree.

Deputy Police Commissioner Herbert F. Mulloney confirmed to the public what was already widely known among law enforcement officers — that much of the bloodshed could be traced to the McLean and McLaughlin gangs. "We think that sometimes a killing is to show personal strength. One gang wants to show another that it is strong, so they kill a member of a rival gang,"[39] Mulloney said. Although these comments were elementary to the situation, they were made to show that the public was not at risk, unlike the Boston Strangler murders.

Raymond Patriarca had been following the Boston mob war from afar for a number of years. At first, the New England Mafia boss was more than happy to remain on the sideline while the Irish gangs rubbed each other out. In Patriarca's mind, the cannibalization of Irish gangsters would lead to greater control of the Boston area rackets for the Italians. However, Patriarca was eventually forced to step in when the war started to cut in on his business. Both the Winter Hill Gang and the McLaughlin Brothers Gang saw their profits plunge while their soldiers went to the mattresses, hiding out in apartments while only venturing out onto the battlefield for short periods of time. The gangs could not run their bookmaking operations that way. This shortage of steady cash forced the McLaughlins to shake down other Boston bookies, including those who paid a hefty tribute to Jerry Angiulo. Feeling the financial pinch and unwilling to take on the McLaughlins alone, Angiulo called upon Raymond Patriarca to settle the mob war once and for all. Patriarca told his associates that he would declare martial law if the killings did not stop. The Mafia boss called on Henry Tameleo to order a sit-down between Buddy McLean and the surviving McLaughlin brothers, Punchy and Georgie.

The warring factions met at the Ebb Tide Lounge in early January 1965. Buddy McLean entered the club with a few of his men, while the McLaughlin brothers came through a side door. The air was thick with tension and the hardened memories of friends and loved ones lost on both sides. Standing in the center of the room, Henry Tameleo immediately noticed that both Georgie and Punchy McLaughlin were carrying small paper bags.

"What have you got in the bags?"[40] Tameleo asked the brothers.

"We got our guns . . . we're not going to come in here unarmed with *them*," Punchy said, motioning to McLean and his men.

The underboss was outraged. "You bring your guns to a peace meeting? Get out of here, all of you get out! Go kill each other!"

Tameleo immediately reported back to Patriarca and explained that Buddy McLean, whom the Office had done much business with, and whom the Man liked personally, was willing to negotiate a peaceful settlement to the mob war, while the McLaughlin brothers appeared ready to continue the battle inside the confines of the Ebb Tide Lounge.

Tameleo suggested that the Office finally choose a side in the Irish mob war, and Patriarca agreed. The Mafia would back Buddy McLean and the Winter Hill Gang and try to exterminate anyone associated with the McLaughlin Brothers.

A month later, in February 1965, Georgie McLaughlin, now wanted for the murder of William Sheridan, the innocent man he had killed at a Roxbury party, was arrested by Special Agent Dennis Condon, who received a $150 incentive award from the FBI for his "outstanding work in investigating and apprehending the top ten fugitive."

One McLaughlin Gang member who had been marked for death since the fall of 1964 was Edward "Teddy" Deegan. Deegan had outlived friends Harold Hannon and Willie Delaney, but just barely. In September 1964, Deegan shot and stabbed twenty-two-year-old Anthony Sacramone, a former boxer whose body was found outside a housing project just a few miles north of Boston in Everett, Massachusetts. At first, police believed Sacramone had been murdered in a case of mistaken identity and that his killer was looking for a man by the same name who had been recently released from prison. The real story was that Deegan and Sacramone were affiliated with opposing gangs; Deegan was tied in with the McLaughlins, while Sacramone answered to Winter Hill. Yet, in accordance to the many subsets of the Boston underworld, these men were also partners in crime, and both had been robbing local bookies, which had become a McLaughlin Gang trademark. The two were sitting in a parked car when an argument erupted over drugs, as both were known users. Deegan stabbed Sacramone in the neck and later shot him.

The murder did not sit well with Barboza or Jimmy Flemmi. For whatever reason, Flemmi had a soft spot in his dark heart for the Sacramone kid and had nothing but disdain for Teddy Deegan, who had not paid back a loan of $300 to the Bear. Flemmi wanted to whack Deegan. After all, he had killed men for much less. Word about Flemmi's deadly intentions quickly reached FBI special agent H. Paul Rico, who on October 18, 1964, just one day after Sacramone's murder, sent a memo to the special agent in charge of the Boston office that was then forwarded to J. Edgar Hoover, stating that he had learned from an informant that Flemmi wanted to kill Deegan. The memo was followed by another a few days later, stating that Deegan had been told by Boston Mafiosi Peter Limone that Flemmi was on the prowl, looking for payback on the $300 loan, and that he was prepared to kill Deegan for it. Both Rico and his partner, Dennis Condon, already had full knowledge that Flemmi was a cold-blooded killer. Since May 1964, both agents had drafted nearly a half-dozen memos suggesting that Flemmi wanted to be considered the best hitman in the area and had already committed several murders, including the decapitation of Francis Benjamin. Yet this information did not stop the FBI from jumping into bed with the Bear.

o o o o o o o o o o o o o o o o o

During the winter of 1965, both Rico and Condon massaged their relationship with Flemmi, no doubt educating him on what they knew about his murderous career. Blackmail was a tactic that was used effectively by both sides. The feds were looking to turn Jimmy Flemmi into a double agent. They would overlook the Bear's murderous exploits, thus giving him a license to kill, while also extracting from him useful information needed to take down Patriarca and the Mafia. In early March 1965, FBI director J. Edgar Hoover received a memo from the Boston office informing him that Flemmi had been designated a target in the Top Echelon Informant program. During this same time, Flemmi was also putting the final touches on his plan to kill Teddy Deegan. Normally, the Bear, in his typical devil may care way, would have murdered Deegan without blinking twice. But now he needed the permission of Raymond Patriarca himself. Concerned that Flemmi's murders were drawing too much heat from authorities, Patriarca had decreed that all murders committed by Jimmy Flemmi now had to be approved by the boss.

Flemmi's erratic behavior had been first noticed by underboss Jerry Angiulo, who sat him down and told him that Patriarca had a high regard for his abilities, but that he did not use enough common sense when it came to killing people.

"You can't kill someone just because you had an argument with him,"[41] Angiulo explained to Flemmi.

However, the Bear was hell-bent on taking Deegan out, so he was forced to travel to Providence to present his case to Patriarca. Flemmi brought Barboza down for the meeting. The Bear and the Animal arrived in Providence's Federal Hill section at midmorning on March 3, 1965. They grabbed a quick breakfast and a cup of coffee at a local diner and waited to be summoned by the boss. Patriarca told his men that he didn't want the notorious Boston assassins to be seen entering his headquarters, so they would have to meet someplace else. Patriarca selected a nearby garage and ordered Flemmi and Barboza to wait there for his arrival. The Mafia boss entered Badway's Garage just after 11:30 a.m. and returned to his office at approximately 12:15 p.m.

During the forty-five minutes in between, Flemmi vigorously pleaded his case.

"The kid [Sacramone] didn't have to be killed," Flemmi told Patriarca. "He's a sneak [Deegan], and I don't fuckin' trust him."

Flemmi must have laughed at himself when he delivered this line. Unbeknownst to both Barboza and Patriarca, Vincent Flemmi was negotiating a deal to become a top-echelon informant for the FBI. For Barboza, it was the first meeting with the Boss of Bosses in the New England mob.

Henry Tameleo made the formal introduction.

"This is Joe Barboza," he told Patriarca.[42]

Joe extended his hand. "My pleasure, Mister Patriarca."

"Call me Raymond," said the Man.

Barboza examined Patriarca closely. This was without question the most powerful man he had ever met. Joe was a student of mob history and had studied Patriarca's rise to power. Now he was studying the Mafia don's features and was taken aback at how sickly the Man appeared. Patriarca had deep bags under his eyes, over an ashen face. Patriarca was of medium build but looked smaller because of the stooped arc of his narrow shoulder blades. His mouth was a black hole of bad teeth and rotted purple gums, the result of his diabetic condition. If this was the face of power, Barboza briefly questioned whether attaining such power was worth it in the end. But men like Barboza could hardly understand the amount of stress Patriarca was under. He was the CEO of a large company where a rough fourth quarter could land you either in prison or on a slab at the morgue.

Although Patriarca was unaware of the FBI gypsy wire in his office, he knew that the feds were gunning for him now more than ever before. His rival, Bobby Kennedy, was no longer in office, after having both his power and commitment to public service briefly rocked by the assassination of his brother, President John F. Kennedy. Still, Kennedy had helped lay the groundwork in the war against Patriarca and others in organized crime, and now the torch had been passed to young federal agents like H. Paul Rico and Dennis Condon, who were willing to bend any rule and break any law in the U.S. government's campaign to destroy the mob.

For Barboza, if there was any advantage of being on the outside looking in, this was it. Joe, Flemmi, and their associates were considered independent contractors by the Office. They had not taken a blood oath and were not tethered to *La Cosa Nostra* in a way that they could never break free if they had to. If you swore your allegiance to the Mafia, men like Raymond Patriarca owned your soul. The benefit of being an independent contractor meant that you were not in the daily crosshairs of a demanding and deadly boss. Several made men in the New England Mafia had a reputation of being lazy and content, which did not bode well for their long-term survival. Patriarca knew this, and those around him knew that he was willing and able to prune the trees of his organization. When discussing his Mafia soldiers, Patriarca once said, "They did something ten years ago and they figure they don't have to do anything but play centerfield for the rest of their lives."[43]

Just as Barboza was beginning to empathize with, if not feel downright sorry for, the boss, his eyes locked in on the massive ring perched on Patriarca's bony finger. It was white gold embedded with a row of four large diamonds. It was the biggest ring Barboza had ever seen. He followed Patriarca's finger like a dog eagerly waiting for his master's command as the Man waved it around the room to accentuate each point he was trying to make. Whatever Patriarca told them must have been open to interpretation. Barboza and Flemmi were under the impression that they had been granted permission to kill Deegan, but Patriarca in later conversations with his closest advisors would vehemently deny giving them the green light. What is clear, however, is that the assassins returned to Boston that day with Teddy Deegan number one on their hit list. During the drive back north, Flemmi nudged his friend in the passenger seat.

"You didn't have much to say in there. What were you thinking?"

Barboza smiled at his friend. "I was thinking how I could bite his finger off and get that diamond ring."[44]

On March 10, 1965, FBI director Hoover was notified in a memo that Barboza and Flemmi had met with Patriarca to ask permission for the Deegan hit. The memo also stated that Flemmi had been with Barboza during the murder of Joseph Francione several months prior. This information did nothing to sway the FBI's decision to align themselves with the Bear. Two days later, on March 12, 1965, Vincent "Jimmy the Bear" Flemmi was officially designated a Top Echelon Informant and assigned to Special Agent H. Paul Rico. Several hours later the bullet-riddled body of Edward "Teddy" Deegan would be found in a dark alleyway in Chelsea, Massachusetts.

Deegan

It was Teddy Deegan's greed that killed him. In early March 1965, a North End hood named Charlie Moore told Deegan about the Lincoln National Bank in Chelsea, which was a prime target for a big score. Moore explained that the finance company, which was located on the second floor of the building, kept a pile of money in its safe and that they would have access to the building after hours, thanks to Moore's brother—a local cop who had agreed to leave the back door of the building open for a cut of the cash. The offer was too good for Deegan to pass up. He had been waiting for a score like this for some time. Deegan's pockets had been a little lighter recently as a result of the murder of his former partner, Harold Hannon, at the hands of Barboza and Buddy McLean. Deegan jumped at the chance and quickly pulled in his friend Anthony "Tony Stats" Stathopoulos to help him on the job. Tony Stats offered to be the wheelman for the robbery, so that meant Deegan would need a third man to help him open the safe. He called on another friend, Wilfred "Roy" French, whom he had used on some previous burglary jobs. French was also a bouncer at the Ebb Tide Lounge. Deegan was confident that his three-man crew could pull off the score, and he also believed that they would encounter no resistance, which is why he decided to leave his gun at home.

On Friday night, March 12, 1965, Tony Stats borrowed his brother's Pontiac and called Deegan, who then phoned French at the Ebb Tide Lounge.

"You ready?" Deegan asked.

French told him yes, and the two decided on a meeting place where Tony Stats would pick him up for the job. Roy hung up the phone and returned to the bar, where Barboza, Flemmi, and five associates—Romeo Martin, Nicky Femia, Francis Imbruglia, Ronnie "The Pig" Cassesso, and

Freddie Chiampi—were all waiting. French told the Animal that everything was a go. Barboza and his crew went out the back door of the Ebb Tide toward Romeo Martin's car, while French took off for his rendezvous with Deegan and Stathopoulos.

Barboza opened the trunk of Martin's car and reached for a bulletproof vest and a bag of disguises. Joe applied a phony mustache and put on a pair of horn-rimmed eyeglasses while Cassesso did the same. The Animal had strategically mapped out the hit on Teddy Deegan with the forethought of a field general. He would use two cars for the job; one to block traffic and another to make a hasty retreat from the scene. Neither vehicle was known to police, unlike Barboza's own Oldsmobile Cutlass, which was dubbed "the James Bond car" by local cops because it was equipped with a hi-tech alarm system and a mechanism that spewed thick black smoke from the tailpipe. Femia was ordered to take one car and park it around the corner from the Lincoln National Bank. He had the vehicle in position to make a hard right and stall it in the middle of the street, thus blocking the route from the Chelsea police station if he had to. Barboza, Flemmi, Cassesso, and Martin placed the other car in position down the street at a parking meter between Broadway and Luther Place with its front wheels turned out to the street ready for a speedy getaway. Barboza and his team had also bent back the plates on the front and back of the car, leaving only a few numbers exposed. The men were sitting in the car with the motor running when Barboza noticed a man in a topcoat and scally cap walk by the vehicle and stop a few paces ahead. The man turned around and headed back their way.

"What does this motherfucker want?' Joe asked aloud.[45]

The man leaned down and rapped on the window, giving Barboza a good look at him.

"Hey, your plate is bent," the man said.

Barboza's stomach tightened. The passerby with the keen eye happened to be a well-known Chelsea police captain named Joseph Kozlowski.

Barboza's crew didn't take any time answering Kozlowski. Instead, Romeo Martin pulled out onto Broadway with tires screeching and took off down the street. Kozlowski didn't think too much of it. It was just another Friday night in Chelsea. He was not on duty at the time, so he didn't pursue. However he did get a good look at the driver and the man in the backseat of the vehicle as it drove away. Martin took a quick left turn and parked the car further away from the alley. The men then doubled back and got into position in the darkness.

Roy French stepped off the curb in nearby Revere when he saw Tony Stats pull up in his brother's Pontiac.

"You guys bring any weapons?"[46] French asked as he climbed into the car.

Both men said no. Deegan was armed only with a screwdriver.

They proceeded to the finance company at Fourth Street and Broadway in Chelsea.

Chelsea police officer James O'Brien was on patrol in the area that evening and walked by the alley in back of the bank at around 9:00 p.m. He failed to notice that the back door of the building had been left slightly ajar but did notice that the lights in the back alley had been turned off, so he turned them back on and continued on his beat. Moments later, someone turned the lights out again.

The burglars arrived at the location thirty minutes later and parked on the opposite side of the street. Tony Stats stayed in the Pontiac as Roy French and Teddy Deegan climbed out of the vehicle, crossed the street, and disappeared into the pitch-black alleyway. Tony Stats scanned the street for potential witnesses but saw no one.

His eyes then reverted back to the alleyway, where he suddenly saw several muzzle flashes light up the dark alley and heard a volley of gunshots. Seconds later Roy French ran out of the alley to the sidewalk on the opposite side of the street, where the getaway car was parked. French looked directly into Tony Stats's eyes and simply shrugged his shoulders. At that moment, Joe Barboza walked out of the alley wearing a dark coat and carrying a .357 Magnum in his left hand.

"Get him too!" came a voice from deep within the alleyway.

As Barboza lifted the revolver's long barrel in his direction, Tony Stats slammed his foot down on the gas pedal and sped away from the scene with his head low. Barboza had selected the .357 Magnum as his weapon of choice that evening because he believed it could penetrate the door of Stats's borrowed Pontiac. However, Barboza was denied a side shot at the vehicle and instead had to line up his target from behind. Knowing that he could not get a clear shot, Joe decided against pulling the trigger.

Tony Stats got away and drove around for several hours before turning up at the home of his lawyer, Al Farese. Stathopoulos, who clearly was not thinking straight, told Farese that he had accompanied Deegan and Roy French on a score in Chelsea and that the cops now had Deegan. Farese picked up the phone and dialed the Chelsea Police Department.

"Is it true that you have Deegan?" Farese asked the night watch commander.

"Yes, we have him with a hole in his head," the commander replied.[47]

Farese decided it was best to take the shaken Stathopoulos back to the scene of the crime, which was now crawling with law enforcement. Once there, they met up with Chelsea police captain Robert Renfrew, who escorted them into the alley. The body of Teddy Deegan lay near the back door of the finance company. He had been shot six times by three different guns.

When asked by Renfrew what he knew about the shooting, Stathopoulos said nothing. The next day, on the advice of attorney Al Farese and another local mob lawyer, John Fitzgerald, Tony Stats visited the Chelsea Police Department, where he was shown photographs of several gangsters including Barboza, Flemmi, Roy French, Romeo Martin, and Ronnie Cassesso.

"These are the guys that did it, am I right?" asked one investigator.

Again, Tony Stats refused to talk.

"Look, they killed Deegan and they're gonna kill you too."

The investigator told Stathopoulos what he already knew, yet there was no way that he could convince the gangster to cooperate. Tony Stats left the Chelsea Police Department without offering any information on the murder of his friend. He and Fitzgerald then drove over to Al Farese's office, and Stathopoulos was shocked to find Roy French there. French had also been questioned in the murder. He had been picked up by police at the Ebb Tide Lounge hours after the shooting. French had done little to cover his tracks. He had blood stains on his shirt sleeve and right shoe and had not thought to change out of his clothes after the murder. Since French had not been formally charged with the crime, he was let go. Now both he and Stathopoulos were staring at each other across the lawyer's office. Tony Stats did not know what to say, but he mustered up something to fill the dead air.

"How'd you get away?" he asked French.[48]

"Over fences and through backyards," Roy replied.

Fitzgerald attempted to cut through the tension by pointing out that Stathopoulos had not cooperated with Chelsea police in their investigation. He then instructed the men not to be seen together. Although he did not say it, the request was fine with Tony Stats, who knew that French had set Deegan up for murder and, by extension, himself too.

Stathopoulos should have fled the area that day, but instead he went home to his apartment and drew the shades and locked the door. Tony Stats stayed in seclusion for several days — his only forays outside were to call John Fitzgerald from a payphone down the street. One night his wife borrowed his leather jacket for a trip to the corner store. As she stepped out onto the street, a car pulled up next to her and continued slowly beside her. She turned and looked at the men inside the car, who then pulled away and parked down the street. The wife kept walking, picked up her groceries, and returned quickly to the apartment. She entered her home shaking and motioned to her husband to look out the window. Tony Stats lifted the shade slightly and saw the vehicle, parked at the end of the street. At that moment, he realized that it would be unhealthy and unwise to leave the apartment again until the police made their arrests.

Chelsea Police investigators presumed they would wrap up this case quickly. Police captain Joe Kozlowski came forward and described the mysterious car that had pulled away from him about an hour before the murder.

"I walked behind the car and saw the rear number plate with a Massachusetts Registered number 444," Kozlowski told his colleagues. "The right half of the plate was folded towards the center obstructing the other three digits. I then walked to the driver's side of the car and rapped on the window. As I did this the driver took off at a fast rate of speed and took a screeching turn to the right on Broadway. I observed that the man in the back was stocky, had dark hair and a bald spot in the center of his head."

Kozlowski had just described the balding Bear. He also identified

Romeo Martin as the driver of the vehicle. With this eye-witness testimony and the blood discovered on Roy French's clothing, the investigation was progressing smoothly, and detectives had no doubt that other dominoes would soon fall.

The FBI had even more evidence at its disposal. On March 15, 1965, Special Agent Rico typed a memo stating that he had been informed five days prior to the slaying that Raymond Patriarca had put the word out that Deegan was to be "hit" and that a dry run had already been made. Rico also mentioned that a close associate of Deegan's had agreed to set him up. On March 13, the day following Deegan's murder, Rico wrote another memo, describing in detail how it had all gone down.

> Informant advised that [Vincent] "Jimmy" Flemmi contacted him and told him that the previous evening Deegan was lured to a finance company in Chelsea and that the door of the finance company had been left open by an employee of the company and that when they got to the door Roy French, who was setting Deegan up, shot Deegan, and Joseph Romeo Martin and Ronnie Cassessa [sic] came out of the door and one of them fired into Deegan's body. While Deegan was approaching the doorway, he [Flemmi] and Joe Barboza walked over towards a car driven by Tony "Stats" [Anthony Stathopoulos] and they were going to kill "Stats" but "Stats' saw them coming and drove off before any shots were fired. Flemmi told informant that Ronnie Cassessa [sic] and Romeo Martin wanted to prove to Raymond Patriarca they were capable individuals, and that is why they wanted to "hit" Deegan. Flemmi indicated that they did an awful sloppy job.

This memo was later disseminated to Chelsea police captain Robert Renfrew. The information backed up the evidence Chelsea police detectives had gained from their own network of reliable informants. Chelsea police lieutenant Thomas Evans told his superiors that he had learned through an informant that Roy French had received a call at the Ebb Tide at around 9:00 p.m. on March 12, 1965, and after a short conversation left the lounge with Joe Barboza, Jimmy Flemmi, Ron Cassesso, Romeo Martin, Nicky Femia, Francis Imbruglia, and Freddie Chiampi. The men returned to the Ebb Tide approximately forty-five minutes later, and Romeo Martin was overheard telling Roy French: "We nailed him."

On March 19, 1965, James Handley, the special agent in charge of the Boston office, advised J. Edgar Hoover that Barboza, Flemmi, French, Martin, and Cassesso were responsible for the Deegan murder. According to Handley's report, Roy French walked in behind Deegan as they were gaining entrance to the building and fired the first shot into the back of his head. Cassesso and Martin then opened fire on Deegan, hitting him five more times in the body.

° ° ° ° ° ° ° ° ° ° ° ° ° ° ° ° ° °

Once news of the Deegan hit reached the Office, Raymond Patriarca was outraged. He had not given Flemmi the okay for the murder. Patriarca had told the hitmen not to take any action until he received a thumbs up or thumbs down from Jerry Angiulo. The Boston underboss insisted that he had given no such order. In fact, Angiulo was convinced that Flemmi was a stool pigeon. Angiulo was not aware of the relationship the Bear had built with the FBI but had received information that Flemmi had a close relationship with a Boston police detective named William Stuart. Angiulo told Patriarca that the two had been seen in New York City together. The Boston underboss wanted the Bear hunted down and killed.

Jimmy Flemmi needed some advice. so he reached out to his brother Stevie. The two met at the Mount Pleasant real estate office on Dudley Street in Roxbury.[49] Stevie Flemmi owned the building, so the Bear knew that he would be safe. The brothers were joined by their childhood friend and fellow gangster Frank Salemme, also known as Cadillac Frank for his love of fancy cars. The Rifleman wanted some answers for himself. He had known Teddy Deegan for a long time. In fact, the two had pulled off some breaking and entering and burglary jobs together. Their most daring job was robbing the Brookline home of Harry "Doc Jasper" Sagansky, a former dentist who became one of the biggest bookies in America. Because Sagansky lived in a high-rise, Flemmi and Deegan had to rappel their way down from the roof. The Flemmi brothers got into a heated argument as Jimmy tried to convince Stevie that Deegan was killed because he was aiding and abetting members of the McLaughlin Brothers Gang. Jimmy also mentioned the fact that his friend Barboza, Ronnie Cassesso, Roy French, and Romeo Martin had committed the murder, but denied having any involvement himself.

Neither Stevie nor Salemme believed it. Still, the Rifleman had to protect his brother from those who wanted to put him behind bars and those who wanted to put him in the ground. Stevie was as vicious as his younger brother, but twice as smart. He knew that Jimmy had created a major problem, and he also knew that there were two men who could help him get out of it. A few days later, Stevie asked Barboza to meet him at Walter's Bar in Dorchester to discuss an urgent matter. Joe got ahold of crew members Chico Amico and Nicky Femia and the three of them drove from East Boston to Dorchester to meet the Rifleman. Flemmi jumped into the backseat of Barboza's car and gave him the news.

"This is red hot. The law has a bug on Jerry Angiulo's phone and so do we,"[50] the Rifleman explained. "I listened to the tapes myself and I heard Jerry say he was gonna have you killed no matter what."

"What else did you hear?" Joe asked.

"Everything points to the fact that he is paying to have you killed. I got in touch with you as quickly as I could."

Stevie Flemmi made no reference to his brother, who was the real target of the Mafia's scorn. In an attempt to protect his Top Echelon Informant, H. Paul Rico worked behind the scenes with Stevie Flemmi to convince Barboza that the Mafia was gunning for him. In a battle between Angiulo and Barboza, Rico, a chronic gambler, was putting his money on the Animal.

After the conversation with Stevie Flemmi, Barboza sought the counsel of his mentor Henry Tameleo. The two met at a mob-run joint called the Tiger Tail Lounge, and Barboza could hardly contain his outrage. He understood that he had made himself a target because of the Deegan murder, and that investigators were shaking the trees of the Boston underworld for information, thus causing problems for everyone.

"I can't help the heat I get from the law," he told Tameleo.[51] "People are trying to kill me and until these people are gone or don't want to kill me no more, I have to say Fuck the law. I'd rather have the heat and be alive than have no heat and be dead."

Barboza's anger was apparent as his eyes began to well up.

"Don't mistake these tears in my eyes for fear, because they're not."

Tameleo asked Barboza to calm down and then got right to the root of the problem.

"What's bothering you?"

"Jerry Angiulo is trying to kill me."

"Where did you hear this?" Tameleo asked.

"Friends of mine got it from the law and from tapes of a bugged phone conversation they heard themselves."

Tameleo asked Barboza if he had heard the tapes. Joe told him no, but that the information came from his friends.

"Jerry couldn't plan a hit without Raymond's say so, and if Raymond knows about it, then I'd know about it," Tameleo explained. "If Jerry does a hit without Raymond's okay, Jerry dies."[52]

Tameleo promised Barboza that he would step in and prevent any move against him. Joe wasn't quite convinced, so he reached out to his friend Buddy McLean. The Winter Hill boss quickly summoned thirty of his most capable gang members for a meeting with Joe at McLean's Somerville headquarters.

"I want everybody here to know that I'm sending word to Raymond that Joe is my partner," McLean told his men. "If anybody tries to kill him, I'll try with my life to stop it, and if he dies I'll avenge his death."

Barboza was relieved to hear these words, because he understood how powerful they were. He knew that even the mighty Patriarca would think twice before tangling with Buddy McLean and his band of experienced killers.

Joe Barboza was taken off of Jerry Angiulo's hit list, but his friend Jimmy Flemmi was not. If the Mafia was tracking the Bear, Jimmy Flemmi wanted to make sure they knew exactly what they were up against. He placed a phone call to Angiulo's top muscle, Larry Baione, and laid his chips down.

"There's too many of us for you, Jimmy," the Mafia soldier warned Flemmi.[53]

"I promise you this," the Bear countered in a controlled fury. "Before I get it — nine of you will be dead, and you might be in the bunch!"

Flemmi would not make good on his threat. On the night of May 3, 1965, the Bear was en route to a meeting with Barboza when he was shot while leaving his Roxbury home. He had walked outside with his hand in his side pocket, his fingers wrapped tightly around his gun. He knew that Angiulo and Baione would be coming for him, he just didn't know when.

Flemmi was heading for his car when he noticed three men approach from across the street. Before he could draw his weapon, the assassins opened fire with two shotguns and a pistol. The impact knocked Flemmi off his feet momentarily before he somehow managed to get up and fire back while staggering. Flemmi collapsed seconds later with eight bullet holes in his chest, stomach, and side.

Barboza learned about the shooting when he arrived in Roxbury's Dearborn Square about an hour later. A friend of Flemmi's ran up to Joe's car and said there had been some trouble at the Bear's house. Joe called the home immediately and was informed by a crying babysitter that Flemmi had been shot. Barboza followed Stevie Flemmi and Wimpy Bennett to City Hospital, where a doctor informed them all that Flemmi's chances for survival were marginal at best.

Hearing this news, the Animal went ballistic. He kicked the wall, shouted obscenities at the top of his lungs, and shoved aside anyone who tried to calm him down. Barboza was hell-bent on driving over to the North End to massacre Angiulo and every member of his crew. Boston police understood that they had a potential bloodbath on their hands, so they decided to round up Barboza, Stevie Flemmi, Bennett, and others who wanted to exact immediate revenge.

Stevie Flemmi learned a few hours later that his brother was going to live, but that did little to cool anyone down. A short while later detectives brought in Connie Hughes, who was a triggerman for the rival McLaughlin Brothers Gang and who Barboza believed might have carried out the contract on the Bear. Joe spent the next several minutes trying to figure out a way to get close to Hughes so that he could kill him right in the middle of Boston Police headquarters. Barboza knew that such an act could land him in the electric chair, but at the moment his fury could not be tamed. Wimpy Bennett tried to calm the Animal down and told him that Connie had an airtight alibi for the shooting. Bennett believed that Connie's brother Stevie was more likely the culprit. The Hughes brothers were the tip to the McLaughlin Gang's spear. Two of the most feared men in Charlestown, Connie and Stevie Hughes worked as a team, although they were never seen together in public unless they were getting brought in by police for questioning.

Barboza got as close to Connie Hughes as he could and told him that

Jimmy Flemmi was going to live, and that Joe was going to kill whoever was involved in the botched hit.

Police kept the Animal in a cage for six hours, while they released Connie Hughes and escorted him safely back to Charlestown. Barboza's plan for revenge would have to wait until he got the full story as to what had happened from the Bear himself.

Joe got to visit his friend a week later in the hospital and was horrified by what he saw. Flemmi had tubes running out of his lungs, and there was a wire net inside his stomach to hold the intestines in. The Animal was surprised to hear his wounded friend arguing with his brother Stevie about a guy who owed him money. Barboza could only smile.

"You're all right, you bald-headed fuck, when you can start worrying about money,"[54] he told his injured friend. Joe asked him to recount the assassination attempt.

Flemmi told him that Wimpy Bennett was right — one of the shooters was indeed Stevie Hughes. The hit squad also included Punchy McLaughlin and another pug ugly named Jim O'Toole.

Hughes and McLaughlin both had shotguns, while O'Toole was armed with a pistol. The Bear said that he was struck by the shotgun blasts, causing him to flip over and somehow land back on his feet with his gun still in his hand. Flemmi said he fired off several shots himself as O'Toole unloaded his pistol while running away. Barboza absorbed the information as he stared down at his friend on the hospital bed and could only envision the Hughes brothers lying side by side on slabs. Flemmi's chest and stomach were a roadmap of stitches and bandages. The Animal and the Bear were evil cold-blooded killers and should have been natural rivals, but instead they shared a predator's bond and a friendship that no one else could explain.

For the next seven nights, Barboza and his crew waited in the bushes near Connie Hughes's house, but neither brother appeared. Joe would have continued the stakeout, but he'd gotten himself thrown in jail after a fight outside the Ebb Tide. Coincidentally, Anthony Stathopoulos just happened to be in the next cell. Tony Stats refused to leave his cell while Barboza was there. However, he tried to cozy up to the Animal in an attempt to save his own neck. Tony Stats told him that Connie Hughes visited a bank in the North Shore Shopping Center the first of every month to cash his veteran's check. Once he was sprung from jail, Barboza ordered his associates Guy Frizzi and Chico Amico to stake out the parking lot. Sure enough, the men spotted Hughes as he was coming out of the bank. Amico wanted to shoot Connie then and there, but Frizzi persuaded him to wait until Hughes got back on the highway. That turned out to be a big mistake. Frizzi followed Hughes to the highway but could never get close enough for Amico to unload his M-1 carbine from the backseat. Hughes spotted his rivals and took them on a high-speed chase through nearby Chelsea. Amico managed to fire one shot, which blew out the back window of Connie's car. Hughes escaped the attempt without a scratch. Once Barboza learned of this, he hit the roof. He'd have to take care of Connie Hughes himself.

But the Animal would have his own problems. That same evening, while Barboza lay waiting for Connie Hughes in an alleyway near his home, a figure stumbled upon him in the darkness.

"You'll leave with more than you came if you don't leave right now, mister,"[55] Joe warned him. The man followed the instructions and walked back down the street. When the man passed a street lamp, Barboza was shocked to see that it was Connie Hughes. Connie jumped into a car, and Joe and his crew followed. The Animal positioned himself in the passenger seat with a rifle. He ordered his driver to pass alongside Hughes's vehicle as he peered inside, spotting not only Connie Hughes but his brother Stevie as well. Unfortunately for Barboza, he could not clear the rifle quickly enough to get a shot. Instead, the Hughes brothers opened fire, piercing the windshield and the passenger-side door and narrowly missing Barboza. The Hughes brothers disappeared into the darkness, leaving the Animal behind to contemplate the day-long comedy of errors.

Turning Up the Heat

Out of frustration and no doubt a little embarrassment, Barboza suspended the pursuit of the Hughes brothers, at least for the time being. Joe understood that the law of averages was on his side — the Animal only had to be lucky once, while the Hughes brothers would have to be lucky every day from now on. With his friend the Bear hospitalized and out of commission, much of the contract business would flow Joe's way during the upcoming months, and he planned to make a killing in every sense of the word.

His first order of business was to take out a sixty-five-year-old Jewish gangster named Sammy Lindenbaum, who also went by the name "Sammy Linden" in mob circles. Lindenbaum had been a longtime rainmaker for the mob thanks to a profitable and well-organized loansharking business. Lindenbaum had recently been funneling a considerable amount of money to the McLaughlin Gang to help fund their efforts to murder members of Winter Hill. Following a newly established protocol, Barboza traveled to Providence to seek permission from Raymond Patriarca. As in the Deegan case, the Man proved once again to be economic in his words and hard to pin down on his position. By no means was this a sign the Mafia boss had become aloof; instead Patriarca probably knew that the feds were out there somewhere listening to his every word, and he did not want to be captured on tape approving Lindenbaum's murder. Although Patriarca believed this was a good strategy for self-preservation, it did lead to miscommunication with button men like Barboza. The Animal left the meeting thinking that he had been given the license to kill.

Soon news traveled to the well-connected Lindenbaum that he had been marked for death. The wanted man quickly reached out to his old friend and semiretired Mafia don Joe Lombardo. Although Lombardo had given up control of *La Cosa Nostra* in the New England area years before, he still maintained considerable influence with Patriarca. Lombardo reached out to his successor and underboss Henry Tameleo and explained that he had a great deal of cash tied up in Lindenbaum's criminal enterprises and that he would take a financial hit if the contract were carried out. Patriarca was never one to let bloodshed get in the way of business. Out of respect for Lombardo, the Office got word back to Barboza that he was to call off the hit against Sammy Lindenbaum.

The feds had followed these negotiations closely. The FBI's gypsy wire—BS 837C*—had recorded much of the back and forth in this "on again—off again" mob murder in the making. Boston special agent in charge James Handley sent a memo to his fellow SACs in Connecticut and New York, along with Director Hoover, telling them that Lombardo was angry over Barboza's close association with the Flemmi brothers and that the Animal had been with Jimmy Flemmi when they killed Teddy Deegan.

With the Lindenbaum hit off the table, Barboza set his sights on another human target. The Animal returned to Providence for a sit-down with the *Padrone* at his headquarters inside the National Cigarette Service Company and Coin-o-Matic Distributors. It was not the first meeting of the two men, but it would be the most memorable. Barboza had long admired Patriarca for his no-nonsense yet even-handed approach in dealing with his soldiers. Patriarca, though, remained leery of the Portuguese hitman from New Bedford. He knew the Animal didn't have any limits and that he didn't play by the rules of engagement; this didn't sit well with Patriarca. Barboza entered the warehouse and showed his respect by taking off his ever-present dark sunglasses. After a quick pat-down by his soldiers, Patriarca ushered him into his small office, where Barboza meticulously described how he planned to kill a very reclusive mob associate who owed him money.

"He lives in a three-family house,"[56] he told the boss. "So what I'm gonna do is, I'm gonna break into the basement and pour gasoline all over the place, after which I either get him with the smoke inhalation or I just pick him off when he climbs out the window."

Barboza also told Patriarca that he'd cut the phone lines so the mobster couldn't call the fire department and that he would have three gunmen watching the other sides of the house.

"Does anyone else live in the house?" Patriarca asked.

Barboza nodded his head. "His mother," he replied.

"You're gonna kill his mother too?" the boss asked incredulously.

"It ain't my fault she lives there," the Animal shrugged.

This didn't sit well with Patriarca; even he had a set of rules to live by—and innocent family members were strictly off limits, especially someone's mother. The Mafia boss immediately canceled the hit. The Animal had proved to be too vicious even for a cold-blooded killer like Raymond Patriarca, who began consulting privately with Tameleo about the best way to deal with Barboza. The two agreed that there were only two ways to deal with a vicious animal—you cage it or you kill it.

Was Barboza serious about his willingness to murder another man's mother? Or was he attempting to sell Patriarca on the notion that he was crazy and therefore should be left alone? Joe's devotion to his own mother and his disdain for violence against women in general suggest the latter. He most likely knew that he was beginning to fall out of favor with the Office and wanted Patriarca to understand just how far he was willing to go to conquer his enemies. If the Man made a move against the Animal he would do it at the risk of his own family's safety.

Barboza most likely shared this strategy with his closest friend, Jimmy Flemmi, and no one else. Joe was a constant presence in Flemmi's hospital room as the killer continued to recover from his gunshot wounds. The Bear also had another semiregular visitor—H. Paul Rico, who would slip into the hospital after hours when the two could be alone. During one late-night meeting, the special agent explained the details of Flemmi's confidential relationship with the bureau.

"You're not an FBI employee,"[57] Rico told him. "But you will furnish information *only* to the bureau."

Rico was making a veiled reference to Flemmi's relationship with Boston police detective William Stuart. From this day forward, the Bear would be serving one master, not two.

Rico also stressed emphatically that Flemmi was never to contact the FBI directly. All information and correspondence would be handled by Rico himself.

The Bear responded with his pledge to assist the bureau and help put away the gunmen who had tried to kill him. Rico had only a cursory interest in taking down the McLaughlin Brothers Gang; instead he planned to use the Bear as bait to trap much larger game — *La Cosa Nostra*.

Developing Jimmy Flemmi as a Top Echelon Informant was the epitome of high-risk, high-reward for the FBI. Both Rico and his boss, James Handley, explained to Hoover that Flemmi maintained direct contact with Patriarca and other major New England Mafia members and could potentially be an "excellent informant." On the flip side, however, they informed the director that Flemmi had killed seven people, including Francis Benjamin, George Ashe, and Teddy Deegan, and from all indications was going to continue to commit murder.

In a memorandum sent directly to J. Edgar Hoover on June 9, 1965, Handley wrote: "Although the informant will be difficult to contact once he is released from the hospital because he feels that the McLaughlin group will try to kill him, the informant's potential outweighs the risk involved."[58]

While his friend Jimmy Flemmi had the invisible protection of the federal government, Joe Barboza was virtually alone, and the walls were beginning to close in. It would only be a matter of time before someone got pinched and flipped on the Teddy Deegan murder. Joe was sure that most members of his hit squad would protect him and refuse to implicate him if they were ever arrested for the slaying. The one member of his gang that he still had questions about was his friend Romeo Martin. Romeo had enjoyed all the trappings of the gangster lifestyle and had proved capable on the street; still, the Animal's instincts told him that Martin could not be trusted. In July 1965, several months after the Deegan murder, Martin found himself playing golf with Vincent "Fat Vinnie" Teresa and Richie Castucci, a nephew of Arthur Ventola and a part owner of the Ebb Tide Lounge. The golf outing was meant to be a leisure gentleman's outing for the newly married Martin, who was planning to travel the next day to Florida for his honeymoon. After walking the golf course in the hot summer sun, the men retired to the Ebb Tide in early evening for a steak dinner and cocktails.

Martin had been on edge for much of the day and finally revealed to Teresa and Castucci that he and Barboza had gotten into a serious argument following a recent job in which they had been paid to bust up a nightclub whose owner had not been paying tribute to Patriarca and the

Office. Joe and his crew were getting paid by the Mafia to protect their clubs and hand out beatings to rival club owners at joints like the Living Room on Stuart Street in Boston and Alfonso's Lonely Hearts Club in Revere. Club protection and plundering provided Joe with another steady revenue stream to add to his already lucrative loansharking and contract business. The scam worked this way: Barboza and his crew would enter a club and immediately begin tossing chairs around, smashing bottles and mirrors, while smacking around anyone who dared to stop them. The victimized club owners would then run to Henry Tameleo and offer the Mafia money to protect their business from Barboza. Joe would get 25 percent of the take from each club, and he made sure that every penny was accounted for. On the last job, Martin had shaken the club owner down for more money than he was supposed to and foolishly tried to pocket the extra cash without telling Barboza. Joe quickly got wind of the bait and switch and told Romeo that he would be gunning for him. This of course made little sense to Martin. Barboza was truly an animal, but he would rarely commit murder over a few dollars. The fact is, the missing money had only reaffirmed in Joe's eyes the fact that Martin could not be trusted. Teresa and Castucci had no idea how the game was actually being played, so they told Martin not to worry about it, that Barboza had considered him a good friend and that he would eventually cool off. Fat Vinnie then reminded Romeo that he had left his golf clubs in Teresa's car.

"I'll get my bag and I'll come back and have one more drink with you,"[59] Martin told Teresa as he headed for the door. "Then I'm going to get my wife and we'll take off."

Martin strolled out of the club probably thinking that his friends were right — that he had overacted to Barboza's threats. Romeo Martin quickly learned just how serious Barboza was when he entered the parking lot and saw that Joe and his pal Ronnie Cassesso were waiting for him.

Martin tried to flee but he was snatched by the Animal and thrown in the back of a waiting car. Barboza drove to an undisclosed location where he shot Romeo Martin five times. Although it was believed by many in mob circles that Barboza had murdered Romeo Martin because of a squabble over a few bucks, no one dared confront Joe about the issue. In fact, both Barboza and Cassesso served as pallbearers at Martin's funeral.

Following the murder of Romeo Martin, the red-hot Boston mob war went cold for the remainder of the summer, but flared up again in a major way in October 1965, thanks in part to Paul Rico and the Boston office of the FBI.

It was no secret that the remaining members of the McLaughlin Gang all had big targets on their backs, especially after their botched hit on Jimmy Flemmi. Barboza wanted the McLaughlin brothers and the Hughes brothers wiped out, and so did the Bear's brother Stevie. In the Rifleman's eyes, Punchy McLaughlin, the gang's new boss, was unfinished business. He had first tried to kill Punchy several months before in November 1964. The Rifleman had convinced another gangster to lure Punchy to the parking lot of Beth Israel Hospital, where the two were supposedly going to discuss business. The gangster never showed. Instead, Punchy was met by Flemmi and "Cadillac Frank" Salemme, both disguised as Hasidic rabbis and both carrying weapons. One of the men fired a shotgun blast that tore apart Punchy's jaw. Before Flemmi and Salemme could fire a few more shots into McLaughlin for good measure, they were forced to flee after the loud noise of the shotgun drew a slew of potential witnesses from nearby buildings. Punchy was badly wounded, but he somehow survived. In August 1965, the Rifleman and Salemme tried to kill Punchy again, this time sniper-style, while the gangster was driving down a rural road outside of Boston. Flemmi fired several shots from high atop a nearby tree. One bullet struck Punchy's right hand, which later had to be amputated. One could say that Flemmi and Salemme were killing Punchy slowly over time, but they were certainly frustrated by the latest botched attempt, and so was Special Agent Rico.

Paul Rico had been gunning for the McLaughlin brothers in his own way since he found out that they had called him a "fag" during a conversation that was captured by a gypsy wire. Rico had planned to murder at least one of the brothers himself. When Rico and Condon had discovered where fugitive killer Georgie McLaughlin was hiding out in the winter of 1965, Rico had no intention of bringing the man to justice. Instead, Rico wanted to kill Georgie and had asked Stevie Flemmi for an untraceable gun that he could use as a throwdown to make it appear as if McLaughlin had drawn his weapon first. The plan was scrubbed when Rico could not get the full support of his FBI raid team. Five agents had agreed to the plot, but a sixth agent could not be convinced. H. Paul Rico knew that there would be no questions of conscience among his underworld friends. The FBI man had provided Flemmi and Salemme with valuable information about Punchy's whereabouts, including the address of his girlfriend. The two mobsters began trailing McLaughlin and found their third opportunity to strike on October 20, 1965, when Punchy made plans to support his brother Georgie at his murder trial. Since he could no longer drive, the one-handed gangster's girlfriend drove him to a West Roxbury bus stop where he would travel by bus and then by subway to the courthouse in Boston's Pemberton Square.

As he stood waiting for the bus with six other commuters, Punchy gripped a small brown paper bag he had been carrying. Inside the bag was a handgun. Suddenly, two cars came into view. The first vehicle carried two hitmen, one behind the wheel and the other in the backseat. The second car, a four-door Chevy, pulled up across the street. The Chevy would be used as a crash car to delay any pursuit of the killers as they tried to flee. Wearing wigs and heavy makeup, Stevie Flemmi and Frank Salemme stepped out of the first vehicle and ran toward Punchy with weapons drawn. McLaughlin turned and ran. With his one good hand, he tossed the brown paper bag concealing his gun to a frightened woman who was waiting in line for the bus. His killers closed the gap quickly and fired five shots into his body, hitting his heart, lungs, liver, and spleen. The last bullet was fired at close range and pierced his scrotum. Punchy McLaughlin fell dead in the street. His luck had finally run out.

Police quickly began rounding up the usual suspects including Joe Barboza, who had been spending a lot of his time recently trying to figure out a way to kill Punchy's brother Georgie, who was being housed at the Charles Street Jail during his murder trial. Barboza had hoped to shoot Georgie from an apartment window overlooking the prison yard about seventy-five yards away. The problem was that the youngest McLaughlin brother refused to leave his cell out of fear that he would be assassinated. Once it became known that the turtle would never poke its head out of its shell, all focus was shifted to Punchy. The hit on Punchy had been carried out by Flemmi and Salemme, but investigators believed that the Animal had most certainly participated in the planning, considering the fact that a crash car had been involved. Also, Barboza's James Bond car had fit the description of the vehicle used by the killers. When police searched Joe's car, they found a suitcase filled with wigs and makeup. Barboza told the cops that the case had been left behind by a girlfriend who worked as a showgirl and actress. Joe was kept at the station for eleven hours until several female witnesses were brought in with the hope that they could positively identify Punchy's killers. Barboza was asked to stand in front of a one-way mirror. Cops ordered him to stand still, but the Animal refused. Instead he paced back and forth, growling at the people he knew were standing on the other side of the glass. "You'd better be fucking sure,"[60] he yelled. No doubt rattled by the thinly veiled threat, the women told investigators they were not sure whether Barboza was one of the men in either of the two cars. The murder of Punchy McLaughlin would go unsolved, at least officially.

McLaughlin's murder would be avenged several days later in shockingly brazen fashion. On October 19, 1965, Joe Barboza called mob boss Buddy McLean at the Tap Room, McLean's Winter Hill headquarters, and told him that he was running down some good information on the whereabouts of McLaughlin Gang hitman Stevie Hughes. McLean was excited to hear the news, and the two friends exchanged pleasantries and insults and both promised to get together soon.

"Be careful and keep your right hand high, Seagull,"[61] McLean told Barboza before he hung up the phone.

Several hours later, at approximately 1:05 a.m., Buddy McLean and two bodyguards, Americo Sacramone and Anthony D'Agostino, who were both on parole, strolled out of the Peppermint Lounge on Winter Hill. They passed the abandoned Capitol Theatre, where Stevie Hughes was waiting with an automatic rifle. Hughes ambushed McLean on the street and fired four shots, striking both bodyguards. Buddy grabbed his men and tried to drag them behind his 1965 Buick and out of the line of fire. Hughes rushed forward and took aim once more. He raised the rifle toward the back of Buddy's head and fired. As McLean collapsed on the sidewalk, Hughes escaped through the back of the shuttered theater to a waiting car with his brother Connie at the wheel. Buddy McLean was rushed to Mass General Hospital, where he died thirty hours later. Buddy had $1,400 in one pocket and a .38-caliber revolver in the other. "Mc-

Lean was living on borrowed time," said Somerville police chief Thomas O'Brien. His bodyguards survived the attack but were later returned to prison on parole violations.

Barboza learned of the shooting in the early morning hours as he was leaving a bar in Boston's West End. He could hardly believe the news. He rushed over to the Tap Royal, where several Winter Hill Gang members were swapping information about the hit and planning their next move. Once Joe had found out that Stevie Hughes was the likely gunman, his anger could only be matched by the guilt he felt for not having killed Hughes when he'd had the chance. The Irish good-bye for James "Buddy" McLean was the biggest ever seen in Somerville. The streets around Kelliher's Funeral Home were lined with cars as politicians, mobsters, and union officials alike gathered to pay their final respects to the founding father of the Winter Hill Gang. Detectives in plain clothes walked up and down Broadway, writing down the registration numbers of all the vehicles. Inside the funeral home, McLean's bronze casket was surrounded by bouquets of red roses and hundreds of Mass cards. The coffin cover was kept closed, as Buddy's face had been partially torn off by the rifle blast. Instead, mourners were greeted by a beaming photograph of the Winter Hill boss and also by his widow, Jean, and their teenaged son, who kept vigil stoically next to the casket.

Barboza entered the funeral home and met friends with a somber nod as he made his way down the receiving line. He shook the son's hand and hugged McLean's widow gently, not wanting to wrinkle her black dress or mess her perfectly quaffed platinum hairdo. Joe also offered his pledge of support for the gang's new boss, Howie Winter. As Barboza filed out of the funeral home a detective pulled him aside. "Hey Joe, who's in there?" he asked.

"A lot of people I don't know,"[62] the Animal said as he walked toward his James Bond car and drove away.

o o o o o o o o o o o o o o o o o

The next morning, three hundred people turned out for Buddy McLean's funeral Mass at St. Polycarp Parish in the heart of Winter Hill. The church was surrounded by a large detail of uniformed police officers armed with shotguns. The side and back doors of the parish were also locked during the service, just in case the Hughes brothers decided the funeral would be a perfect opportunity to wipe out the rest of McLean's gang.

A week later, a high-ranking member of the Winter Hill Gang received a large floral arrangement with an elegant black ribbon. There was no name on the card, but he knew it had come from Stevie and Connie Hughes and the message was clear — You're next.

Raymond L. S. Patriarca. The Godfather of the New England Mafia, who was both idolized and later reviled by Joe Barboza. *Courtesy of the Massachusetts State Police.*

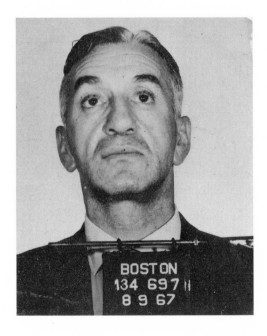

Gennaro "Jerry" Angiulo. The Boston underboss bought his way into La Cosa Nostra by handing Raymond Patriarca an envelope stuffed with $50,000. *Courtesy of the Massachusetts State Police.*

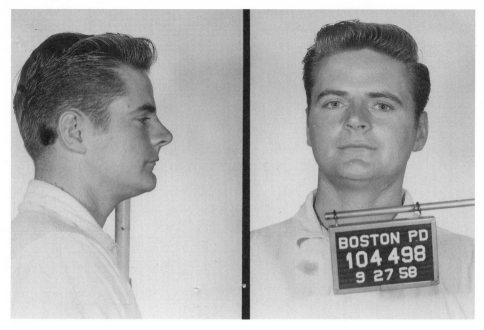

Buddy McLean. Boss of Somerville's Winter Hill Gang, McLean presided over one of the bloodiest mob wars in American history. *Courtesy of the Massachusetts State Police.*

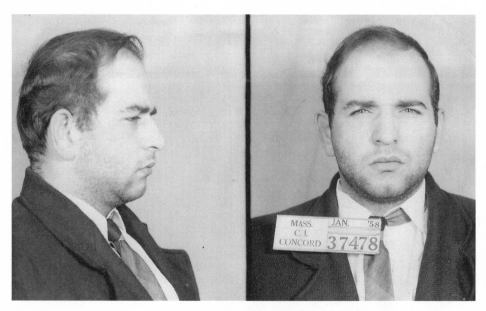

Vincent "Jimmy the Bear" Flemmi. A cherubic psychopath whose goal was to become the number one hit man in New England. *Courtesy of the Massachusetts State Police.*

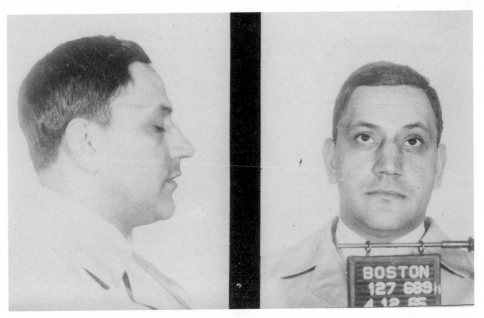

Arthur "Tashi" Bratsos. A trusted soldier in Barboza's crew, Bratsos met a violent end inside the Nite Lite Cafe in 1966. *Courtesy of the Massachusetts State Police.*

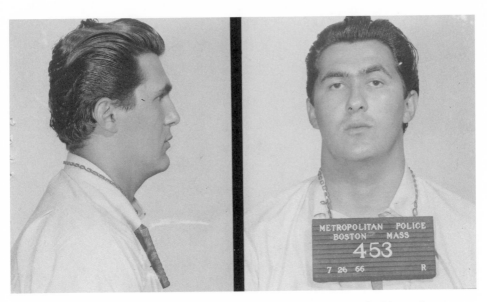

Chico Amico. Barboza loved Chico like a brother and vowed revenge for his murder at the hands of La Cosa Nostra. *Courtesy of the Massachusetts State Police.*

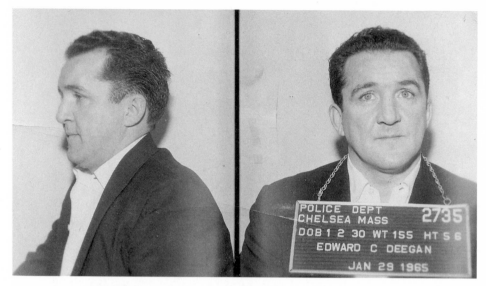

Edward "Teddy" Deegan (*mugshot*). A small-time burglar and killer whose murder of Anthony Sacramone put him at odds with the Animal. *Courtesy of the Massachusetts State Police.*

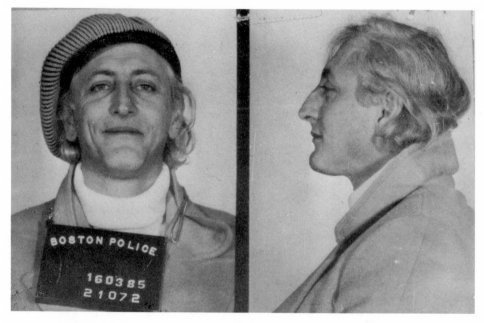

Joseph J. R. Russo. Known as a flashy dresser and a "bleeping genius with a carbine," Russo was sent to San Francisco to hunt down the Animal. *Courtesy of the Massachusetts State Police.*

The Deegan murder scene. One of the most significant gangland slayings in American history, Teddy Deegan's murder in March 1965 would trigger a decades-long court battle, resulting in one of the largest judgments against the federal government in history. *Courtesy of the Massachusetts State Police.*

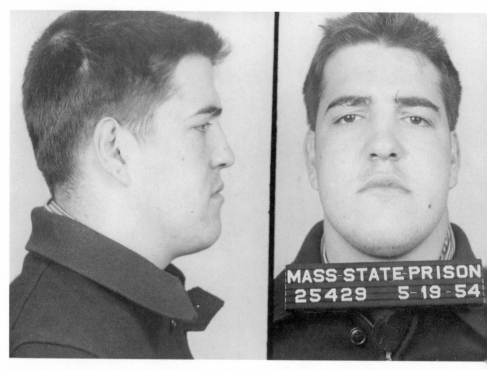

Joe Barboza, age 22. The former leader of the Cream Pie Bandits, Joe "The Animal" Barboza spent much of his early years in reform school and behind bars. *Courtesy of the Massachusetts State Police.*

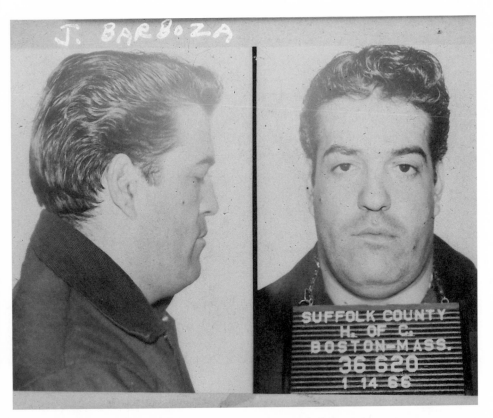

The Animal in 1966. The FBI convinced Barboza to provide false testimony in two major mob trials in hopes of destroying the New England Mafia once and for all. *Courtesy of the Massachusetts State Police.*

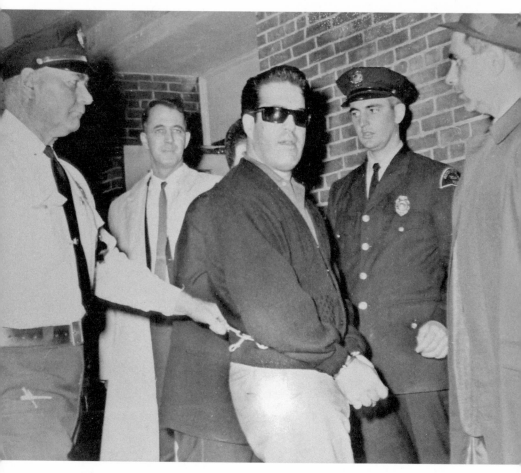

When Animals Attack. Joe "The Animal" Barboza became the first man ever placed into the Federal Witness Protection Program. *Courtesy of Kevin Cole.*

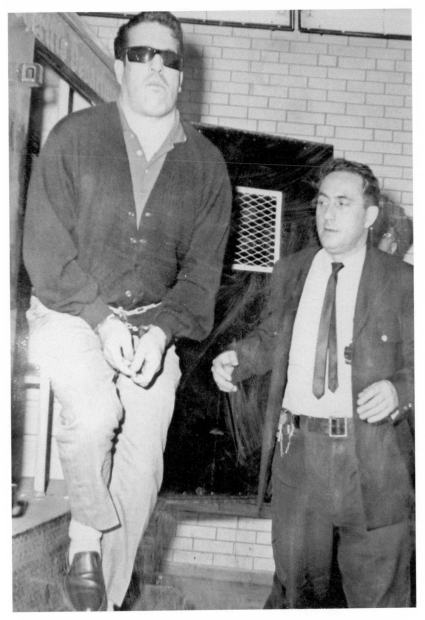

When Animals Attack. Photos of Barboza would go uncredited in newspapers because photographers were afraid of reprisal from the Animal. Here, Barboza lunges at Boston Herald photographer Kevin Cole for snapping his picture. *Courtesy Kevin Cole.*

Thacher Island. Barboza and his family were guarded on Thacher Island, off Rockport, Massachusetts, as he prepared his testimony against Angiulo and Patriarca. Patriarca sent a hit squad to the island in hopes of silencing the Animal.

The Mafia could not reach Barboza, so assassins tried to kill his lawyer John Fitzgerald with a car bomb in January 1968. *Courtesy of Howie Carr, author of* Hitman.

The powerful bomb blast snapped powerlines and damaged windows in the neighborhood near Fitzgerald's law office. *Courtesy of Howie Carr, author of* Hitman.

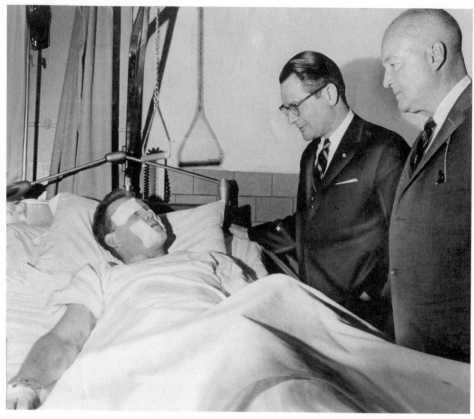

Fitzgerald in hospital. Surgeons spent nearly six hours operating on Fitzgerald, whose right leg had to be amputated three inches below the knee. *Courtesy of Howie Carr, author of* Hitman.

The Mickey Mouse Club

In the fall of 1965, H. Paul Rico and the FBI had come to the realization that their ignoble experiment with Jimmy Flemmi had failed. The feds had decided they would happily turn a blind eye to Flemmi's crimes as long as he did not get caught, but the Bear could not keep up his side of the bargain. Flemmi had recently become a fugitive after failing to show up for court after he was charged with shooting a man named John Cutliffe. Unlike most of Flemmi's victims, Cutliffe had survived to tell the tale and could positively identify the shooter. "In view of the fact that informant Jimmy Flemmi is presently a local fugitive, any contacts with him might prove to be difficult and embarrassing,"[63] Agent Rico stated in a memo to his superiors. "In view of the above, this case is being closed." Two months later, the Boston FBI office sent a follow-up letter to Director Hoover letting him know that Jimmy's brother Stevie Flemmi was being designated as a Top Echelon Informant who could provide them with valuable information about the Mafia's growing allegiance with the McLaughlin Brothers Gang (or what was left of it). This purported alliance was of course far from the truth. Raymond Patriarca had long respected Buddy McLean and the Winter Hill Gang and had nothing but contempt for their Charlestown rivals, who were now led by Connie and Stevie Hughes. But Paul Rico hated the McLaughlins, and J. Edgar Hoover hated *La Cosa Nostra*. By creating an allusion that both sides were now working together, Rico believed that the FBI would provide him with additional resources to destroy the McLaughlins once and for all.

While Paul Rico was moving his chess pieces around to stack the board in his favor, Joe Barboza remained on the front lines of the war—looking to strike first and prevent his enemies from taking him down. Barboza was now giving much more thought to his own personal safety. The sheer act of leaving his home had become a highly coordinated operation. He used a motorcade of three cars and communicated with members of his crew by two-way radio. Police detectives followed him every night, but the Animal soon found ways to shake their tail, especially on nights when he had to perform his blood work.

Barboza's next target was a small-time hood and part-time bartender named Ray Distasio. Distasio worked for the McLaughlin Gang, and he had once helped Punchy McLaughlin hunt Buddy McLean before both were subsequently murdered. This was not the reason Distasio was now on Joe's hit list, however. Joe was given the contract to kill Distasio because the mobster had borrowed $15,000 from the Office and had made little attempt to pay it back. "You'll get your money when I have it," Distasio defiantly told the Mafia. Barboza found out that Distasio lived in a small house behind a school in the suburb of Medford. The original plan was to ambush Distasio when he walked out of his house. Joe and two members of his crew showed up one morning and waited in the adjacent schoolyard for Distasio to show himself, but the marked man had given them the slip. Several hours later, at approximately 5:00 p.m., Barboza and his crew, which now included fugitive Jimmy Flemmi, arrived at the Mickey Mouse Lounge on Revere Beach Boulevard where Distasio was working as a bartender. Joe pulled his car up on the sidewalk in front of the bar and stepped out with Flemmi and two others. Joe had another member of his crew waiting in a car down the street — ready to block traffic in case the cops came. Barboza ordered one of his men to stand guard near the entrance with a carbine as he, Flemmi, and another man went inside. Joe flipped the hood of his sweatshirt over his head and covered his eyes with a pair of dark sunglasses. As they entered the lounge, Flemmi wrapped his arms around his wide frame and shook. "Brr . . . it's cold,"[64] he said, while keeping his head low. Distasio, who was standing on the dance floor, looked up and smiled. At that moment Barboza appeared from behind Flemmi holding a .38 pistol. Distasio looked up in horror and ran back toward the bar where his friend John O'Neil was standing. Barboza caught Distasio in midstride, cutting him down with one bullet.

"I don't wanna die," O'Neil screamed as he took off in the opposite direction across the dance floor toward the front door at the far end of the bar. Barboza and Flemmi gave chase, pausing just long enough to pump a few more bullets into Distasio's head. Joe had not planned on killing O'Neil, but he felt that he had no choice. The Animal closed the gap on the fleeing O'Neil and raised his pistol. Barboza tried to pull the trigger but the weapon jammed. He then pulled out a backup gun, an airweight snubnose .38, and shot O'Neil once in the arm. O'Neil screamed in pain, grabbed his arm, and stumbled forward. Barboza shot him again in the same arm. Badly wounded, O'Neil fell to the ground. The Animal stood over the man, pointed his weapon, and finished the job.

Barboza and Flemmi spilled out of the Mickey Mouse Lounge, jumped into their getaway car, and sped over the General Edwards Bridge spanning the Saugus River toward Lynn. Joe pulled into a shopping center and switched cars. He continued on toward the Charter House Motel and dumped the murder weapons in some nearby weeds.

When police arrived at the scene a short time later, they immediately ruled out robbery as a motive for the slayings. There was more than $100 that sat untouched in two cash registers, and the victims' wallets had been undisturbed. Detectives found Distasio lying face down on the floor, while the body of his friend O'Neil was discovered two feet from the front door. Detectives surmised that the man had been trying to flee. They were right. Police also found bullet casings scattered on the floor and two slugs embedded in the wall. O'Neil had been shot three times, while Distasio had been shot at least five times; most of the bullets were lodged in his skull. "This was a professional job," one police official told the *Boston Globe*. "Whoever killed these men knew exactly what he was doing."[65]

Although he had yet to be charged with the murder, the *Boston Globe* implicated Barboza almost immediately. The day after the hit, the *Globe* published an article suggesting that "the Animal and his Beasties" had committed the crimes. The article also painted John O'Neil as a devoted father of five and innocent bystander who was simply in the wrong place at the wrong time. It was true that O'Neil had been murdered as a matter of circumstance. He may have been a bystander, but by no means was O'Neil innocent. In reality, O'Neil was a gunrunner who supplied weapons to Distasio to sell to other members of the McLaughlin Gang.

Barboza was outraged when he read the article, despite the fact that it was mostly accurate. Joe even threatened to sue the newspaper but was talked out of it by fellow mobster and friend Wimpy Bennett.

Detectives were also scrambling to figure out if the hits at the Mickey Mouse Lounge were connected to another gangland murder earlier that same day in Boston. In certain ways they were, as all the murders had involved Jimmy "the Bear" Flemmi. Stevie Flemmi had asked his friend and fellow mobster, twenty-four-year-old Johnny Martorano, to grant him a favor. The Rifleman had heard that two mob associates, Bobby Palladino and John Jackson, were planning to testify that Jimmy Flemmi had been involved in the murder of a woman, Margie Sylvester, the year before. The thirty-five-year-old blonde divorcee had been stabbed to death and her body rolled up in a rug and stashed above a bar called Luigi's on Washington Street. Johnny Martorano's brother had already been indicted as an accessory after the fact. Jimmy Martorano ran the bar and had replaced the rug used to entomb Sylvester's body. Martorano was confident that his brother would not flip on the Bear, but the same could not be said for Palladino and Jackson.

Johnny Martorano found Palladino at a blackjack game on Blue Hill Avenue and asked him to take a ride in his green Cadillac El Dorado convertible. Palladino got in the passenger seat while Martorano slid into the backseat. A friend of Johnny's was behind the wheel. Once the car began moving, Palladino panicked and drew his gun. He fired a wild shot at the driver and missed, instead blowing out the driver's side window. Johnny Martorano whipped out his revolver, pressed it to the back of Palladino's head, and fired. Johnny then ordered his friend to keep driving toward the North End, where they would dump the body. They pulled Palladino's bloody remains from the Cadillac and left the corpse next to a steel girder outside the Boston Garden. Later Martorano tossed his own bloody clothes down a sewer and torched the car. The next morning a news photographer snapped a photo of Palladino's body that later found its way onto the pages of *Life* magazine. The Palladino murder infuriated Mafia underboss Jerry Angiulo, not because he had any warm feelings for the gangster, but because the killers had dumped his body in the North End, just a few blocks from Angiulo's headquarters. The Palladino murder was the first gangland hit of Johnny Martorano's notorious career, which would span three decades. During that time Martorano would kill nineteen more people for his friend Stevie Flemmi, for the Mafia, and for his future partner — James "Whitey" Bulger.

Joe Barboza would supply members of his own crew to help Johnny Martorano take care of the other witness in the Sylvester murder a year later. John Jackson, an African American, had been a part-time bartender at the lounge where Margie Sylvester was killed. Martorano and Barboza cohort Tommy DePrisco trailed Jackson to his girlfriend's apartment on Queensbury Street in the shadow of Fenway Park. Martorano hid behind a fence and shot Jackson as he stepped out of his car. The murder weapon, a shotgun, had been purchased hours before with a phony license at Sears Roebuck.

The murders had been committed to protect the Bear, who also had other legal problems to worry about. Jimmy Flemmi had finally been captured hiding in a closet in an apartment in Brookline and put on trial for the shooting of John Cutliffe. Flemmi was found guilty of armed assault with intent to murder and was shipped off to Walpole State Prison. Flemmi was also being eyed in the recent shooting of a McLaughlin Gang member named Maxie Shackleford, who had been wounded in the right arm while sitting in a parked car. A witness came forward and told reporters that he had seen "bullets flying everywhere" and that the gun battle had lit up the sky like the Fourth of July. When pressed by police to give up the name of the man who had shot him, Shackleford stayed true to the code. He told detectives that it was a misty night and that he couldn't see anything. The witness had no such problems, however. He had written down the license number of the getaway car, which matched an automobile owned by the Bear.

∘ ∘ ∘ ∘ ∘ ∘ ∘ ∘ ∘ ∘ ∘ ∘ ∘ ∘ ∘ ∘ ∘ ∘

The Animal avoided prosecution for his major crimes such as the murders of Ray Distasio and Teddy Deegan, but he found himself in and out of court on lesser offenses — offenses that still carried jail time. In January 1966, Barboza was put on trial for assaulting a police officer, illegal possession of a firearm, possession of marijuana, and disturbing the peace. Through some legal maneuvering on the part of his lawyer, a young attorney named F. Lee Bailey, Barboza was convicted only of the least serious charge —

disturbing the peace, and was given a six-month jail sentence at the Deer Island House of Correction near Logan Airport. While behind bars, Barboza was put on trial again, this time for resisting arrest and fleeing police.

"He was speeding your Honor,"[66] Barboza's mob lawyer Al Farese explained in court. "He was fleeing police officers who thought he was someone else."

The judge nodded and looked at Barboza. "If he had lived a better life, he wouldn't be fleeing."

"He changed his name to Baron so that he can change his life," the lawyer pointed out.

This drew a laugh from the judge. "Mr. Farese, when Barboza changes we'll all be on the moon," the judge replied. Barboza was given a $35 fine and ordered back to Deer Island. Three more gangland murders were committed while Joe was behind bars. One victim was Barboza's former training partner, Tony Veranis. In the words of Marlon Brando in *On the Waterfront*, Veranis coulda been somebody. He coulda been a contender. As a boxer, Veranis was one of the best welterweight prospects ever to come out of Massachusetts. He had fifteen hard-fought wins under his belt, with most victories coming by knockout. But he had also taken a beating in the ring, and the mileage began to show when he started complaining of severe headaches. In his next bout, Veranis was knocked down in every round and was later rushed to the hospital, where he fell into a coma. He recovered just enough to get back into the ring once again, but his best days were clearly behind him. He soon hung up his boxing gloves and fell into a life of crime.

Veranis was a minor criminal who carried major debts with the mob. He was constantly fending off loansharks that had come to collect what they were owed. One gangster continually stiffed by Veranis was Barboza crew member Tommy DePrisco. Veranis, who was fearless and oftentimes drunk, ran into DePrisco's friend Johnny Martorano at a club opening in late April 1966. The former boxer boasted that he had just kicked DePrisco out of South Boston with his tail between his legs. Veranis told Martorano to fuck off and then reached for his gun. Martorano, who was every bit as capable as Flemmi and Barboza, drew first, shooting Veranis in the head and killing him with one shot. The former boxer's body was later dumped in the Blue Hills of Milton.

A month later, talk of Veranis's murder would subside as the Winter Hill Gang was able to hook a much bigger fish. The Hughes brothers were still on the streets and running the show for the McLaughlin Gang. Stevie Hughes had survived a recent ambush at the hands of Wimpy Bennett but had had to have his spleen removed. Stevie had been shot in the chest as he and Connie stepped out of a car across the street from Connie's home in Malden. Wimpy Bennett fled quickly and so did Connie Hughes, leaving his brother on the street and bleeding badly until help arrived. Stevie of course gave detectives no information regarding his assailants. Brother Connie told police that that Stevie had "been shot, period."[67]

Connie was not going to allow the law to settle this dispute. Instead, he hit the streets looking for revenge and looking for information on the whereabouts of Bennett and Howie Winter, the newly minted boss of the Winter Hill Gang. On May 25, 1966, Connie and an associate were inside a Charlestown bar grilling a young gangster for information. When the kid refused to talk, Connie took out a long knife and stuck it into his leg. The interrogation took more than an hour, and another bar patron, a young gangster named Brian Halloran, managed to get word out that Connie Hughes was inside and demanding answers. The Winter Hill Gang mobilized quickly and had two cars in position outside the tavern when Hughes finally departed in the wee hours of the morning. Connie Hughes jumped into his car and drove toward the Mystic River Bridge. The Winter Hill Gang followed. Connie did not appear to notice the tail. Instead, he paid the bridge toll and kept going. The killers drove through the toll gate and sped forward surrounding Connie on his right and his left. They opened fire on the car in the center lane, riddling it and the driver with more than sixty bullets. Connie Hughes was struck twice in the head, killing him instantly. His head hit the steering wheel as the car careened from the center lane toward a bridge abutment where it caught fire. The killers kept going. Moments later, a passerby, thinking he had stumbled upon a horrific accident, stopped his car and rushed over to the wreck. He pulled Connie's body out of the vehicle just before it exploded into flames. It was then, in the pale light of the roaring fire, that the motorist noticed that Connie had been shot several times.

The newspapers once again tried to tie Barboza to the murder. One reporter claimed that Connie had been given a contract to kill an inmate on Deer Island but that the inmate had somehow managed to strike first. Although he was not named in the article, it was implied to those in the know that Barboza was indeed the inmate in question. When Joe was notified about the hit on Connie Hughes, he celebrated with a filet mignon that he had stolen from the warden's refrigerator and later some marijuana. As Joe stretched out in his bunk with a joint, he smiled and thought of his friend Buddy McLean, whom he had now avenged, at least in the public's mind.

In March 1966, Special Agent H. Paul Rico was assigned exclusively to the development of Top Echelon Informants. He also received glowing praise from his superiors, who stressed that Rico had "exceptional talent in his ability to develop informants and his participation was considered outstanding." A year later, Joe Barboza would help to enhance Rico's reputation tenfold.

The Hit Parade

Less than a month after the fiery murder of Connie Hughes, another Boston gangster would also die in his car. The hit on Rocco DiSeglio was a classic case of what can happen when you bite the hand that feeds you. DiSeglio was yet another in a long line of boxers turned mobsters in the New England underworld. DiSeglio had first come to the Mafia's attention during his brief prizefighting career when he proved all too willing to take a dive for the mob. But after his boxing career, DiSeglio felt that the Mafia owed him more than just a debt of gratitude. When Mafia money and opportunity didn't flow Rocco's way, he began to hold up mob-controlled dice games around Massachusetts. DiSeglio worked from the inside, making sure the doors to the joint where the high-stakes games were played were left unlocked. When Jerry Angiulo found out about the robberies, he pulled in one of the robbers and gave him an offer he couldn't refuse. Kill DiSeglio, or be killed yourself. The robber quickly accepted the assignment and lured DiSeglio into a car ride of which he would not be coming back. The robber shot DiSeglio three times in the head, tearing apart half of his face. Another bullet traveled through the back of his head and exited out of his eye socket. The body of Rocco DiSeglio was dumped, along with his wife's Ford Thunderbird, in the Ipswich River Wildlife Sanctuary in the idyllic town of Topsfield, Massachusetts. Although he had not taken part in the hit, Barboza knew all about it. In fact, Angiulo had originally blamed Barboza for the dice game stick-ups, claiming that one of the robbers bore a resemblance to Joe's associate Chico Amico. Hours after the shooting, Barboza called an Irish cop he knew and told him where to find DiSeglio's body.

When Joe was finally released from Deer Island in the summer of 1966, his crew had grown to include not only the Frizzi brothers (Connie and

Guy) and Chico Amico but also Tommy DePrisco, Nicky Femia, and Arthur "Tashi" Bratsos. Femia was all brawn and no brains, but as loyal as a German shepherd. Tashi Bratsos was also brought aboard because of his loyalty to Barboza and because he had a brother who was a police officer. Like all mobsters, Barboza understood the benefit of having an informer from the other side of the law. One man whose loyalty had now come into question was Guy Frizzi, who had been with Barboza the longest. The other crew members hated him, and Guy had a habit of beating women, which did not sit well with Barboza. Frizzi felt the growing tension and decided to take a sabbatical to California.

"You've had a five-month vacation," he told Barboza. "Now it's my turn."[68]

While Guy Frizzi was vacationing out West, a girlfriend approached Barboza with a warning. She told Joe that Frizzi had been talking behind his back constantly and that Guy believed that he should be the leader of the crew, and that he should be the one traveling down to Providence to confer with Raymond Patriarca. This was all Joe needed to hear. Guy Frizzi would leave the gang quietly, or he would leave in a coffin.

"I'm buying you out," Barboza told Frizzi.

Tashi Bratsos bought Frizzi's end of the shylocking business for $15,000 with an agreement to pay an additional $10,000 in the future. At first, Frizzi refused to sell and went around to the gang's customers begging them to come with him. But the customers were loyal, and, more important, fearful of Barboza. Guy Frizzi took the cash and left the gang with a chip on his shoulder and a score to settle with the Animal.

While Guy Frizzi could be both conniving and vicious, he still knew how to run a bookmaking business and, equally important, he knew how to steer clear of the law. This could not be said of Barboza's other crew members, who were too quick to decide a dispute with a knife, a gun, and even their mouths. This lack of discipline would continue to plague Barboza. Shortly after his release from jail, Joe was picked up on a phantom gun charge while at a club in the South End. The Sahara Club was raided by cops one night and a gun was found in the back office. Police fingered Barboza for the weapon and placed him in cuffs. Joe knew the charge was bullshit so he kept his cool, which could not be said for his friend Chico Amico.

"You can't leave him alone, can you?" Amico shouted at the officers as they placed Barboza in a waiting cruiser. "You won't be satisfied until they find some of you on the streets with your heads blown off!"[69]

Boston police officers did not take kindly to the overt threat, so they kept Barboza in stir for several hours before they let him go. Immediately afterward they went looking for Amico, who managed to escape but not before spraining his ankle in flight.

When Barboza finally caught up with Chico, he squeezed the bad ankle until the man screamed out in pain. "You and your big mouth," the Animal scolded him.

Amico should have heeded Joe's warning. Instead, he brought heat on the gang once more when he stabbed a man outside the Tiger Tail Lounge in Revere. The victim, twenty-three-year-old Arthur Pearson, had become embroiled in a shouting match with the club's bouncer when Amico, Barboza, and Nicky Femia entered the fray.

"We don't like you, guy," one of the men whispered into Pearson's ear from behind. Pearson also felt something sharp against his back.

After the dust had settled, Pearson left the bar only to find Barboza's crew waiting for him outside. Without a word, Chico Amico stepped forward and stabbed Pearson in the stomach. The victim was rushed to the hospital while police rounded up the usual suspects, which in this case meant Amico, Barboza, and Femia.

Pearson survived the attack and gave a statement to police while lying in his hospital bed. He told investigators that all three men had been involved in the stabbing in some way. Pearson also said that two of them walked over to him while he was lying on the ground and warned him not to talk or he would be killed. The victim was happy to share his story with police at the hospital, but when it came time to testify before a grand jury Pearson suddenly grew silent. Barboza's threats were real, as was the $10,000 he had given the victim's father to ensure his silence. The case was eventually dropped, but Joe's faith in the competency of his crew grew even more suspect.

In July 1966, as some were beginning to question the control Raymond Patriarca had over the rackets in New England, the Man answered his doubters in a big way. Patriarca had learned that a bookie named Willie Marfeo had gone into business for himself on Federal Hill in Providence.

This was a major no-no. To make matters worse, Marfeo had refused to pay tribute to Patriarca. When the Man sent underboss Henry Tameleo to warn Marfeo that he had better pay up or else, Tameleo was greeted with nothing more than a slap in the mouth. The insult was a slap in the face to Patriarca, who sent out the order that Marfeo had to go. The only question now was how to do it. Marfeo knew all the muscle that Patriarca employed, so it would be nearly impossible to get a jump on the bookie with local hitmen. Patriarca decided to bring in an outside assassination squad for the job. The boss provided the killers with weapons, cars, and an escape route. He also selected the best possible place to find Marfeo flatfooted. The assassins caught Willie Marfeo enjoying a slice of pizza at a joint called the Korner Kitchen on Atwells Avenue in Providence. After ordering all the patrons to lie down on the floor, the killers grabbed Marfeo and shoved him into a phone booth. They closed the door, raised their guns, and unloaded on the bookie — killing him with four gunshots to the head and chest. The Marfeo hit proved to those inside law enforcement, and inside the mob, that Raymond Patriarca's bite was still every bit as deadly as his bark.

Two years later, in April 1968, the Man ordered the murder of Willie's brother. Rudy Marfeo shared his brother's stubborn streak and had also been interfering with Patriarca's gambling business. Adding to the size of the target on his back was the fact that Rudy had sworn revenge against his brother's killers. For this gangland hit, Patriarca did not subcontract the violence; instead he used five of his own men, including Maurice "Pro" Lerner. The assassins found out that Marfeo always did his grocery shopping at a certain market on Pocasset Avenue in Providence. The killers had conducted surveillance on the grocery store for several weeks while trying to determine the right time to strike. The delays frustrated Patriarca. "I don't want to hear anymore stories," he told one of the hitmen. "I just want him (Marfeo) killed."[70]

On a bright Saturday afternoon soon thereafter, the hit squad donned Halloween masks and followed Rudy Marfeo and his bodyguard Anthony Melei into the market, where they opened fire with a carbine and sawed off shotgun. The killers fled in a stolen car that they ditched in the parking lot of a nearby golf course. After wiping the stolen car clean of fingerprints, the assassins drove away in a maroon Buick.

Sibling loyalty often proved fatal in the New England mob. What the Marfeo brothers had found out, the Hughes brothers would soon learn. Stevie Hughes would outlive his brother Connie by only four months. Each man had a criminal career that had spanned over two decades. Police in Charlestown had been chasing after them since they were in knickers. For the Hughes brothers, crime was a family tradition that had been passed down by their father, Stevie Sr., a shipyard electrician who had served time at Walpole for possession of a machine gun. Crime was in their blood, and it was also in their neighborhood. Most of Connie and Stevie Hughes's early capers, which included robbery and car theft, were committed with their childhood friends Bernie and Punchy McLaughlin. The McLaughlins and the Hugheses were peat from the same bog. Now three of them were dead, George McLaughlin was on death row, and Stevie was the only one left on the street to ensure the gang's survival.

Everyone understood that a successful hit on Stevie Hughes would bring an end to one of the bloodiest gang wars in American history. There were no shortage of volunteers as members of the Winter Hill Gang, the Mafia, and others all offered themselves up for the plum assignment. Stevie Hughes knew that he was vastly outnumbered and that his time was running out. He asked his close friend Sammy Lindenbaum (Sammy Linden) to make peace with Barboza and the other mob killers. The Animal would never accept such a deal, knowing that Stevie Hughes had killed Joe's friend and mentor Buddy McLean. "Tell him to go fuck his mother,"[71] Joe told Lindenbaum.

Barboza was surprised that Lindenbaum had reached out to him, as the loanshark had been on Joe's hit list just the year before. Raymond Patriarca had wanted Lindenbaum killed, and the contract had originally been assigned to the Bear. But after Jimmy Flemmi had been ambushed and shot, Barboza felt that it was his responsibility to see the assignment through. He had asked Lindenbaum for a tour of his house overlooking Revere Beach. Lindenbaum had just put the place up for sale, and Barboza said he was interested in buying. The Animal's real plan was to lure his victim to the home and kill him inside with no witnesses. When Lindenbaum arrived at Barboza's East Boston headquarters to pick him up for the tour, he brought two small dogs with him — a red flag for the Animal, who knew the damned things would yip and yap and draw attention once

Joe had clipped Lindenbaum. As he was trying to figure out a way around the situation, Barboza got a call from his friend Ronnie Cassesso, who had participated in the murder of Teddy Deegan. Cassesso told Joe that the Office had revoked the order but that no reason had been given by Patriarca. Joe later discovered that the Man wanted to keep Lindenbaum alive just long enough to borrow $80,000 from him, with no intention of paying it back. Joe Lombardo had also wanted to keep Sammy alive because he was deemed good for business.

Lindenbaum was a walking cash machine, with money on the streets of at least twenty cities and towns in Massachusetts. Along with running numbers, the squat, dough-faced crook was also a popular abortionist who could "fix" a problem for as little as $450. Sterilization and safety were foreign concepts to the sixty-seven-year-old Lindenbaum, who would correct his medical mistakes by simply making the patient disappear. Now, a year after the hit was called off, it was back on, and with any luck the mob would rid themselves of Lindenbaum and Stevie Hughes at the same time.

The Pearson stabbing case was still unfolding, and Barboza was under pressure by his lawyer to stay out of trouble. When Joe learned that Lindenbaum's demise was imminent, he skipped town for New York and left the hunt to fellow predators Stevie "the Rifleman" Flemmi and Cadillac Frank Salemme.

The two killers pounced on their prey on a Friday afternoon in late September 1966. Lindenbaum and Stevie Hughes had just enjoyed a long lunch after making the collection rounds in Lawrence and were traveling along busy Route 114 just two miles from the town of Middleton when a black sedan appeared virtually out of nowhere. The car overtook Lindenbaum's Pontiac Tempest at the top of a hill near the Three Pines Inn. The passenger-side window of the black sedan was rolled down and sticking out of it was the barrel of an M-1 rifle. The gunman opened fire with at least seven shots. One bullet ripped the fingers off Lindenbaum's hand. Screaming in pain, he let go of the steering wheel and the Pontiac veered dangerously close to a steep embankment. Stevie Hughes reached inside his trench coat for his own gun but was cut down by bullets. The 1965 Pontiac Tempest hit the embankment and plummeted ten feet into a swamp. The black sedan kept going. The manager of the Three Pines

Inn heard what he thought was a car backfiring and looked out a window. When he saw that the guardrail had been torn down, he yelled to a waitress to call the police for help. The manager then rushed outside, crossed the street, and maneuvered his way down the steep embankment to the wreck, where he discovered that not only had both men been killed but that they had been shot several times each. When a tow truck finally arrived to haul the car away, the driver discovered Lindenbaum's two dogs, a Chihuahua and a mutt, alive and hiding under a seat.

Sammy Lindenbaum was carrying more than $1,000 at the time of his murder. Stevie Hughes had roughly half that amount, but police also found a newspaper clipping in his pocket dated March 16, 1966, describing how he had barely survived an ambush outside his brother's Malden home. News of Hughes's death came as no surprise to the Charlestown cops, who had known him during his brief and violent life. "They [Stevie and Connie Hughes] went the route," veteran Charlestown police detective John Donovan told the *Boston Globe*. "The brothers had been too close to the McLaughlins to expect anything but a gangland death."[72]

Police from Charlestown to Somerville to Boston and beyond were bracing themselves for a reprisal, but the murder of Stevie Hughes served as a death blow to the McLaughlin Gang. The Boston mob war was now unofficially over. Of course there would be more gangland slayings, but none would be blamed on the blood feud between Somerville and Charlestown. Joe Barboza had survived the purge unscathed, and he was now in position to fill the power vacuum left wide open by the war. Virtually all of Barboza's enemies and friends were gone — either dead or in jail — and now he was one of the only men standing in the way of the Mafia's total control of the Boston rackets. The Animal weighed these options heavily in his mind. Would he attempt to seize the brass ring and all the risk and reward that went with it? Barboza was a pathological killer, as were most of his comrades in arms, but there was also a practical side to his personality. He recognized and understood his limitations better than anyone. Joe knew that he was not equipped to handle the rigors of running a big organization. Joe's skills were ill suited for pulling strings from behind a desk like Raymond Patriarca. Barboza had to be on or near the front lines of the battle. He was General Patton to Patriarca's General Eisenhower. If anything, Joe thought the void left behind after the

McLean-McLaughlin feud would solidify his standing with the Office. The Mafia needed someone who could manage the growing number of independent contractors whose only allegiance was to the all-mighty dollar. Henry Tameleo was growing old, and Jerry Angiulo had not done enough to earn the respect of the Boston underworld. Barboza believed that he was now a major step closer to his dream of becoming the first non-Sicilian to join the ranks of *La Cosa Nostra*.

Double Cross

The Animal could dream all he wanted, but Raymond Patriarca had other plans. The Irish mob war had cost the Office countless millions in lost revenue. The Wild West had shipped East during the war, and what was once a mob boom town had now become a ghost town as the steady flow of money slowed to a trickle. Fear of violence had kept people away from gambling parlors, race tracks, and mob-controlled bars. Patriarca and his underbosses Henry Tameleo and Jerry Angiulo needed to get business moving again, and a gunslinger like Barboza had become a burr under their saddle. The same was true with law enforcement. Suffolk County district attorney Garrett Byrne had made it a top priority to take Barboza off the streets. Cops began harassing the Animal at every turn. Joe stopped driving his "James Bond" car, as it had become a magnet for police. They had even given the automobile its own code — 66. The Animal had to adapt to his new environment, so he began traveling by cab and subway; when he needed a car, he made sure that he never used the same vehicle twice. He also relied more heavily on tipsters to keep him one step ahead of the law. One evening in the fall of 1966, Joe received a phone call from a detective friend who told him that police were staking out his headquarters and that they planned to arrest him the minute he was on the move.

"The heat's on. They wanna catch you, Nicky (Femia), and Chico (Amico) with guns," the detective whispered into the phone. "The word is out to get you guys off the street one way or the other."[73]

At the time, Joe was driving a friend's black convertible, which had a trunk loaded with handguns and an M-1 rifle. Barboza ordered his men to dispose of all the weapons before they picked him up for a ride into the city. Normally he would not venture away from his headquarters unarmed, but the mob war was over now and the heat from law enforcement was indeed on. Police spotted the black convertible later that night as Joe and his crew pulled up to a local bar. Officers jumped out of their vehicles with weapons drawn and ordered Barboza out of the convertible. A detective working with the district attorney's office was also on the scene. The police officers shoved Barboza up against the side of the car and searched his body. They did the same with Nicky Femia and Chico Amico but found nothing. An exhaustive search of the car found the same. Barboza smiled as he stood by watching the spectacle. After about an hour, the frustrated officers were forced to let Joe and his men go on their way. Barboza made sure that the tipster got an extra $100 for his effort.

A few days later, Barboza was having a drink with his crew and counting his blessings at the Intermission Lounge on Washington Street in Boston. A friend walked by Joe's table and motioned him to meet outside. Once there, the friend informed Joe that a mob killer was on his way to Boston to take him out.

Fuck him, Joe thought. *He can die like the rest.*

The friend said the contract had been paid by Rudy Marfeo, who blamed Barboza for his brother's murder in Providence a few months earlier. Joe began to connect the dots in his mind. Why would Marfeo blame him for a murder that had been so clearly orchestrated by Raymond Patriarca? *Maybe Patriarca himself is behind the bait and switch,* Joe thought. By blaming Barboza for the hit on Willie Marfeo, Patriarca could get Joe killed without having to order the hit himself. For the first time in a long time, the Animal felt vulnerable. He hadn't been carrying a gun for the past two weeks and contemplated borrowing one from his friend. Finally, he decided against it. If the cops found a gun on him now while he was still on bail in the Pearson stabbing case, they could toss him in jail and forget about him. The Animal would have to send one of his men to find this mob killer and take care of him.

Joe left the Intermission Lounge with Nicky Femia, Tashi Bratsos, and another associate, Patsy Fabiano. They all got into Tashi's gray Cadillac and began driving down Washington Street headed for Revere. Joe noticed a vice squad car following them.

"Get rid of anything hot," he told his men. Joe lowered the window slightly and tossed out three marijuana cigarettes. He also ripped up a piece of paper with the names and addresses of two mobsters he was looking to do business with in Florida and Detroit and sprinkled them like confetti on the sidewalk. The gray Cadillac reached Congress Street in Boston and Barboza thought they were in the clear. When the vice squad car ordered Bratsos to pull over to the curb, Joe had little worry. In fact, he told the officer to fuck off as he approached the vehicle.

"If you want anything from me, take me to the station and I'll call my attorney," Barboza said defiantly.[74]

The cop informed Joe and his men that they were all getting booked on suspicion. Joe laughed in his face and strode happily over to a waiting police wagon. Barboza's laissez-faire attitude quickly changed when he noticed the look of worry on Tashi's face.

"What's the matter?" Joe asked.

"I just remembered there's a .45 in the glove compartment,"[75] Tashi responded.

Barboza shot up from his seat like a bottle rocket. "What?"

Bratsos explained that the gun belonged to Tommy DePrisco and that he had forgotten it was in the glove compartment. Joe could not believe that Tashi could be so stupid.

"We had time to throw away a cannon, let alone a pistol. You realize the law will try to blame me?"

Once at the station, Barboza refused to be fingerprinted. He figured that it was a waste of time, as police already had his prints on file. Joe also complained that his rights had been violated, because the car had been searched without a warrant. The cops just shook their heads and laughed. Finally, one officer told Barboza that they had found the gun in the glove compartment. Joe was right about one thing; the cops would try to tie the weapon directly to him. But there was more. Police also claimed that they had found an M-1 rifle and a knife in the vehicle. Barboza was convinced that officers had planted the other weapons in the Cadillac after they had whisked him off to jail.

District Attorney Garrett Byrne now had the Animal right where he wanted him. Byrne released a statement following the arrest in which he called Barboza "the biggest killer in the Commonwealth." Later, at the arraignment, Byrne claimed that police were tipped off by a reliable informant that Barboza was on his way to a hit on the night in question, and that he was armed to the teeth. The D.A. also told the judge that officers saw Barboza pass the handgun to his pal Nicky Femia to hide. Because of the gun charge and the pending court action in the Pearson case, bail was set high, at $100,000. Nicky Femia was held on half the amount, while Bratsos and Fabiano were released. Barboza and Femia were transferred to the Charles Street Jail, where Joe waited to find out whether he was truly on the outs with the Office after all. It was customary for the Mafia to pay for the release of its top members and associates through bail bondsmen, but Garrett Byrne sent out word that Barboza was off limits and that his office would lean heavily on anyone who tried to free him.

The warning gave Patriarca just the cover he was looking for. The Man did not want Barboza running the streets anymore than Byrne did. The Animal had been a useful tool for Raymond Patriarca to strike terror in the hearts of his enemies and to handle the jobs that his own people did not have the stomach for. The boss understood early on that this was not a sustainable relationship. "Someday, we'll have to whack him out," Patriarca told his closest associates. He had not planned to move on Barboza this quickly, but an opportunity had presented itself, and Patriarca was not one to pass it up. With the Animal in stir, the Office could now dictate the time and place of his execution. Barboza was behind bars, but he was not beyond the reach of the Mafia. The key was making sure that no one came up with the $100,000 cash bail to uncage the Animal.

Since parting ways with Guy Frizzi, Joe had surrounded himself with soldiers he believed would be loyal to him. That loyalty was now being tested as he sat in the notorious Charles Street Jail. The jail had once been home to Sacco and Vanzetti, Malcolm X, and even a German U-Boat captain named Freidrich Steinhoff, who had committed suicide inside the prison by opening his arteries with broken pieces of his sunglasses. The place would have been frightening and ominous to a newcomer, but Barboza had been living behind prison walls for much of his life. For him, Charles Street Jail was as good a home as any. He did miss his wife, Claire, and their young daughter, Stacy, who had been born a year into their marriage. The Barbozas, or "Barons" as they were now called, since Joe had officially changed his last name, lived in a rented house on a quiet street in the town of Swampscott just over the border from Revere. He had fought hard to keep both sides of his life — the domestic and the deranged — from crashing into each other. Claire had a basic understanding of how he made his money. In fact, she had been drawn to the excitement early on, but now she was the mother of a little girl, and it was her job to shelter the child from harm. Joe felt the same way. He was a man capable of extreme cruelty, yet he would melt into a puddle around Stacy. He wanted to win his freedom so that he could get back to her, and he would have to rely on Tashi Bratsos, Chico Amico, and Tommy DePrisco to make that happen. The Animal also knew that he'd been set up, and he'd have scores to settle once he was back on the outside.

Bratsos visited Barboza at Charles Street. Clearly feeling responsible for his boss's predicament, Bratsos told Joe that the crew had hit the streets to raise bail money and had collected a little over $70,000.

"The Office has promised to supply the difference," Bratsos told Barboza. "You'll be out in a couple days tops."[76]

The Animal did not share his friend's enthusiasm and warned him to be careful. On the night of November 15, 1966, ten days after Barboza's arrest, Tashi Bratsos and Tommy DePrisco walked into the Nite Lite Café on Commercial Street in the North End. Larry Baione was Jerry Anguilo's top enforcer. He told Barboza's crew to bring all the cash they had raised to bail out the Animal, and they would then make up the difference. Bratsos and DePrisco had managed to raise $82,000 and were promised they would receive another $18,000 at the meet. Barboza's men should have recognized the setup a mile away, but their devotion to Joe was no substitute for intelligence. As Bratsos and DePrisco entered the Nite Lite, they were immediately surrounded by Baione and eleven other Mafiosi who informed them that the Office would provide no charity for the Portugee nigger rotting in the Charles Street Jail. Knives were pulled and guns were drawn. Baione and his men pounced on Bratsos and DePrisco, who did not stand a chance. The two men were beaten, stabbed, and shot. Bratsos took two bullets in the head, while DePrisco was shot four times in the skull at close range. Their bodies were stuffed into Bratsos's Cadillac and driven to South Boston, where the vehicle was abandoned in a vacant lot at the corner of A and West Fourth streets. *La Cosa Nostra* had chosen Southie in an attempt to blame the murder on the Irish.

Unfortunately for the Mafia, too many gangsters had been involved in the murders, and the story of what happened inside the Nite Lite filtered out through the evening. Several mobsters, including Wimpy Bennett, phoned in tips to the police. The Cadillac, with the butchered bodies of DePrisco and Bratsos occupying the front and back seats, respectively, had been discovered in the early morning hours, and now police were racing toward the North End. The owner of the bar was a Mafia soldier named Ralphie Lamattina. They called him "Ralphie Chong" because he looked more Chinese than he did Sicilian. When officers arrived at the Nite Lite, they caught Ralphie and his men in mid cover-up. Lamattina was busy removing shattered mirrors and hanging pictures on the walls to hide the bullet holes, while another man furiously tried to scrub blood off the floor.

When Patriarca was told about the hits, he hit the roof. He told Larry Baione that he should have buried the bodies instead of dumping them in South Boston. "No bodies, no case to worry about," said the boss. Jerry Angiulo also found himself in Patriarca's crosshairs, since it was his men who had handled the murders so sloppily. Angiulo saved his own neck by convincing Ralphie Chong to turn himself in and plead guilty to a charge of being an accessory after the fact. Angiulo assured Patriarca that Ralphie would stand up for the "family" to prevent a long, drawn-out investigation. Still not satisfied, Patriarca called a meeting in Boston with Angiulo, Larry Baione, Ralphie Chong, and others, including former underboss Joe Lombardo. Two mob lawyers were also present for the sit-down at Giros Restaurant. Patriarca could not be seen meeting with these men, so he sent Henry Tameleo to mediate. Lamattina still needed some convincing, so Angiulo promised him that he could fix it so that he would receive a light sentence. The underboss also stressed to Ralphie that if he didn't go along with the plan, he would not survive the afternoon. Lamattina avoided the death sentence by standing before the judge and pleading guilty. He admitted to the judge that he had wiped up blood and disposed of a blood-soaked carpet, replacing it the next day. He received two consecutive sentences of five to seven years, each at Walpole.

Chico Amico, one of the last Barboza crew members left standing, called a meeting of his own with Wimpy Bennett, Stevie Flemmi, and others at a pool room in South Boston. Words of revenge were thrown around the room, but no one seemed willing to step up and take care of the situation. Frustrated by the lack of action, Amico challenged his associates to band together and take on the Office. Wimpy Bennett stepped forward as the voice of reason. He told Chico that such a move would mean suicide for them all. It would be like a commando unit waging war on an entire division. The Mafia had an unlimited supply of soldiers spread across the United States, while the independent killers of Boston numbered in the dozens. They would have to plot their revenge more strategically. At the close of the meeting, Bennett pulled Chico aside and urged him to kill Larry Baione. Chico glanced around the room at Stevie Flemmi and other members of the group. He then asked Wimpy whether these men would back him up if he went after Baione, who was considered the New England Mafia's number one killer.

"They'll be with you after you make the move on Baione," Bennett informed him. "I guarantee it."[77]

Chico did not fully trust Bennett, but he felt that he had no other choice. It was kill or be killed now for Barboza's crew. Amico began hunting for Baione at the mobster's favorite haunts, such as the Bat Cave, a tavern on Friend Street, or any number of clubs in Chinatown. Chico even traveled to Baione's home in the town of Franklin but could not catch up with the elusive Mafiosi. While tracking Baione, Chico could not help but think that there was another setup in play. Wimpy Bennett had never been shy about voicing his hatred for Larry Baione. Bennett wanted Baione dead for his own reasons but was unwilling to pull the trigger himself. Instead, he had convinced his surrogate assassin to do it for him. Chico vowed to kill Baione but now had his sights set on Bennett as well. In a letter smuggled into Charles Street Jail addressed to Barboza, Chico wrote: "I'm gonna do my best, Joe, but if I die, I want you to cut that motherfucker's head off and put it on my grave."[78]

Amico had a right to be suspicious. Unbeknownst to him, Bennett had met privately with Patriarca and promised the Mafia boss that he had nothing to fear from him, that Wimpy would not make a move against the Office. Wimpy Bennett's treachery was not the only double-cross in play. Guy Frizzi, Barboza's disgruntled former partner in crime, had also sold his soul to the other side. He recruited another hood named Louis Grieco to lure Patsy Fabiano, who was free on bail, into an ambush in Revere. Grieco had been a bona fide hero during World War II, having seen combat in the Philippines, where he was awarded a Bronze Star and Purple Heart. Grieco survived the war but nearly lost his leg to a gunshot wound. The injury placed him on permanent disability when he returned to the states, where Grieco made his money repossessing automobiles for banks before beginning a more lucrative career in the mob. Together, Grieco and Frizzi made a formidable pair.

Patsy Fabiano would not have stood a chance in a firefight against either man, and fortunately he didn't have to. Unlike Tashi Bratsos and Tommy DePrisco, Fabiano could tell when a trap was being set. He had originally agreed to accompany Bratsos and DePrisco to their ill-fated meeting at the Nite Lite Café but had pulled out at the last minute. A few days later, after agreeing to meet Frizzi in Revere, Fabiano decided to drive by and case the rendezvous spot about an hour before the scheduled meeting time. Upon spotting Grieco there lying in wait, Patsy pressed his foot against the gas pedal and took off. Frizzi and Grieco tried to give chase but they never caught up with Fabiano. Patsy kept a low profile following the incident and had implored his friend Chico Amico to do the same. Chico would not listen. He figured that he would always be looking over his shoulder for Larry Baione, so he decided that it was best to strike first. On December 7, 1966, Amico and his friend Jimmy Kearns walked into a bellydancing club called Enrico's, which was owned by Baione. Their target was nowhere to be found, but Chico did spot one of Baione's relatives. He walked up to the man and slapped him hard across the face. "That's for Larry," Chico told him. Amico had grown sick and tired of chasing Baione all over town. Tonight, he would initiate the confrontation. He mentioned to those in the bar that he and Kearns were headed to Alphonse's Broken-Hearts Lounge in Revere. When Amico and Kearns got into their car, a phone call was made from Enrico's to Alphonse's.

Chico arrived at the second location expecting a bloodbath. He entered the bar and kept one hand in his pocket and his fingers on his gun. But no one paid any attention to Amico and Kearns as they sat at the bar and sipped their drinks. Guy Frizzi sat at the other end of the bar and refused to look up his former friends. Finally, about fifteen minutes later, Chico decided to leave. He would have to bring the fight to Baione some other night. As Amico and Kearns entered the parking lot, someone inside the bar walked over to the window, pushed aside the curtains, and rapped hard on the glass. The man then walked back to the bar and raised his drink in a toast. "Well, that's the last you'll see of Chico," he said proudly. Frizzi, who had introduced Chico to Barboza years before, raised his own glass in salute.

As Amico and Kearns drove away, they were followed by another car with Wisconsin plates. Inside the car was an East Boston Mafiosi named J. R. Russo, who was armed with a carbine. Russo rolled down the window and leaned out with the weapon pointed at the back of Jimmy Kearns's car. The young Mafiosi fired one shot through the back window. His aim was perfect, and the bullet struck Chico in the back of his head, killing him instantly. The kill shot did not exit through the front of Amico's skull; instead it pushed his eyes forward out of their sockets, giving him a look in death that resembled a Chuck Jones cartoon character. Russo fired another shot that struck Kearns, who was driving, in the back. Despite the injury, Jimmy Kearns kept his hands on the steering wheel until he finally lost control of the vehicle and ended up over an embankment and in a field.

Barboza was pulled from his cell at the Charles Street Jail at 3:00 a.m. the following morning and led downstairs to a conference room, where two detectives were waiting.

"We've got some bad news for you, Joe," said one of the officers.

Joe understood that it was the kind of bad news that could not wait for morning. Someone had been killed — someone very close to him. For a moment, he thought of his wife and daughter. When he was told that Chico Amico had been murdered, the news hit him nearly as hard. Barboza's body went limp as he sat across from the detectives. He had just lost his best friend. Chico wasn't just a partner; he had been like a kid brother to Joe. He had idolized Barboza and had shown the kind of loyalty that was truly rare in mob circles. That loyalty had cost Chico Amico his life, and the Animal decided at that moment that he would have his vengeance. But before he could plot against his enemies, he had to protect Fabiano, who was no doubt next on the hit list.

"Get Patsy Fabiano off the street," Joe told the detectives. "He don't know how to handle himself against these type of people and they'll kill him."[79]

Fabiano was brought in and placed under protective custody. Meanwhile, Barboza wanted to put the Mafia on notice. Through a jailhouse conversation with a well-known mob lawyer named Joe Balliro, the Animal spread word that he was going to kill everyone who might have been connected to Chico's murder—and that group included Jerry Angiulo, Larry Baione, and *the Man* himself, Raymond Patriarca.

The Mafia boss responded by mobilizing a small army of killers to go after Barboza. A rumor had been circulating that Joe was close to making bail, and plans were now underway to ensure that his first day of freedom would also be his last day on earth. Henry Tameleo had thirteen men on standby ready to fan out across the Boston area upon word of Barboza's release. They were to take up position inside local mob hangouts and even along highways and roads usually frequented by the Animal near his home in Swampscott. Tameleo then recruited Guy Frizzi to perform the ultimate betrayal. Frizzi would offer to pick Barboza up from jail. If the Animal accepted, Frizzi would lure Barboza into a deadly ambush. Tameleo did not account for the fact that Barboza did not trust Frizzi and would no doubt decline the ride. Ultimately the plan had to be scrapped anyway, because the district attorney refused to let Barboza out on bail. This also meant that D.A. Byrne would have to fast track his court proceedings.

In late January 1967, Barboza, Nicky Femia, and Patsy Fabiano were all found guilty on weapons charges. Joe received a prison sentence of four to five years for possession of a gun and a knife. Moments after the judge's gavel sounded, Barboza was shipped off to Walpole under heavy security. Once there, he was reunited with the Bear in the maximum security section. Flemmi welcomed his old friend with some encouraging news. He told Joe that a move was being made against Wimpy Bennett. This was music to Joe's ears, as he felt that his former mentor had betrayed him and was now worthy of death. Death came in the final days of January, when Wimpy Bennett was confronted with allegations that he was skimming money from Stevie Flemmi's gambling operation. A meeting was called, and Wimpy's bookkeeper pointed the guilty finger his way. Bennett denied the accusation but nobody believed him. Wimpy Bennett had always been a thief and a liar, and now he was going to have to pay for past sins. Stevie Flemmi pulled out a pistol and shot Wimpy under the right eye. They buried Bennett's body at a shooting range in the town of Hopkinton, Massachusetts, near the starting line of the Boston Marathon. The Bear was among the first to learn about Wimpy's demise. "The fox that bit us is dead," he told Barboza.[80]

One enemy was now gone, but many more remained. When Ralphie Chong Lamattina arrived at Walpole to serve out his sentence for the Nite Lite murders, Barboza tried to make his life a living hell. Joe, who was now working on the chow line in the prison cafeteria, told Ralphie Chong that he had smuggled a vial of tasteless poison into his cell. Barboza did not threaten Ralphie directly, but the insinuation worked. The North End gangster passed on every dish Joe served and soon stopped eating altogether. One afternoon, Barboza crept into Ralphie's cell when he was taking a nap. When Ralphie opened his eyes, he was shocked to find the Animal standing over him with a meat cleaver.

"Don't flinch or move your hands," Barboza told him. "I know you got a knife under your pillow but before you reach it, I'll sink this cleaver into your greasy head."

Joe demanded that Ralphie tell him exactly what had happened at the Nite Lite on the evening that Tashi Bratsos and Tommy DePrisco were murdered. Ralphie Chong had no choice. He spilled his guts but afterward received no reprieve from Barboza, who told him that he was marked for death. "But not now," he hissed at the shaking gangster. "I want you to worry, but I swear I'll kill you." The Animal spit in Ralphie's face and then left the cell. Petrified, Lamattina told prison officials about the threat and was transferred to another prison the next day.

Deal Makers

While H. Paul Rico was still considered the Golden Child of the Boston FBI office, his partner Dennis Condon had fallen out of favor with his superiors. Condon had recently been written up for failure to properly disseminate information that had been obtained by an informant who had told him that a particular suspect in another FBI case carried a machine gun and was considered crazy. Although no disciplinary action was taken, it was a mark on his record, and the FBI agent was now in desperate need of a win. In early February 1967, Stevie "the Rifleman" Flemmi was approved as a Top Echelon Informant for the FBI. Soon afterward, he began making frequent trips to Walpole State Prison to speak with his brother and with Joe Barboza. Serving as an envoy for Rico and Condon, Stevie told both the Bear and the Animal that the feds had Jimmy Flemmi dead to rights for the murder of Edward "Teddy" Deegan. Stevie told them about a key witness: Chelsea police captain Joseph Kozlowski, who had observed a stocky man with dark hair and a bald spot in the center of his head in the back of the getaway car on the night Deegan was killed. With witness testimony from a cop, there was little doubt that Vincent "Jimmy the Bear" Flemmi would be convicted of the crime and sent straight to the electric chair. There was one intriguing alternative, however. The Rifleman told his brother and Barboza that the FBI would be willing to cover up their respective roles in the Deegan murder and possibly help reduce their sentences if they were willing to cooperate in their war against *La Cosa Nostra*.

"Tell the FBI to go fuck themselves," Barboza said.[81]

The Animal had committed just about every egregious crime there was, but he still lived his life under a certain code of conduct. Barboza's commandments were simple: never hurt women and children and never snitch on your friends or even your enemies. Despite his falling out with the Office, Joe's natural enemy had always been law enforcement. Any assistance given to the FBI would violate all of the unwritten rules of the mob jungle. Joe Barboza was no Joe Valachi.

Stevie Flemmi begged Barboza to listen to the FBI's offer. The feds wanted the Rifleman to convince his brother or Barboza to flip. Stevie applied more pressure on Joe because he knew that if his brother publicly cooperated with law enforcement, his own neck would eventually be slit. This frightening realization was also compounded by the fact that the Bear would make for a horrible witness. On a credibility scale of from 1 to 10, the Bear was at zero. Barboza could at least be an eloquent and engaging speaker at times. His story would be much more believable than Jimmy Flemmi's.

"Think about it," Stevie implored Barboza. "What do you owe the Office after the way they've treated you?"

Joe did think about it, long and hard. The Mafia had killed his friends, stolen his bail money, and framed him on a gun possession charge that had landed him at least four years in prison. They had taken away his power and left him with nothing.

"Okay, I'll meet with the FBI."

Dennis Condon and H. Paul Rico entered Walpole on March 10, 1967, for their first meeting with Joe Barboza. Rico introduced himself and then his partner. Barboza recognized Rico immediately, as he had seen him at the track several times before.

"I'll talk to you if you agree not to testify against me for whatever I've said," Joe told them.

"We'll respect your confidence," replied Rico.

Barboza had been burned by law enforcement before and decided to share with them the story of a Boston police lieutenant who had promised him one thing only to deliver something else.

"I've always tried to make a living outside of the law," Joe explained. "If anyone in law enforcement could prove that I was doing wrong, I'm willing to pay the consequences. However, when you find that a police officer that you know fingered scores, acted as a lookout when scores were being pulled, and divided up the proceeds from these scores, turns around and manufactures evidence and testimony against you, you have a feeling that maybe you the criminal have played by the wrong standards."[82]

Barboza stressed to Rico and Condon that he planned to target this police officer for retribution when he was eventually released from prison. This was the Animal's way of saying—Fuck with me and I'll fuck with you.

"Look, you probably suspect what's happened in most of the gangland murders that have happened in this area," he told the federal agents. "But I *know* what's happened in practically every murder that's been committed. But one thing I won't do is give you any information that would allow the Bear to fry."[83]

Rico and Condon agreed to the terms. Joe also wanted a guarantee that he would receive any additional time tacked onto his concurrent sentences for the gun and knife possession.

"If I'm left in here too long, my wife will leave me and I'll probably commit suicide."[84] Barboza demanded protection for his wife and little girl because he knew that Patriarca would view them as his Achilles' heel. The FBI agents swore that they would keep Claire and Stacy out of harm's way. Joe Barboza was putting his own safety and that of his family in the hands of two men he had never met before. It was a calculated risk to be sure, but he had been gambling one way or the other all of his life. Yet, still conflicted about his decision to turn stoolie, Joe decided that he would use his meeting with the FBI as leverage in a last-ditch effort to strike a truce with Patriarca. He wrote the mob boss a letter and had it smuggled out of Walpole. In the note, Barboza wrote that he would not cooperate with the feds if the Mafia promised to leave him alone and let him disappear with his family once he was freed from prison. It was a Hail Mary pass that was quickly knocked away by Patriarca. Upon reading the letter, the boss called Barboza a "dirty nigger bastard" and vowed to kill him—inside or outside of prison. Word quickly got back to Joe that he was indeed a dead man walking. The decree of murder left him no choice. The Animal had to go all in with the FBI.

"Yes, they [the Mafia] would never let me out if they could stop it," Barboza wrote later in his memoir. "They know they'd have to kill me if I got out and they know I'd take plenty of them with me. That old fool [Patriarca] in Rhode Island misinterpreted my respect for fear. Fear him? I didn't fear tougher guys than Raymond Patriarca. Besides, I'd learned to accept dying a long time ago as my friends all around me died in the gang war. I've got nothing left but my mouth with which to fight now. I'd be a fool to keep quiet on the theory that twenty years from now, when I'm 55, I could get out and get even. No, now while I'm young is the time to get even. I'll bring them in the can with me since I can't get out to them and when I get them here, we'll get on with it."[85]

Barboza sat down again with the agents two weeks later, this time at the Federal Building in Boston and this time in the presence of his lawyer, John Fitzgerald. For legal counsel, Joe had hired several attorneys during his criminal career, including F. Lee Bailey and Al Farese. But when it mattered most, he trusted Farese's partner, John Fitzgerald, more than anyone. Fitzgerald was loyal to Barboza. Like Chico Amico, the attorney idolized Barboza and had seen his own status rise through his connection to the "biggest killer in the Commonwealth." Fitzgerald acted like a mobster in lawyer's clothing. Despite being married, Fitzgerald had his own harem of gangster molls that he squired around Boston in Barboza's James Bond car, which he had purchased from Joe the previous year. Barboza had made Fitzgerald's career, and Joe believed that the lawyer would protect his interests.

In the second meeting with Rico and Condon, Barboza said that he had come to the conclusion that they had a common enemy in "the Italian organization," as he called it.[86] Joe shared his belief that the Mafia would try to kill him in prison or when he got out.

"Either way, I'm a dead man," he stated. "They can reach into local law enforcement agencies and obtain any information in their possession."[87]

It was different with the FBI, Joe explained. Unlike local cops, the bureau was committed to the all-out destruction of *La Cosa Nostra*, and Barboza pledged that he was now committed to the effort also. He told the agents that he had even asked Patsy Fabiano to join the fight. He said that Patsy had been inside the Nite Lite Café during the massacre of Bratsos and DePrisco and had witnessed Larry Baione fire the first shot at Tashi. Barboza promised that he and Fabiano would also furnish names of the other shooters involved to District Attorney Garrett Byrne.

"I hope the district attorney appreciates my help and will gimme a break on the two cases still pending against me," Barboza said, playing his cards closely.

Rico and Condon nodded their assurances.

"What do you have on Raymond [Patriarca]?" asked Rico. "He's our number one target."[88]

"I'm acquainted with him and I've seen him on a number of occasions."

The agents asked whether those meetings had been set up through underboss Jerry Angiulo.

Barboza shook his head no. "I never asked Jerry's permission. I went straight to Raymond and that aggravated Angiulo. Jerry's the biggest money-maker that Raymond has. He has about a million bucks in shylock business on the street and gives 50 percent of his profits to Patriarca."

Barboza then provided a few details about the murders of Teddy Deegan and Willie Marfeo. Unbeknownst to Joe, the FBI already knew much about the hit on Deegan. In fact, Rico and Condon were busy developing their own version of the gangland slaying that they hoped Barboza would one day reveal to a jury. Barboza's information regarding the Marfeo murder was something entirely new. Of course everyone had suspected that Patriarca was behind the deadly shooting that occurred just a block from his office, but the Animal had now promised the feds a direct link to the Man. This was exactly what the FBI had been working toward when it first created the Top Echelon Informant program. It was one thing for a gangster like Joe Valachi to testify before Congress, where very little was at stake beside one's reputation. It was another thing entirely for a witness like Joe Barboza to take the stand in a criminal trial where the defendants could lose their freedom and even their lives. The feds needed someone like Barboza to connect all the dots for a jury and to help bring Raymond Patriarca to justice once and for all. Both Condon and Rico felt their balloon pop when Barboza told them that he would provide his information behind closed doors but never in front of a jury.

"Since the Mafia is doing everything in its power to hurt you, don't you feel that justice could be done by testifying?" asked Condon.[89]

"If I ever testified, you people would have to find me an island and make a fortress out of it," the Animal replied.[90] Instead, he implored the agents to convince his pal Patsy Fabiano to testify. "I can protect him while he's in jail," Barboza promised. "Once he's freed, Patsy could hide out until I'm released from jail and I'll continue to protect him then."[91]

Rico and Condon failed to see the logic. Barboza wanted his friend to testify so that he himself would not be labeled a rat by the press. Joe had worked to cultivate his own image over the years and did not want it tarnished beyond repair. The agents had a major dilemma on their hands. After sending Barboza back to Walpole, they discussed ways in which they could force Barboza onto the witness stand. Both men came to the conclusion that more pressure had to be applied to their reluctant witness. At Barboza's urging, Rico met with Patsy Fabiano and pressed him for information about what he had seen during the Nite Lite Massacre, but Patsy insisted that he was never there.

"I only spoke with Bratsos by phone and later drove by the Nite Lite and saw their cars parked outside," Fabiano stated.

Rico jotted down the information and passed it along to Barboza, who tried to persuade the agent of his own truthfulness. "Either Patsy's afraid to testify or I was misled."

H. Paul Rico knew that he had caught the Animal in a lie. In a memo sent to his superiors, Rico wrote: "This office is aware of the distinct possibility that Barron [Barboza], in order to save himself from a long prison sentence, may try to intimidate Fabiano into testifying to something that he may not be a witness to."[92]

Rico was not discouraged by the falsehood, however. All criminals lied, this he knew. But some crooks proved better liars than others, and Barboza had just demonstrated the power of his persuasion. He could lie with conviction, and Rico knew that this personality flaw would serve them both well as this game continued to play itself out.

J. Edgar Hoover had now expressed great interest in the Barboza case, and the agents provided the director with daily updates on the negotiations. The Animal also presented Dennis Condon with an opportunity to improve his own image within the bureau. In a performance appraisal in late March 1967, Condon was given an excellent rating with a special emphasis on how he "handled complicated matters in an able and capable fashion." The appraisal further noted that Condon was dependable and enthusiastic, with an outstanding knowledge of the hoodlum and gambling element of Boston.

Meanwhile, the hoodlum element of Boston continued to settle scores. In mid-April, Jerry Angiulo sent three of his men after Joe Lanzi, one of the informers who had tipped off police to the Nite Lite Massacre. The enforcers shot Lanzi as he sat in the front passenger seat of their car and then drove his body through Medford in the early hours of the morning, looking for a place to dump the corpse. Unfortunately the killers were spotted by police, so they tried to ditch the car and flee on foot. One of gunmen could not get out of the car fast enough and was arrested on the spot. The other two men managed to escape but were eventually captured a year later.

The hit proved that the New England Mafia was back in the murder business big time after having sat on the sidelines for the majority of the Irish gang war. This was not good news for Barboza, who was now convinced that *La Cosa Nostra* would be coming for him en masse. Law enforcement still wanted its pound of flesh also. The Animal found himself back in court, where he was arraigned on the broad charge of being an "habitual criminal."

"The Suffolk County D.A. is trying to crucify me," he told Rico and Condon.

Barboza also believed that the Mafia had conspired with local law enforcement to "bury him in jail."[93] It was the opportunity the feds had been waiting for.

"If these people are trying to do this to you, don't you feel it would be fair in the interest of justice if you testified against them?" asked Condon.[94]

Barboza answered the question with a question.

"What if I testify against the Office and the government isn't able to convict those I testified against, would the fact that I cooperated still be brought to the attention of the prosecutors and the judge who'd be imposing a sentence on me?"[95]

Condon and Rico explained that before they could discuss the matter with the U.S. Attorney's Office they had to find out in detail exactly what Barboza could testify to.

What the agents wanted was for Barboza to provide information about Raymond Patriarca's involvement in the murder of Willie Marfeo.

"Sometime over the past two years, the date I can't remember, I called Henry Tameleo in Providence," Joe explained. "I asked if he'd be around that day and he told me to come down on Tuesday because George and I want to talk to you. "George" is the name Tameleo always gave on the phone when he was talking about Raymond."[96]

Barboza told the agents that he and Ronnie Cassesso went down to

Providence to meet with Tameleo and Patriarca and were told that Marfeo had been running a crap game on Federal Hill that was drawing too much attention from police. When ordered to shut the game down, Marfeo slapped Tameleo and told him to go fuck himself.

"We want this guy whacked out," Patriarca told Barboza.[97] The Man then suggested that Barboza and Cassesso disguise themselves as butchers complete with butchers' coats and a truck in order to catch Marfeo off guard, as the wily mobster was always on the look-out for potential assassins. After getting a tutorial on Marfeo's favored hangouts, Barboza returned to Boston, where he would draw up plans to begin casing Marfeo on the street. The next day, however, Joe was told to put the hit on hold, as Tameleo had just been arrested on some charge and there was too much heat. Days and soon months went by and no one brought up the name Willie Marfeo again, so Barboza forgot all about it.

"About a year later, a guy mentioned to me that Marfeo had been shot and killed inside a telephone booth in Providence. I ran into Henry Tameleo later and he told me that everyone in the place where Marfeo was whacked out were plants of theirs. He said that a guy in a baseball cap nailed Marfeo and that the guy was a good guy and did a good piece of work for us."[98]

The details about the Marfeo murder were just what the FBI had been waiting for. Rico and Condon were drawn to the fact that Barboza had traveled from Massachusetts to Providence to discuss the proposed hit. This placed the case in a whole new category thanks to Bobby Kennedy's ITAR statute, which made interstate travel in aid of racketeering a federal crime.

The noose was already tightening around the neck of Raymond Patriarca. In early May 1967, a Patriarca soldier named Louis "the Fox" Taglianetti was put on trial for tax evasion in Providence. His lawyers pressed the FBI to turn over whatever evidence they had in the case, and, much to their chagrin, the feds handed over everything including files filled with memos regarding the wiretaps on Patriarca's Atwells Avenue headquarters. The news came as a shock to Patriarca and the public at large. Newspaper reporters openly questioned whether this marked the beginning of the end to Patriarca's reign as New England's undisputed organized crime kingpin.

The wiretaps had captured details of several Mafia murders, including Taglianetti's hit on a hired killer named Jackie "Mad Dog" Nazarian. Mad Dog had been responsible for one of the most notorious mob murders in U.S. history—the assassination of Murder Incorporated chief Albert Anastasia as he sat in a barber chair at New York City's Park Sheraton Hotel in 1957. Nazarian had signed his own death warrant, however, when he began mouthing off that he would make a more efficient, more fearsome crime boss than Patriarca. The Man answered the challenge by having Nazarian shot five times. Also highlighted in the evidence was the unusual correspondence between Patriarca and his unrequited prison pen pal Paul Collicci, who was serving prison time in Massachusetts for a robbery that had involved Patriarca.

Collicci wrote:

Hello Boss, Do you notice how I respect you and call you boss? But do you have to leave me in jail? I wrote to you and Henry [Tameleo], but I didn't get an answer. . . . But dear boss, get together and get me a new lawyer and a new trial. Because I would like to be on the street. . . . Please don't tell me you people are broke, because I know better. If not, tell me so and we can all be together here and have a good time. . . . I'm reading a novel, Oliver Twist, and it's all about a man named Fagin. He was a man who sent kids out to steal and then would steal from them . . . Bye, Big Boss

PAUL.[99]

Collicci had described the right Charles Dickens classic, but the wrong character. Patriarca was no Fagin, but instead shared character traits with a more dangerous *Oliver Twist* character, the murderous Bill Sykes. Collicci discovered this for himself when he was later gunned down in Quincy, Massachusetts.

No doubt influenced by the treachery of gangsters like Collicci, the wiretaps showed that Patriarca expressed a growing concern about the character of the men being recruited into the mob. "Don't look for toughness alone in a man, but look for guys who have brains and don't talk," he told one subordinate. "Be careful who you bring in. Together we survive, alone we die."

Lawyers for Taglianetti argued that the evidence obtained by the FBI against their client should be thrown out because it was obtained through the use of an illegal wiretap. The harder the attorneys fought for Taglianetti, the more trouble they brought for their client. Instead of getting sentenced to a few years in prison for tax evasion, Louis "the Fox" got the death penalty, with Raymond Patriarca serving as judge, jury, and executioner. Just a few years after the wiretaps were made public; Taglianetti was shot dead while bringing his girlfriend back to his Cranston, Rhode Island, home.

The wiretaps had caused irreparable damage to Patriarca and his control over the New England Mafia, and law enforcement officials feared that he would become even more dangerous and violent as he tried to cling to power. A week after the wiretaps were made public, Joe Barboza was brought before a grand jury to testify about what he knew about the Marfeo murder and the murder of Rocco DiSeglio, in which he implicated underboss Jerry Angiulo. But Barboza was still wrestling with his conscience. If he testified before a grand jury, there was no going back. He would be branded as a rat for all time. Instead of spilling his guts to the grand jury, Joe surprised both Condon and Rico when he suddenly got a case of cold feet and invoked his Fifth Amendment right to protection against self-incrimination. The FBI agents had fueled Joe's anger and then rushed him in front of the grand jury before he had fully prepared himself for this life-altering decision. But the Animal wasn't ready for his close up just yet. Barboza was sent back to Walpole, where he was visited once again by Stevie Flemmi, who finally persuaded him to fight back against Patriarca, a man hell-bent on destroying him. After serious contemplation, Joe told the federal agents that he was ready to confront the Mafia and his fear of being labeled a turncoat.

Barboza returned to Boston under heavy security on May 11, 1965, where he provided ninety minutes of testimony before the grand jury. Following the appearance, he was taken down a private elevator and placed in the back of an unmarked police car. Knowing the methods used to kill other mobsters, including Connie Hughes and Joe's best friend Chico Amico, Barboza felt particularly vulnerable in any automobile, even a police car. Once in the backseat of the vehicle, Joe rolled himself off the cushioned bench and onto the floor, where he would be out of an assassin's direct line of fire. That is how the feared mob killer would be forced to live his life from now on—in hiding. The Animal would have to adapt to his changing environment. The predator would now have to retreat to the shadows in order to save himself and his family. There was no turning back.

There is no hiding place. No where to run,

no where to escape

◦ FOREIGNER

Deegan Part II

Following Barboza's testimony, a convoy of police vehicles escorted him back to Walpole without incident. Word of his betrayal had not been leaked to the public, but it soon would.

Law enforcement officials feared that this news would inevitably trigger a bloodbath within the walls of Walpole State Prison, where Raymond Patriarca maintained a high level of influence over inmates and, in some cases, prison guards. A decision was made by Suffolk County district attorney Garrett Byrne to transfer Barboza from Walpole to the Barnstable House of Corrections on Cape Cod to ensure his safety. Joe's wife, Claire, and their daughter, Stacy, were also placed under the protection of the U.S. Marshal Service. John Partington, the U.S. Marshal whom Raymond Patriarca had once referred to as a boy scout, was assigned the task of protecting Barboza's family at their home in Swampscott. Claire Barboza was suspicious of Partington from the outset and asked him to define the parameters of the arrangement.

"What's expected of me, and what are you going to do?" she asked.[100]

Partington shrugged and honestly told her that this kind of arrangement was new to him also, and that they would have to make it up as they went along. Claire Barboza was not at all what Partington had expected in a mob wife. She was petite and refined and looked no different from the wife of a banker, doctor, or lawyer. It was hard for Partington to fathom that this somewhat elegant woman was married to a murderous animal. The marshal felt the same way about Stacy. How could someone so evil also produce something so beautiful? The youngster reminded Partington of Shirley Temple with a head full of curls that joyously bounced like a circus parade as she walked. Unlike her mother, Stacy Barboza was taken with the marshal almost immediately. She climbed up on his lap and peppered him with questions that were mostly geared to her cat Oby. Partington had not been aware the child had a pet, and as harmless as the cat appeared, it could pose a problem with the family's protection. The marshal understood that the stakes were extremely high with this assignment and that the Office would go to any lengths to prevent Barboza from testifying further. If they somehow managed to kidnap Joe's daughter, there is no doubt the Animal would do anything they asked in hopes of getting her back safely. If by chance Stacy followed the feline off property, she would be at risk of being abducted. Partington would have to place Oby under house arrest during the course of this assignment. He had thought about taking the cat away but understood that Stacy was attached to her pet, and it was his job not only to protect the family but also to make them as comfortable as possible under his watchful eye.

Partington had second thoughts about the cat soon after, when it escaped into the neighborhood. The marshal had to send other members of the protective detail from street to street, but they had no luck corralling the fugitive feline. At day's end, Oby finally returned with a mouse in its mouth and placed it at Partington's feet. The marshal made up his mind right then that the cat would stay. He faced other problems, however, from his own colleagues, who constantly complained about protecting a mobster's family. Partington had to remind them that little Stacy Barboza had never harmed anyone and deserved to be kept out of harm's way. He also had to remind himself not to get too close to Claire Barboza. Even a hint of impropriety would be hard to explain away to his fellow marshals and to Claire's husband. With that in mind, Partington recruited students from nearby Radcliffe College to serve as matrons, and also convinced his own wife, Helen, to stay with them so that Claire would have someone to talk to and confide in if she felt the need.

Meanwhile, Joe was having his own difficulty adjusting to his new home at the Barnstable House of Corrections, overlooking the cold waters of Cape Cod Bay. Barboza was housed in protective custody all by himself in the women's section of the prison. Soon after his arrival, he was visited by his lawyer, John Fitzgerald. The Animal had been reduced to tears because of the way he had been characterized by the newspapers. The media referred to him as a canary, stoolie, and turncoat. For a mob killer like Joe Barboza, these were the worst insults imaginable. The gangster's code had meant something to him at one time, and the tears of frustration proved it still did.

"They [the media] shout for law and order, they pressure the police for action, but when they're handed on a silver platter someone willing to stand up and do what most Americans are afraid to do, they call him names," Barboza later wrote in his memoir. "Don't they realize that these names of "Songbird" and "Canary" only help organized crime by discouraging other potential witnesses from coming forward? Is that what they really want?"[101]

The Animal took his case directly to the public. He struck up a cozy relationship with James Southwood, the *Boston Herald* reporter who had broken the story about his incarceration on Cape Cod. In July 1967, the pair worked together on another story developed to aid Barboza in the public relations war against the media and the mob. Under the banner headline "A Letter from Barboza: Why I Decided to Tell All," the Animal attempted once again to win people over to his side of the case.

I am not looking for slaps on the back or kind words. All I want is to be left alone. Leave my family alone. I have a job to do and a duty to do in taking the stand against these people [*La Cosa Nostra*]. Living with the thought of the peril and dangers I face where my life is concerned is enough — without the newspapers' pressure (and it seems hypocrisies) on their part to write like that when they, the reporters, are the ones that stir a notion that [*La Cosa Nostra*] is trying to show the younger element that look up to them in awe and admiration just what type of people they are. Younger inmates in Walpole and Concord would do anything to get in with these people, figuring that they would become big men. The Office likes them to believe this because then they bleed every single favorable effort from these disillusioned kids and men — then they throw them a crust of bread. I can cite many many cases. But I'll name two as an illustration. One person whose first name is Jackie, or was because he's dead, killed in the neighborhood of 25 people for them. He is dead now. Who did it? They did! I have a dear friend named Tony. He busted legs, arms, stabbed people for them. They sure took care of him [financially], so much so that he had to take a state job just to support his family. I'll give you one more. One guy took a federal prison sentence to save a friend in the Office. . . . The same person he protected put a bullet in his head. I could go on and on, but I won't. I am just trying to say, don't pat me on the back. I don't want no rewards. Just leave us be and thank God somebody is coming forward to expose these people. . . . I can't stop the reporters from writing things about me because there are rotten apples in almost every barrel. But if they think it'll stop me from standing up against these people, they are wrong because life or no life, I am going to take the stand against these people for the future [Jackies and Tonys], hoping they will see through them and stay away from them.[102]

Barboza's words rang true to an extent. Reporters were always quick to demonize criminals who furnished law enforcement with information needed to do their jobs more effectively. However, Joe's attempt to paint himself as a martyr was baseless for the sheer fact that he was still trying to strike a deal with the Mafia. He provided Fitzgerald with a list of mobsters that he was prepared to testify against if they didn't work to get him back on the streets. Joe also demanded $50,000 from Patriarca himself for lost wages, as his bookmaking business had dried up since he had been in jail. Fitzgerald passed along the message, which was partially rebuffed by the Office.

"Patriarca says he'll put the money in escrow," Fitzgerald told Barboza.

They were not discussing a simple real estate transaction here. Escrow meant nothing to Barboza. Joe said that he wanted the money now or there would be no deal. Fitzgerald presented the counter offer but was again turned away.

"I want him to know . . . to spend every night shitting his pants, this bastard," Patriarca told his subordinates. "Who does he think he is? He'll kill this guy and that guy? I'm a fag, he says. I'll get him. He talks that way about me. I'll straighten him out."[103]

Barboza later admitted to both Condon and Rico that he had asked John Fitzgerald reach out to Patriarca and Angiulo to let them know of his plans to testify against them.

"I felt that I was doing the right thing by letting them [the Mafia] know," Barboza told the agents.[104]

He made no mention of the offer to rescind his testimony for fifty grand. If the Mafia would not come up with the cash to right Barboza's financially sinking ship, he would have to lean on his new friends in the FBI.

"I've got $23,000 in shylock money owed to me by a guy in East Boston," he informed Condon and Rico. "Can you get it for me?"[105]

The agents would not give Barboza a definitive answer. Joe then changed the subject to his difficult transition at the Barnstable House of Corrections.

"My cooperation is causing me big problems," he told the agents. "I'm confined all by myself, which is like solitary confinement. I can't even exercise, which is what the other inmates are all allowed to do. If Patriarca wants me dead down here, he'll probably just poison my food."[106]

The agents told Joe that they would discuss his situation with the Barnstable sheriff. Pressure was also mounting on the home front. Claire Barboza felt that she too had been relegated to solitary confinement, and she was beginning to climb the walls of her Swampscott home. Despite her refined appearance, there was no doubt that Claire was attracted to the dark side. Why else would she marry the New England mob's most prolific killer? During one particular weekend, she begged John Partington to take her out to dinner—at the Ebb Tide Lounge. This was the equivalent of bringing a hen into a fox den. The young marshal told her that it was a bad and potentially very dangerous idea. However Claire was adamant, and Partington needed to do all he could to keep her happy while her husband was sitting in a jail cell on Cape Cod. He discussed the idea with his team, and they came to the conclusion that the danger would be minimal since Mrs. Barboza would be heavily guarded; the last thing the Mafia would ever attempt would be a gunfight with federal agents. Partington also wanted to show the mobsters that he and his team were not afraid of them. This bravado could easily have blown up in Partington's face. Fortunately for him, they enjoyed their dinner at the Ebb Tide without incident as U.S. marshals positioned themselves around the restaurant and also in the parking lot. Following dinner, Claire asked Partington to join her for a stroll along the Revere Beach boardwalk. She had enjoyed a few cocktails during dinner and was a bit tipsy when she let her guard down and opened up during their walk. Claire Barboza mentioned how "peaceful" it had been without her husband in the house, and began to question their future. They were treading in dangerous waters, this

Partington knew. If Claire were to leave her husband, there would be no way that Joe would go through with his testimony against the Mafia. His family was the only thing that kept him tethered to the FBI. Partington promised her that "Uncle Sam" would take good care of her and her family. Hearing this, Mrs. Barboza said that it wasn't the federal government that was concerning her most at the moment — it was her husband.

"You don't know him, John," she warned Partington. "You think you do, but you don't."[107]

The Animal got in touch with his wife soon after, and she told him that the U.S. marshal's protective detail was much too restrictive and that she was nearing a mental breakdown. Claire also told him that she would be willing to break all ties with her friends and family and move down to Cape Cod so that she and Stacy could not be found by anyone outside the FBI.[108] She naively believed that moving eighty miles southeast would keep her beyond the reach of Raymond Patriarca.

Any thoughts of breaking out on her own vanished on June 20, 1967, when Patriarca, Henry Tameleo, and Barboza's old friend Ronnie Cassesso were indicted by a federal grand jury on charges they had conspired to engineer the murder of Willie Marfeo. Barboza himself was charged as a coconspirator. Although the FBI would utilize intelligence it had gathered from the three years of bugging Patriarca's office, the most damaging evidence against him would come from the man he had called — nigger. In a memo drafted by the U.S. Attorney's Office, Assistant U.S. Attorney Edward Harrington discussed Barboza's key role in the proposed prosecutions of Patriarca and Tameleo:

> The establishment of the agreement [to commit murder] will not be based on circumstantial evidence or inferences arising therefrom but rather the very agreement itself will be testified to by one of the individuals [Barboza] who was to participate in its execution. The overt acts which took place in Massachusetts are especially appropriate in a case involving a gangland assassination in that it has always been one of the essential factors in perpetrating a successful "hit" that the contract be given to an out-of-state "torpedo" as a means of minimizing the chance of detection of the assassination and thus lessening the risk that the individual who planned the assassination be traced.[109]

Federal agents moved swiftly, arresting both Patriarca and Tameleo, while Cassesso was notified of the charges while serving time at Norfolk Prison. The special agent in charge of the Boston FBI office petitioned Director Hoover in a written memorandum for quality salary increases for both Condon and Rico, as the indictments against Patriarca and others represented "the first major blow to the LCN in New England. Patriarca, as LCN boss and possible commission member, and his top lieutenant, Henry Tameleo, were felt to be beyond prosecution by top state and local police officials based on what for years resulted in frustration in securing witnesses who would testify."

Condon and Rico each received incentive awards of $150 for, as the FBI put it, "developing and skillful handling of several confidential sources of great concern to the Bureau in the criminal field."[110] One lingering problem was the fact that the FBI had never conducted a full investigation into the background of its star witness. Director Hoover alerted the Boston office to this issue and demanded that Barboza be put through a rigorous vetting process. Obviously, a killer like the Animal had real skeletons in his closet, but Hoover wanted everything laid out on the table in order to help mitigate questions about Barboza's character that would undoubtedly be raised by Patriarca's defense. A report compiled by Boston FBI agent Thomas Sullivan and sent directly back to Hoover stated that Barboza had murdered both Joseph Francione and Romeo Martin and was responsible for the massacre of Ray Distasio and John O'Neil at the Mickey Mouse Lounge in Revere. The memo also suggested that Barboza had "bumped off" Teddy Deegan. J. Edgar Hoover did not blink when faced with the Animal's murderous past. Instead, the grisly details only elevated Barboza's status in the director's eyes. The major task now was keeping him alive through the trial.

Boston Herald crime reporter James Southwood had recently broken the story that Barboza was now being kept in solitary confinement at the Barnstable House of Corrections and that only two FBI agents had access to him. The Animal's secret location was no longer a secret, and he feared that it would only be a matter of time before Patriarca sent out a hit squad to finish him off.

"The big people like Angiulo, Baione and Patriarca won't handle it themselves," he told Condon and Rico. "Instead, they'll farm it out to some of the suckers they have working for them, guys willing to do hits to ingratiate themselves with the Office."[111]

Barboza stressed once again that Patriarca could pay somebody to poison him. He also wasn't impressed with the security at the prison and felt like a sitting duck. He warned the agents that an assassin could walk right into the jail and kill him if they wanted to. The Animal put his concerns on paper in a letter to the U.S. Attorney's Office in which he explained that he would not testify unless something was done about the situation:

> To Whom it May Concern:
>
> Why is it that because of doing something nobody has dared to do, am I being punished? You people spend hundreds of thousands of dollars checking on Raymond and came up lame. But I came forward "not denying to help myself too" & for coming forward & putting my life in & out of danger, also having to run for the rest of my life with my family, I still from the same people I am working with have been put away so tight that I am being punished. I am here 24 hours a day with all kinds of pressure all alone. I might add that I am like a sitting duck up here because I am not too hard to be had. In fact it is easy. But you people don't want to be bothered. The food at Walpole was 100 times better than here. I could see my wife two times a week at Walpole for 2½ hours a visit. Because of maybe testifying & with all the newspaper talk, I can't sell my house & if I do I lose 3 or 4 thousand dollars. The people with my wife sit in my dining room worth $3,000.00 and make it their clubhouse. And then after telling my wife to move to the Cape and the feds would pay all expenses, now it can't be done. Everything I have been promised in the start turned out to be lies. Ask Mr. Rico if I am guilty of the 4 to 5 years I am doing & the talk heard all over the city concerning how I got framed. . . . I'll either be killed or will have to kill to save myself. I put my faith in you people . . . but whether I get on the stand is up to you people. You broke every promise you made me, caused me to be punished. . . . Is this how you're going to treat my family & I after this is all over? Well I've always been considered a cuckoo anyways & believe me, before I'll be used and played for a "Mickey the Dunce," I'll refuse to testify. . . . You take everything away from me,

leave me alone with my thoughts, make me lose money on my house, drive my wife crazy, break promises & yet you expect me to testify because you have me fenced in. . . . Before I'll be used like this I will not testify. So put me in the Can framed, & get somebody else. . . . My life is ruined, even if I was freed. Because I have to run all my life. I am no threat to the law because I'll be too busy running. . . . I don't think I'm asking for too much. But you people don't want to be bothered. Well neither do I!

JOE BARON[112]

When Barboza handed the letter to Condon and Rico, he also asked them to push authorities to grant him a pardon for the weapons conviction for which he was currently serving time and provide him immunity for the murders of Carlton Eaton, Joseph Francione, Romeo Martin, Ray Distasio, John O'Neil, and Teddy Deegan. The immunity request was shot down immediately, as the so-called Immunity Bill was still being debated in the Massachusetts legislature.

Now alone in his cell without much hope for a pardon, the Animal could only think about those who had wronged him. He had already put the federal government on notice that he would not carry its water unless prosecutors were willing to cut him some kind of deal. Now his thoughts centered on the man he had once respected but now despised. Raymond Patriarca had underestimated him and had undervalued his survival instincts. The Mafia boss was now tucked away in a jail cell probably no bigger than Barboza's. If their battle were a ten-round fight, the first round had gone convincingly to the underdog. Round two was about to begin, and Patriarca would need to advance more cautiously. He asked World War II hero turned leg breaker Louis Grieco to deliver a message to Barboza through attorney Al Farese. Grieco told the lawyer that the Office was now prepared to buy Barboza's silence. They would give him $50,000 plus the $25,000 that had been taken from Tashi during his ill-fated visit to the Nite Lite Café. Grieco also promised that the mob would straighten out the Pearson stabbing case, which was still pending against Barboza. The Mafia would even be willing to prune its low hanging fruit. According to the deal on the table, Barboza could testify against anyone as long as he didn't testify against Patriarca and Tameleo.

Now who's shitting their pants? Barboza thought. The Animal refused Grieco's offer.

"Tell Raymond to go fuck his mother in the mouth," Joe growled.

Next, Jerry Angiulo applied pressure on Jimmy "the Bear" Flemmi to discredit Joe's testimony about Angiulo's alleged involvement in the murder of Rocco DiSeglio and dissuade Barboza crew member Nicky Femia from following his boss's lead. The Bear found himself in a tough situation, because he owed Angiulo $10,000. Convincing Femia not to testify was an easy task, but Flemmi was not about to challenge his best friend, seeing as Barboza had vowed to protect the Bear from prosecution in the Deegan case. In the end Flemmi remained loyal to Joe, and that meant bad news for Angiulo. On August 9, 1967, the underboss was arrested with three other gangsters and charged by District Attorney Byrne's office with organizing the hit on DiSeglio. Knowing that he would be held without bail until his trial, Angiulo showed up for his court arraignment with his toothbrush and shaving kit.

With the hierarchy of the New England Mafia now behind bars, federal and state authorities were in position to strike a death blow against the "Italian organization" in the territories north of Connecticut. The gangland murder of Teddy Deegan was about to resurface in a big way.

Anthony "Tony Stats" Stathopoulos, a key witness in the Deegan murder case, was still hanging around, and there was word on the street that his old friend and accomplice Roy French was now gunning for him. Police detectives played to his fears and convinced Stathopoulos that the best way to stay alive was to help them put French and others behind bars. Like the Animal, Stathopoulos was also preparing to testify before the grand jury. John Doyle, a detective assigned to the Suffolk County district attorney's office, drove Tony Stats down to Cape Cod for a face-to-face meeting with his would-be killer, Joe Barboza.

Stathopoulos and Barboza discussed the Deegan murder while Doyle, Condon, and Rico took notes. The two mobsters talked for several minutes before Stathopoulos finally brought up Jimmy Flemmi's alleged involvement in the murder. Barboza responded with a cold stare.

"I'm keeping the Bear outta this thing," Barboza told him. "Look, he's a good friend of mine and he's the only one who's treated me with respect through this whole thing."[113]

Stathopoulos and Detective Doyle were taken aback by Joe's comments, but Condon and Rico stood unfazed. The last thing the FBI wanted was for one of its informants to go down for a murder rap for a crime he had committed while in the employ of the federal government. The Bear had been a Top Echelon Informant after all. During private conversations, Barboza had suggested they focus on one of Joe's most hated rivals—Peter Limone. Limone was Jerry Angiulo's top bodyguard, and Barboza convinced Condon and Rico that Limone was in line to succeed Angiulo if the Boston underboss was convicted for the murder of Rocco DiSeglio. In truth, Limone would have faced a stiff challenge from Larry Baione for the top spot, but Barboza told the feds that ultimately Limone's brain would outmatch Baione's brawn. Of course Barboza had personal reasons to take Limone off the chess board. Limone was one of the rare few who had never backed down from the Animal. The men had gotten into a heated shouting match on a North End street that to everyone's surprise did not end in bloodshed. Instead, each man went back to his neutral corner, but never forgave nor forgot the other. For Condon and Rico, it also made sense to go on the offensive against Limone, because both agents had been previously told that Limone had warned Teddy Deegan that Jimmy Flemmi was planning to kill him. Together, Barboza and the FBI agents concocted a story to incriminate Limone in the Deegan murder. They tested the story out on the detective from Suffolk County, who appeared to buy what they were selling.

Barboza told John Doyle that he had been approached by Peter Limone to take care of Teddy Deegan.

"He [Limone] came outta the Dog House [Angiulo's North End headquarters] and said he wanted to talk to me. Limone said that a lot of people had been complaining about Deegan killing the Sacramone kid," Barboza claimed. "He also said that Deegan had robbed a bookie in Everett and grabbed $82,000 in action money that belongs to the Office."[114]

Continuing the story, Joe said that Limone offered to pay him $7,500 to "handle the Deegan problem," and that later, Henry Tameleo himself approved the hit.

"Henry told me, yes it's okay. He [Deegan] has to go."

With both Limone and Tameleo now implicated by Barboza for the Deegan murder, the feds still faced a problem with the actual hit squad itself. They wanted to save both Nicky Femia and Jimmy Flemmi, and that meant replacing them in the getaway car on the night of the murder. Through an informant, Chelsea police believed it had strong information about Femia's involvement. Barboza would have to swap out his friend Nicky with someone else. The question was who? This proved to be a great opportunity for the Animal to settle some old scores. He would simply replace Femia with Louis Grieco. After all, Grieco had tried to ambush Barboza crew member Patsy Fabiano several months back and had also served as Raymond Patriarca's errand boy during botched negotiations with Joe's lawyer, John Fitzgerald.

"How did Grieco become involved in the Deegan murder?" Detective Doyle asked Barboza.

Joe explained that Louis Grieco had reached out to him and complained that his wife was cheating on him and asked Joe to kill her for him.

"Louis told me that he'd return the favor any way I wanted it," Barboza added.[115]

Joe said that he'd recruited Grieco as a triggerman and another associate from the North End to serve as one of the getaway drivers. The biggest challenge facing Barboza and the feds was explaining away the description of a heavyset, bald man given by a key witness—Chelsea police captain Joe Kozlowski. This was the most damning evidence against the Bear, and it could give him a one-way ticket to the electric chair. Was there someone else whom Joe knew that might fit this description? The first man who came to mind was Joe "the Horse" Salvati, a Mafia wannabe from the North End who had been given his nickname because of his ample appetite. Salvati was a part-time fishmonger who also made money unloading trucks and working the door at various neighborhood social clubs. Salvati had three strikes against him in Joe's mind. First, he had witnessed Barboza draw a knife and stab another gangster named Jackie Civetti inside Romeo Martin's North End apartment in 1965. Salvati had pulled Barboza off Civetti, who ran out of the apartment and onto the street, leaving behind a trail of blood. Barboza then grabbed Salvati and pointed the knife to his throat. "You keep your mouth shut or you get worse."[116]

Salvati did keep his mouth shut but made an equally egregious mistake by taking a $400 loan from a Barboza associate and not paying it back.

When the Animal went to collect while Salvati was working the door at a Mafia-owned bar, the Horse told him to go fuck himself. Barboza was tempted to kill Salvati where he stood but thought better of it, only because he was in the North End at the time — enemy territory.

Fuck Salvati, Joe thought. Although the Horse and the Bear shared a similar physical build, Jimmy Flemmi was bald, while Salvati maintained a thick head of hair. Condon and Rico had no solution for this major dilemma. Their plan had hit a wall, and that would mean bad news for Jimmy Flemmi. It would be easy to refute testimony brought forth by a regular citizen, but it would be nearly impossible to contradict statements made by a trained investigator like Chelsea police captain Joe Kozlowski. Suddenly Barboza had an idea. He told Condon and Rico about the elaborate disguises he had used on a number of jobs, including the hit on Teddy Deegan. Joe had worn a fake mustache and glasses to alter his appearance on the night he shot Deegan.

"I'll testify that Salvati was wearing a bald wig," Barboza announced.

It wasn't airtight, but it certainly was the most plausible explanation they had heard thus far. The key now would be Barboza's ability to sell it to a grand jury and later at trial.

Barboza testified before a twenty-one-man secret grand jury in late September 1967 and was then transferred from the Barnstable House of Corrections into the custody of the U.S. Marshal Service. He was removed from his jail cell under the cover of darkness and driven to the airport in Hyannis, where he was to meet his new protector — John Partington. The marshal had flown to the Cape in a PBY seaplane donated for the occasion by the Coast Guard. As he stood on the tarmac waiting for the man they called the Animal, Partington assessed his surroundings. Although the small airport lacked the security of a larger facility, Partington was somewhat relieved to find that a heavy fog brought on by cold, damp weather had decreased the visibility for any potential sniper hiding under the pine trees just beyond the runway. The marshal then returned his thoughts to Barboza. Given all that had been said and written about Barboza, it was crucially important for Partington to establish control over the prisoner right away. The Animal arrived at the airport at midnight and was escorted onto the tarmac surrounded by more than thirty state troopers and local cops armed with rifles. Wearing a porkpie hat and a long trench coat ill suited to his stocky frame, Barboza shuffled forward bouncing on the balls of his feet like the boxer he once was. His appearance reminded Partington of the Raging Bull himself—Jake Lamotta. He also wore his signature wrap-around sunglasses and sported a three-day beard that covered his pronounced jaw.

"Get on the plane," Partington ordered.[117]

"Jesus Christ, where's the rest of the guards?" Barboza asked as he took a deep drag on a cigarette.

Partington motioned to his partner, Deputy Marshal Jack Brophy, who would later protect Patty Hearst among others. "I'm it along with him," Partington explained. "Put out your cigarette and put on your seatbelt."

Barboza mimicked the order. "What're you, a goddamned warden or something?"

Partington laid down the ground rules so that there could be no mis-interpretation. He told Barboza that he was to follow orders or they'd sit on that fucking plane until morning.

The Animal stood his ground and asked Partington to offer his name, which the marshal did.

"Oh, you're the prick on the beach every day with my wife. The other marshals come and go. What's your angle?"

Partington ignored the poke. Instead he reiterated the order for Barboza to get on the plane. The PBY took off in the early morning hours, headed for Boston's Logan Airport. After landing a short time later, Partington placed his prisoner in a car and continued on to the Federal Building.

As they entered the Sumner Tunnel, taking them from East Boston into the city, Barboza noticed a car following them. He alerted Parting-ton, who had the car pulled over. The vehicle was carrying a small flock of reporters who had been tipped off that the Animal turned stool pigeon was being brought back to Boston. The media had its airport spies, and so did the Mafia. Partington knew that he had dodged a bullet, and his goal now was to get his prisoner in and out of the city of Boston as quickly as possible.

After a brief meeting at the Federal Building, Barboza was told that he would be reunited with his family on a secure island in Boston Harbor. The idea sounded very tranquil to Joe, who figured it would be a major improvement over his jailhouse accommodations on Olde Cape Cod.

His mood changed quickly when he landed on Thacher Island. This was no resort; instead it appeared to be Barboza's own personal Alcatraz. There were a couple of weather-beaten cottages that appeared to shake in the harsh winds. Snakes slithered about in search of seagull eggs while the protective birds squawked incessantly, trying to keep the reptiles at bay.

"My wife's gotta live in this shit place? My baby, living here? What the hell are they gonna do? You're bringing my baby out to this goddamned place?"[118]

"It's either here or a ten-by-twelve-foot cell," Partington replied.

Barboza didn't respond. Instead, he stepped down from the landing pad and walked a few yards toward one of the many rocky hills that dotted the island. He stared down at the waves crashing below and thought how easy it would be for little Stacy to slip and fall to her death. He would have to watch her as closely as the guards watched him. Lost in thought, he gazed out at the horizon back toward Boston. It was at this moment more than any other that he realized that he was taking down New England's Mafia Empire and that his enemies would try to destroy him no matter what the cost.

Seeing Barboza exposed as he was on the rocks, Partington rushed over and ordered him down. The Animal didn't respond, so the marshal grabbed his leg. Barboza reacted on instinct and lunged at the marshal, connecting with a left hook to Partington's mouth. He started bleeding from the lip and was momentarily unaware that Dennis Condon and Paul Rico had arrived and wanted a word.

"How's it going?" Condon asked.[119]

Partington wiped the blood from his lip and bit down hard. He told them that everything was just fine.

As they walked toward Barboza's cottage, he whispered into Partington's ear.

"Thanks for not ratting me out back there."

Barboza knew that he had just struck a federal officer and that he could spend an additional ten years in prison for the assault.

"I'm not a rat," Partington replied.

"Yes you are," Barboza pointed out. "But you're a good rat."

There had been little activity on Thacher Island in recent years, and suddenly the rocky atoll was alive again with people coming and going with supplies. The residents living onshore in Rockport and Gloucester buzzed with speculation about what was happening there. Most towns-folk thought the Coast Guard was involved in some new type of training on the island. Yet some people had seen a woman and little girl being escorted by small boat to the mainland in Rockport for a few hours of shopping from time to time. No one could have imagined that they were the wife and daughter of a notorious mob killer who himself was under twenty-four-hour guard on the island once known as Thacher's Woe.

Well I run to the rock, please hide me

◦ NINA SIMONE

Baron's Isle

Barboza had spent the past several months in solitary confinement, and now he was having a tough time transitioning back to life as a husband and father. This certainly wasn't an Ozzie and Harriet type of arrangement, but it had never been. Barboza was no domesticated animal. Previously, when the boredom of married life became too big a burden, Joe would simply vanish for days on end, shacking up with mistresses here and there. He had proved to be more like his father than he would care to admit in that respect. But there were no avenues of escape on Thacher Island, so Barboza had nothing to do but commit himself to being a better family man.

This was no easy task with more than a dozen U.S. marshals constantly hovering around.

Little Stacy Barboza had brought her cat Oby to the island, but there was no swing set and there were very few toys for her to play with. Her mother had allowed her to bring her tricycle onto the island, unaware of just how dangerous it could be. The only thing that her father truly feared in life was that something terrible could happen to his little girl. On Thacher Island there seemed to be a deadly hazard around every corner, and Joe had peace of mind only when Stacy was in the cottage and out of harm's way. On one occasion she asked her father if she could ride her tricycle, and Joe said no. Like most children, little Stacy sought a second opinion, but she didn't go ask her mother. Instead she asked her new friend, John Partington, who told her that it was okay. The marshal was unaware that he had overruled Barboza, and when the Animal saw Stacy riding her tricycle, he yanked her off and ordered her back to the cottage.

"I hate you," she told him with tears streaming down her cheeks. "I want John."[120]

Barboza gave Partington a menacing look. First the marshal had tried to win over his wife, and now he was attempting to take his daughter away from him, at least in Joe's mind.

To Partington's credit, he understood the threat he had posed in Joe's eyes. The marshal tried to make peace by setting up a makeshift boxing gym and allowing Barboza to sit in on the protection detail's nightly card games. But even this had its challenges. Joe sparred with another young marshal who had doubted his argument that a great slugger could defeat a great boxer. The two men met on the landing pad and tapped gloves. The young marshal showed a few flashes of skill as he caught Joe with a straight jab to the face. Barboza seemed to relish the pain. His senses were suddenly alive again. It was the first time in a long while that he'd had the chance to physically dominate someone. The predator pounced and returned fire with a powerful hook to the body. The young marshal keeled over and the match was called. X-rays later revealed that Barboza had broken three of the man's ribs. During a card game, Barboza and Partington had to be physically separated after an angry Joe told the marshal to fuck his mother in the ass.

Partington had thought that reuniting Joe with his family would calm him down, but the marshal also understood the added pressure Barboza had felt thanks to the constant visits from Dennis Condon and Paul Rico. Barboza was brought once again before the secret twenty-one-man grand jury investigating the Deegan murder case in late October. Hours after his appearance, detectives fanned out across the Boston area to make their arrests. They grabbed Roy French across the street from his home in Everett. Joe Salvati was nabbed at the corner of Prince and Hanover streets in the heart of the North End. French knew that his luck would eventually run out, but the arrest came as a complete shock to Salvati, who had played no role in the Deegan slaying. Both men hid their faces from news photographers and other onlookers as they were hauled into the Chelsea police station and booked. Salvati was charged with two counts of conspiracy to murder and one count of accessory before the fact to murder. Henry Tameleo was booked on similar charges in Rhode Island. Roy French was charged with first-degree murder. Soon Louis Grieco and Peter Limone would also be rounded up. Like French, Grieco faced a first-degree murder charge, while Limone was booked on a charge of being an accessory before the fact of murder. Only Roy French had truly taken part in the hit on Teddy Deegan. And while Tameleo and Limone were high-ranking members of LCN and Grieco was a feared mob enforcer, Joe Salvati barely had a criminal record. Barboza and his handlers Condon and Rico looked upon Joe "the Horse" as nothing more than collateral damage in their war against the Mafia.

Focus soon shifted from the murder of Teddy Deegan to the hit on Rocco DiSeglio as the trial of underboss Jerry Angiulo was fast approaching. The two FBI agents were preparing the Animal for his final exam, and that meant spending several hours each week going over his story and filling in any gaps that defense attorneys might successfully exploit. During his grand jury testimony, Barboza had proved himself to be a natural born liar. But would his story hold up against a skilled defense lawyer during cross-examination? Condon and Rico could not gamble on such an eventuality. They grilled Barboza day in and day out until the Animal himself started to believe his own lies. The tutoring sessions were interrupted, however, after members of the media found out where Barboza was hiding.

Townspeople in Rockport and Gloucester were stunned to learn that the government had chosen to safeguard an assassin just off their shore. The Mafia was also surprised by the news, but not shocked by the lengths to which the government would go to protect its star witness. Raymond Patriarca proved that he was willing to match the government's commitment by sending his own assassins into the Atlantic Ocean with the slim chance of silencing the turncoat. Fortunately, vigilant protection by the U.S. Marshal Service and rough boating conditions made the attempt on Barboza's life an impossible feat. Hitman Pro Lerner's dream of reaching the island and going mano a mano with Barboza would have to wait. Fat Vinnie Teresa was a swindler who had never been asked to participate in the Mafia's darker arts, but he did not need to be a professional killer to understand that they had little chance for success aboard the *Living End*. Upon seeing the heavily armed protection detail lined up in formation on the island, Teresa turned the vessel around and headed back to Boston. He later explained the situation to Patriarca, but it did little to quell the Mafia boss's quest for vengeance. If Patriarca couldn't kill Barboza by boat, he and his men would have to wait patiently until he returned to shore. The Man was not in a patient mood, as time was the one thing he could ill afford to lose. The boss was under enormous pressure from his Mafia counterparts around the country, as they looked upon him as the first domino to fall. Joe Valachi's testimony had placed the mob under a microscope, but there were few if no ramifications in a court of law. Barboza was a much different animal altogether. His words and his lies could send LCN leaders to prison. Any success he had might also influence other disgruntled gangsters to turn on the Mafia. *Omerta* would be no more.

The decision was made: Joe Barboza must die before being allowed to testify at trial. But in order for the mob to put down the Animal, they would have to go through John Partington and his U.S Marshals, and those men had an obligation to keep Barboza breathing even at the cost of their lives.

Once the Thacher Island location was exposed, the U.S. Marshal Service decided that it was best to move Barboza and his family back to the mainland. This time they secured a sprawling estate near Freshwater Cove in Gloucester. For the U.S. marshals the move was a major concern, as it would eliminate the added layer of protection provided by the sea. The decision was gleefully supported by Barboza, however, as he felt the island was slowly driving him insane.

The island would have one last laugh on its most notorious guest. On the day of the move, Partington made several trips by helicopter transferring equipment and supplies from Thacher Island to the Gloucester estate. Once Partington felt the new location was secure and ready to hold and protect Barboza, he called for the chopper to take him back to the island to retrieve Joe and his family. By this time, however, heavy fog had shrouded the island, making it impossible for the helicopter to land. Partington had not accounted for the possibility of bad weather. He had shipped all the family's clothes, and more important, their food to the mainland. To make matters worse, there was no heat in Barboza's cottage, and forecasters were predicting an autumn frost. Partington radioed the deputy he had left in charge on the island to notify him that Barboza would have to spend one more night on the island with no supplies and very little comfort.

Upon hearing about the situation, an enraged Barboza grabbed the radio from the deputy.

"You really fucked this up right," he growled at Partington. "John, I'm not blaming you but you fucking left me. My baby, my baby is out here!"[121]

Barboza also threatened to pummel Robert Morey, the top U.S. marshal for Massachusetts, who had originally conceived the plan to use Thacher Island as sanctuary for the mob killer. Morey had planned to meet with Barboza upon his relocation to the estate at Fresh Water Cove. Partington relayed the threat to his superior and tried to dissuade him from meeting Barboza until Joe had a chance to cool down. Morey was unfazed and wanted to remind the Animal that he was not a hotel guest but a prisoner with no rights of his own. The next morning Morey stood stone straight as the chopper carrying Barboza landed on the plush lawn of the Gloucester estate. Barboza leaped from the helicopter like a soldier heading into combat and began making his way toward Morey with fists clenched. Sensing the impending confrontation, Partington grabbed little Stacy Barboza from her mother's arms and handed her over to Morey, the little girl serving as a human shield against her father's rage. Seeing his daughter's bright smile, the Animal uncoiled his fists. *Not here, not now,* he thought. Joe would have to wait for another opportunity to express his anger to Morey. That moment came later in the day in a private meeting at the estate. Barboza unloaded a laundry list of gripes to Morey, who nodded occasionally but showed little or no emotion. When Joe was finished and nearly out of breath, Morey began to speak in a slow and deliberate manner.

"Now Joseph, you have a very nice place here," he said, waving his arms around the lavish room. "You see this place you have here? It's a lot nicer than that Barnstable County jail, right?"

Barboza nodded reluctantly.

Morey's soft voice suddenly grew louder. "Now if you don't like it, your ass can go down to Barnstable."[122]

Morey stood from his chair and walked out of the room, leaving Joe speechless. The U.S. marshal was not one to be fucked with.

"Everything's cool," Barboza bellowed a few seconds later, loud enough for Morey to hear.

The security detail was increased from a dozen men to twenty. The

U.S. marshals ran barbed wire along the seawall and planted flare bombs with trip wires along the tree line. Spotlights were set up outside the four houses on the estate, while four German shepherds, a gift to Joe from the U.S. Marshal Service, patrolled the perimeter.

Their cover was almost blown again when a reporter living nearby got curious and began poking around the estate. The marshals sat the newspaper man down and negotiated a deal with him. They would grant the reporter the first behind the scenes story of exactly what was happening at Fresh Water Cove if the man maintained his silence for the time being. The reporter recognized the potential for a big scoop and signed off on the agreement.

Another agreement was also in the works involving one of the suspects in the Deegan murder case. Lawyers for Louis Grieco were so confident of their client's innocence that they agreed to have him take a polygraph test administered by police. Subjecting a client to a lie detector test is always a risky move, especially when the client is a career criminal. But Grieco had nothing to hide, at least not in this case. He sat down for the polygraph test and calmly answered questions as to where he had been on the night of Teddy Deegan's murder.

"I was in Florida and nowhere near Chelsea on March 12th, 1965," Grieco told police.[123]

The polygraph indicated that the gangster had answered truthfully to the question. The results of the test were problematic for FBI agents Condon and Rico, as was the news that the mob was applying added pressure to Barboza's attorney, John Fitzgerald. First, Fitzgerald's law partner, Al Farese, who represented a number of gangsters, said that he had tape recorded some of his conversations with Barboza and that he was prepared to testify against the Animal for obstruction of justice. Fitzgerald's wife, Carol, then received an anonymous call informing her that her husband had taken up with Dottie Barchard, the notorious gangster moll who had inadvertently gotten her boyfriend Ronnie Dermody murdered a few years before. The same caller also reached out to Dottie and warned her to stay away from Fitzgerald or that she and her children would be killed. Barchard was still married to convict Jimmy O'Toole, and the Office had promised to have the man killed if Fitzgerald would help them weaken Barboza. The attorney had danced too close to the mob's flame for years, and now he was paying a price that could cost him his family and even his life. He met with Paul Rico at a restaurant in Dorchester to relay his growing fears. In Rico's eyes, Fitzgerald was a shaken man.

"Recently, a couple guys came to my office and asked where the 'Barboza braintrust' was,"[124] Fitzgerald confided. "I wasn't there at the time, but my secretary later told me that one of the men was about 5′7″, paunchy and in his mid-fifties. I think it was Henry Tameleo's brother."

Fitzgerald told Rico that he blamed his law partner, Al Farese, for his latest troubles.

"I told Al about what I was gonna do to Patriarca and others for causing Joe and me all of this trouble, and Al turned around and told the Office. Now I'm on the hit parade."

Rico knew that if the Mafia could not get to Barboza or his family — they would go after his closest friends, and at this point Joe had no more trusted confidant than Fitzgerald.

The lawyer was an easy target. Despite the threats, he did not keep a low profile. Fitzgerald refused to be taken into protective custody and instead paraded around the city in Barboza's James Bond car, with one and sometimes two mistresses on his arm. To make matters worse, he continued to confer with mob killers like Larry Baione. The two met at a Howard Johnson's restaurant in Dedham, Massachusetts. Baione had heard that Barboza was trying to bury him along with Patriarca, Anguilo, and the Deegan suspects.

"I need to know what Joe is telling the law," Baione explained to Fitzgerald. "It'll be worth a lot of money to you if you can find out and help me."[125]

Fitzgerald would not budge. "I hold no influence with Joe Barboza," he replied. "I'm only his legal counsel. I don't discuss any of these matters with Joe and I cannot help you."[126]

These were pious statements made by a lawyer who had carved out a successful career as Barboza's personal consigliere. Fitzgerald then leaned forward and whispered a message for Baione to take back to Raymond Patriarca. "You tell that diabetic asshole in Rhode Island that if he doesn't lay off me, I'll testify against him myself."[127]

The harassing phone calls to Fitzgerald's wife and girlfriend began soon after this meeting. Paul Rico knew that blackmail was just the first lever to be pulled by the Mafia, which would soon resort to murder if it didn't get what it wanted.

The mob also targeted Joe's older brother. Don Barboza arrived home one night to find two gangsters parked across the street. He recognized one of the men as Blu D'Agostino, a former bodyguard for slain Winter Hill chief Buddy McLean. Blu stepped out of his car and motioned Don Barboza over.

"I've got some papers for your brother," he said with a telling smile.[128]

Don Barboza did not take the bait. Instead, he ran inside his home, locked the door, and closed the shades. He never saw Blu D'Agostino again.

The Animal was livid when he learned of the threats to both his lawyer and his brother. He had also learned that Jerry Angiulo had hired New York Mafia killer "Crazy" Joe Gallo to drive up to Massachusetts to finish Barboza once and for all. Joe managed to sneak a phone call to Gallo's Manhattan headquarters.

"It's the Animal," Barboza snarled into the phone. "I want you to remember one fucking thing. The distance from New York to Boston is the same as Boston to New York."[129]

Barboza threatened Gallo that he would break out of protective custody, drive to New York City, and cut his head off.

The Animal then put pen to paper in a telegram to Tameleo and Angiulo. With help from Claire, Joe wrote down the biblical phrase *Mene, mene, tekel, upharsin* — which, in the Talmudic explanation, means "The king had been weighed and found wanting, and his kingdom is now divided." According to the Bible, the phrase means, "The writing is on the wall." Either definition would have suited Barboza's purpose. He wanted to put the Mafia on notice that its empire was crumbling. He signed the note simply — *The Animal.*

As autumn turned to winter, the FBI agents increased the number of visits to the estate at Fresh Water Cove, where they prepared the Animal for his close-up before a judge and jury.

A few days before Christmas, Barboza was whisked into Boston for his first face-to-face meeting with Raymond Patriarca since the indictments were handed down. Joe had been asked to testify briefly at a pretrial conference about Patriarca's role in the murder of Willie Marfeo. He got up on the witness stand and performed his song and dance for the judge while Patriarca sat silently at the defense table shooting him bullets with his eyes. Once Joe was finished, the Man ran his thumb across his own neck in a garroting gesture. "You rat," he whispered.

"Go fuck your dead mother in the mouth," Barboza shouted as he sprang from the witness stand and headed toward his former boss. John Partington grabbed him before he could reach Patriarca and escorted him out of the courtroom. To calm the seething Animal's nerves, Partington and his men went out and purchased a stuffed Santa Claus for Joe to bring back to little Stacy. Holding the toy in his beefy palms, a macabre grin spread across the Animal's face.

"You know, I used to buy her a stuffed animal after every hit," he said with pride.[130]

After months of rehearsals, it was now time to lift the curtain. Barboza's first public performance took place in January 1968 at the Rocco DiSeglio murder trial. Joe had implicated Jerry Angiulo and three other mobsters—Richard DeVincent, Marino Lepore, and Benjamin Zinna—in the slaying, and now he had to make his words stick. Barboza wasn't the only one getting his first real shot at center stage. U.S. marshal John Partington had also spent months preparing for his role. The feds had received information that all four doors of the Suffolk County Superior Courthouse were going to be covered by mob snipers, so Partington slipped Barboza into the building at 2:00 a.m. on the first day of the trial. Barboza was surrounded by twenty members of the protective detail, each man wearing hoods with slits for eyes. Partington wanted to make sure that Barboza could not be indentified by any potential gunman. The trip from Gloucester to the courthouse at Pemberton Square in Boston was as tightly controlled as a presidential motorcade. A lead car was deployed several miles ahead to look for potential Mafia roadblocks and to scout for sniper positions on bridges and along roadways. The convoy carrying Barboza followed a route of right turns only, out of fear they could be susceptible to a double road block. Once safely inside the courthouse, marshals provided Barboza with his own water and food to ward off any attempt of poisoning.

The Animal was then cleaned up, given a freshly pressed gray suit, and escorted into the eighth-floor courtroom, where he passed the prisoners box avoiding eye contact with Angiulo and the other men who no doubt looked upon him as the rat he had become. The murder trial was the hottest ticket in town as reporters and spectators alike stood in line for more than an hour to get inside. Each had to pass through a metal detector and was subjected to an additional patdown by police looking for guns, knives, or anything that could be used as a weapon.

Earlier that morning, the sixteen-member jury heard the presentation of forensic evidence gathered from the crime scene. The prosecutor, John Pino, then called Joe Barboza to the stand. Pino took little time zeroing in on the night in question. Pino had spent several weeks coaching Barboza in Gloucester, and it was now time to perform their act before a live audience.

"What did you say to Mr. Zinna, and what did he say to you?"[131]

"I said what are you doing around here at this time? You're up to no good."

"Then what was said?" asked Pino.

"Benny [Zinna] said to Vinny [DeVincent], 'Joe says we're up to no good.'" Vinny said, "We're up to no good for our *own* good."

Barboza then told the jury that Zinna informed him that they were waiting for Rocco DiSeglio and that Joe would read about it in the papers tomorrow. Joe also said that he saw the three alleged hitmen get into a car and spoke to them again hours after the murder. The Animal also contended that Jerry Angiulo had given a kill-or-be-killed order to the other defendants in the case, and that the underboss had marked DiSeglio for death because he had acted as the "fingerman" in several hold-ups of Mafia-controlled gambling games. The Animal performed well under Pino's direct questioning. The real test would come during cross-examination.

Angiulo's lawyers were ready for a firefight. They had received information that Barboza had been in talks with author Truman Capote about penning his life story.

"He's the man who wrote *In Cold Blood*, isn't he?" defense attorney Joseph Balliro asked the Animal.[132]

"I think so."

"Have you ever read it?"

"Ah, no."

Attorney Balliro smiled. "I think you'd like that book, Mr. Barboza."

Balliro then asked Barboza if profit was his true motivation for testifying in the case.

"I only started negotiating a book after they killed my friends," the Animal responded angrily. He did not elaborate on who "they" were. He didn't have to. Everyone in the courtroom knew he was talking about the Office. Still, the judge had the comment stricken from the record. The defense immediately called for a mistrial, but the motion was denied.

Once the trial resumed, Balliro, smelling blood in the water, began where he'd left off.

"Did you expect to receive any consideration from anyone for telling this story?"

The question confused Barboza. "Consideration? What consideration?" he asked.

"Did you expect to get any money?" Balliro shouted. "Did you discuss a book or a movie?"

Joe told the court that he began exploring his literary options long before the murder of Rocco DiSeglio. Balliro refused to allow Barboza any room to pivot away from his line of questioning.

"And it all depended on a guilty finding by this jury, didn't it?"

"I'm up here telling the truth, and I'm not motivated by capital gains," Barboza shouted while pointing directly at the defense attorney.[133]

Balliro turned his back on Joe and waved his hand in the air, dismissing him out of hand.

The gesture dug under Barboza's skin as he trembled with rage on the witness stand. If he could have jumped onto the courtroom floor and strangled Balliro with his bare hands, he would have.

The Animal was in the legal ring with an opponent who could attack him from just about any angle. Balliro had Joe on the ropes now and would have landed a knockout punch had the judge not stepped in and called "time." The Animal was transported back to the Gloucester estate with his ego bruised and his brain battered. Dennis Condon and Paul Rico wondered if Barboza had the mental stamina to finish the trial. They had to come up with a better answer to the question of motive. They bounced around several ideas until they settled on what was the most obvious and what would be the most impactful to the jury—Joe's family.

The next morning when testimony resumed, Barboza made an impassioned plea that his testimony in the DiSeglio case had not been fueled by money, promise of a lighter sentence, or revenge. "I decided to tell what I knew after they threatened my wife and kid," he told the jury.[134]

Although members of the Office had never threatened Claire or Stacy Barboza directly, the implication had been there. Barboza's story may have struck a chord with the media and those others who were merely following the trial for sport, but prosecutors could not gauge how it was playing with the most important audience of all—the jury. The defense had pounded away at Barboza's credibility and at one time during the trial had even suggested that he had committed the DiSeglio murder himself and then blamed it on the defendants.

When it was time for the defense to make its final arguments, Balliro was joined by fellow counsel Lawrence O'Donnell, who made an impassioned speech of his own before the court. He implored the jury to steer away from stereotypes when deciding this case.

"Society is eternally tugged toward the lynch law whenever they decide there is a criminal type," O'Donnell argued.[135] "Through propaganda we are told that all Irish are drunks, all Jews are sneaks and all Italians are gangsters. I don't want any of that in the jury box. Michelangelo would turn in his grave. If that is the basis for your decision, scream it out now." O'Donnell then raised his index finger to the jury before mentioning Barboza by his legal name. "In this case the evidence rests on the word of one man, Joseph Baron, and he should not be believed. A baron has no friends. A baron specializes in victims."

The defense reminded the jury once again of the previous indictments against Barboza and asked the panel once again to question his whereabouts on the night of the DiSeglio murder. "Show me one honest man who has got up on the witness stand and testified to one single iota to the defendants," O'Donnell asked rhetorically as he ended his speech.[136]

Prosecutor John Pino got the last word and made a desperate attempt to distance himself from his star witness and yet preserve his testimony. "This is the case of the Commonwealth against Angiulo, Zinna, DeVincent, and Lepore, and I respectfully direct your attention to that fact. This is not the case of Joe Baron against the defendants. . . . Joe Baron told the truth, and who would know better than a man of Joseph Baron's criminal record?"[137]

The jury received the case on January 18, 1968, and reached its verdict after only two hours of deliberations. Jerry Angiulo and his three fellow defendants were rushed back into the courtroom, where they sat quietly as the judge rendered the verdict. The underboss had cheated death numerous times during his service in World War II, and now sixteen ordinary American citizens—a jury of twelve plus four alternates—posed a greater threat to Angiulo's survival than the Japanese Navy ever had. He would get the electric chair if convicted. In the anxious moments before the decision was read, it is possible that Angiulo thought back to the prophetic words in Barboza's telegram: *Mene, mene, tekel, upharsin.* Would his kingdom be divided among his enemies? But in the end, it was Joe Barboza who had been weighed by the jury and found wanting. His murderous past had made him unbelievable in court. The state's case rested almost entirely on Barboza's testimony, and that was not enough for the jury. The verdict was unanimous—Angiulo and the other three defendants were found not guilty on all charges.

Jerry Angiulo, who had cultivated an image of a strong, stern Mafiosi fought back tears in court. Swallowing hard, he told a flock of reporters, "I don't want to say anything right now. I want to see my mother. She's seventy-three, and this thing has been bothering her."

For the prosecution, the FBI, and Joe Barboza, the verdict was stunning to comprehend. How could a jury let a notorious gangster like Jerry Angiulo walk? And what would this mean for the trials against Raymond Patriarca, Henry Tameleo, and the suspects in the Deegan case? As Barboza was notified of the acquittal, he simply paused and stared out at the wave crests colliding with the rock along Freshwater Cove. "See what ya get for trying to do the right thing?" he muttered to himself.[138]

We like explosions. It's only right we should

◦ DEVO

18

Ka-boom!

If Joe Barboza's fragile mind wasn't shattered yet, it soon would be. He had slipped into a minor depression after the Angiulo trial, and both Condon and Rico did their best to keep his spirits up. They told him that he had performed well during the trial but that the case was the weakest of the three. They promised him that he would get his revenge in the Patriarca and Deegan trials. Barboza was not convinced. Jerry Angiulo had been allowed to walk free, and no doubt the underboss would hunt the Animal until his last dying breath. The FBI agents made almost daily visits to the Gloucester estate to check on Barboza's mental state. John Partington was concerned as well. He had recently found Joe in an off-limits room of the mansion — the kitchen, which was filled with knives and other utensils that could be used as weapons. Barboza's eyes were bulging and his speech was slurred. Partington knew right away that he was under the influence of some kind of drug. At first, Barboza thought the marshal was an intruder. "You motherfucker," he hissed as he moved slowly toward the marshal.[139]

"Joe, it's me, John Partington, and you're not supposed to be in here."

His words shook Barboza out of his semiconscious state. Joe blinked several times and shook his head to clear the cobwebs. He then gave an ominous warning to the man he now considered a friend.

"If you ever see me like this again, John, get the fuck away from me. I'll fucking kill you. Don't forget it."[140]

In an effort to calm his prisoner's nerves, Partington relied on an old horse trainer's trick. One way to soothe a particularly stubborn horse is to place a smaller animal in its stable for companionship. Partington figured the method might work at Freshwater Cove as well, so he surrounded Barboza with a menagerie of pets including several dogs, cats, two canaries, and a wounded seagull that Joe tried to nurse back to health. The small petting zoo lightened Joe's mood for a short while until one of his worst fears was finally realized.

Night had fallen on January 30, 1968, and with it came a cold rain. Folks had been buzzing from Boston to Washington, D.C., all day about Bobby Kennedy's sudden announcement that he would not run against his nemesis, President Lyndon Johnson, in the November election. The former attorney general and current U.S. senator from New York told reporters at the National Press Club that although he questioned Johnson's ability to lead the nation, there was nothing he could do about it because of the president's power over convention delegates. Kennedy agonized over the war in Vietnam and most likely gave little thought to the war he had started against organized crime, which now appeared to be at a stalemate following the Angiulo debacle. Attorney John Fitzgerald was no stranger to war. He had fought to stay alive as a combat soldier in Korea, and now he was fighting for survival at home.

Fitzgerald had just locked up his office at 449 Broadway in Everett, Massachusetts, and had planned to visit his parents' house for dinner before heading home to his family in Westwood. He had vowed to be a better husband since the revelation of infidelity surfaced in an anonymous phone call to his wife, Carol. Deep down, Fitzgerald knew that he would not be able to keep that promise. He was thirty-six years old, successful, and drawn to the action. He had been living his life vicariously through clients like Joe Barboza, but somewhere along the line he had morphed from attorney to gangster himself. He had the car, the women, and now he had the weapons. Fitzgerald carried two loaded pistols and made a mental note to keep them in his car during their dinner visit, so as not to upset his father, who was a retired Protestant minister. After turning the key to lock his office door, Fitzgerald waved good-bye to his partner, Al Farese, and walked across the street to a drug store to use a pay phone. Although he still worked with Farese, Fitzgerald no longer trusted him and did not want him eavesdropping on conversations.

Fitzgerald made several calls, including one to Paul Rico. He left the drugstore and walked swiftly through the driving rain to a vacant lot on Mansfield Street, where he had parked the James Bond car, the black and gold Oldsmobile that was still registered in Joe Barboza's name. The lot was about a half-block away from Fitzgerald's office. Normally he would have parked across the street from his Broadway office, but the lawyer was taking every precaution he could now that he was on the "hit parade." One precaution that he had overlooked when he parked his car earlier that day was setting the alarm. John Fitzgerald got into the Oldsmobile and placed his briefcase next to him on the seat. He then placed the key into the ignition, turned it, and pressed his foot against the gas pedal.

The action ignited two big sticks of dynamite that were hidden under the hood. The car erupted into a huge fireball, launching the hood several feet in the air and propelling the hubcaps out hundreds of feet in both directions. The windshield exploded into a thousand pieces as tiny fragments of glass tore at Fitzgerald's face and jaw. Two nearby power lines were snapped by flying debris, and the impact also cracked the windows of neighborhood apartment houses. One man who lived nearly a block away said the explosion felt like a plane going through the sound barrier. There was a deafening noise and the ground shook. The explosion hurled Fitzgerald against the car door and onto the pavement. His clothing was on fire, his flesh was burning, and it appeared that portions of the car's seat cover were molded to his body. The street resembled a war zone as flames and smoke smothered the area. Lying spread out on the asphalt with his right leg nearly ripped from his body, the lawyer begged for help.

"Help, help. . . . Get me the FBI!" he muttered softly as he slipped in and out of consciousness.[141]

Fitzgerald was rushed to Whidden Hospital, where doctors worked feverishly to save his life. He spent nearly six hours on the operating table and was given twelve pints of blood. A team of orthopedic surgeons could not save the right leg, which had to be amputated three inches below the knee. Fitzgerald was also treated for serious burns to his face and hands.

Back at the site of the car explosion, detectives from the Suffolk County D.A.'s office pulled Fitzgerald's briefcase from the fiery wreck and hurried away from the scene. An explosives expert from the state fire marshal's office later determined that two large sticks of dynamite—three inches thick, sixteen inches long, and weighing eight to ten pounds in total— had been wired to the ignition.

"It is a typical gangland bomb," Inspector Joseph Sainato told reporters. "The whole thing can be installed in a minute. Anybody with any knowledge of explosives and electricity could do it."[142]

Dennis Condon and Paul Rico drove to Whidden Hospital, where they waited with other law enforcement officials along with Fitzgerald's wife and five children for an update on his condition. As Carol Fitzgerald prayed for her husband's survival, Paul Rico privately hoped that he would die on the operating table. For Rico, it was a case of sacrificing one for the greater good of many. The FBI agent knew that Joe Barboza's usefulness would end and he had to prepare for the future. It was a future that was dependent on the steady stream of information supplied by Stevie Flemmi, Rico's newly minted Top Echelon Informant. Flemmi had helped convince Barboza to testify against the mob. If this news ever got out, it would mean an end to Flemmi and, more important, an end to Rico's vaunted program in the Boston area. Flemmi needed to ingratiate himself with the Mafia so they would never question his loyalty. When the Office needed someone to send a message to Joe Barboza, Flemmi and his partner Frank Salemme volunteered for the assignment, no doubt with Rico's full approval. The two men thought they had packed the Oldsmobile with enough dynamite to do the job, but somehow John Fitzgerald had made it out alive, if just barely.

"Joe Baron [Barboza] will be wild about this," Al Farese told reporters when he was notified about the bombing.[143] These words were an understatement. Once the news reached Freshwater Cove the Animal erupted, vowing to kill Raymond Patriarca and anyone else he could get his hands on. John Partington increased security on the Gloucester estate, not only to keep intruders from getting in but also to keep Barboza from getting out and making good on his threat.

The attack on Fitzgerald, which had been carried out in an effort to intimidate Barboza and prevent him from testifying against Patriarca, had the opposite effect on the Animal. The bombing only strengthened his resolve to bring the Man down.

"If I can't get that motherfucker with my bare hands, I'll get him with my mouth," he told Partington.[144]

Barboza also blasted the media and local leaders for their public condemnation of organized crime. "They screamed about law and order and how a lawyer, the father of five and the son of a minister, wasn't safe," he later wrote in his memoir. "The politicians all got in the act. They had pretty much ignored the gang war all those years with the excuse it was just punks killing off punks and good riddance, but now that a lawyer had been maimed and crippled they rose up in wrath and tried to outdo each other in pious indignation."[145]

The trial for Raymond Patriarca and his fellow codefendants, Henry Tameleo and Ronnie Cassesso, began in early March 1968 at U.S. District Court in Boston. U.S. Attorney Paul Markham served as lead prosecutor and used his opening statement to paint a picture of an all-powerful Mafia boss who had targeted Willie Marfeo, a small-time gambler, for operating a dice game that drew too much heat in Patriarca's backyard.

"Henry Tameleo telephoned Baron [Barboza] in 1965 to say that he had a problem that Baron and Cassesso could straighten out,"[146] Markham told the fifteen-member jury that had been impaneled in just forty-two minutes and ordered sequestered during the duration of the trial. "He told Cassesso and Baron that they wanted Willie murdered and they wanted it done right away."

All three defendants listened quietly as they sat at the defense table with their lawyers, two of which, Joe Balliro and Ronald Chisolm, had been members of the successful Angiulo defense team. Patriarca had confidence that his lawyers would be tearing to shreds the testimony that would be provided by Joe Barboza. The sixty-year-old Mafia Godfather felt that he was due for a break after what had been a turbulent period in his life. His wife, Helen, had succumbed to cancer a few years before, and now his criminal empire had been jeopardized by FBI wiretaps and the words of a man he had dismissed as nothing more than a "nigger thug." Patriarca had gone from being viewed as a gangland Lord Voldemort — "a man whose name you ordinarily hear whispered but nobody wants to hear out loud," District Attorney Garrett Byrne had said at one time, to a criminal whose arrogance and sloppiness now threatened to destroy *La Cosa Nostra* in New England.

Joe Barboza was equally confident in his ability to hammer the nails into Patriarca's proverbial coffin. Unlike his testimony in the Angiulo trial, his story about the Marfeo murder was mostly true. The challenge now, though, was keeping himself alive long enough to share it with the jury.

The task would fall to John Partington and his team. It was time once again to bring the Animal out of hiding and keep him out of harm's way.

On the morning of Barboza's scheduled testimony, as many as five

Mafia hitmen were positioned outside the courthouse with orders to kill the Animal before he made his way inside. One assassin, tucked away in a nearby office building, covered the courthouse steps with a sniper rifle. Another killer tried to slip into the courthouse dressed as a policeman. A member of the protective detail discovered five hundred pounds of nitroglycerin that the mob had planned to use to blow up the security convoy. Partington had them all fooled; he had smuggled Barboza inside the building under the cover of night three full days before his testimony was to begin.

Sensing the impending danger, the marshal had Barboza transported by helicopter from Gloucester to the Charles River Esplanade. The chopper landed a few yards away from the Hatch Shell stage, where the maestro, Arthur Fiedler, conducted the Boston Pops every Fourth of July. To avoid any unwanted fireworks, eight heavily armed marshals surrounded Barboza during the short walk from the helicopter to an armored Cadillac. The caravan whisked the prisoner to the courthouse, where Joe and Partington were housed in a basement storeroom that had been reinforced with steel plates for added protection. It was not the first time that Partington had executed an elaborate scheme to protect his charge. During the Angiulo trial, he had Barboza brought to the city on a fishing boat that docked at an isolated pier on Boston Harbor. From there they had traveled in the back of a U.S. Postal Service truck to the courthouse, where they were escorted inside the building along with the day's mail.

The U.S. District Courthouse resembled a military barracks, with bomb-sniffing dogs patrolling every floor. Barboza and Partington slept on cots and waited patiently for their names to be called.

The Animal was called to testify on the second day of the trial and was led into the twelfth-floor courtroom by twelve U.S. marshals. Patriarca sat up and leaned forward over the defense table as Barboza entered the room. The marshals moved Barboza along quickly to avoid a repeat of Joe's last courtroom confrontation with his former boss. As an unindicted coconspirator in the murder of Willie Marfeo, Joe took the witness stand and told the jury that he and Cassesso had been recruited by Tameleo and Patriarca to "whack out" Marfeo. As the public at this time was still unaccustomed to mob lingo, the judge asked Barboza what he meant by "whack out."

"He [Patriarca] wanted him killed," the Animal answered. "There was a lot of discussion about how we were gonna do this and when we were gonna start. They suggested we use a meat truck and wear white coats to look like delivery men, and using a dolly walk into the place where he hung out."[147]

The Trojan Horse method seemed the most logical at the time, as Marfeo had recently increased security at his headquarters at the Veterans Social Club on Atwells Avenue by installing a reinforced door and placing metal bars on the windows.

"He [Patriarca] said he'd take care of us, and I said I'd do it for nothing and Cassesso said the same," Joe added.[148] He explained that providing a free hit for the boss would be good for business and would open up a lot of doors. By that, Barboza surely meant that such a favor might help his campaign for induction into *La Cosa Nostra*.

Under cross-examination, attorney Joe Balliro continued the line of defense that had torpedoed Barboza's testimony in the Angiulo trial. Balliro questioned Joe about a recent letter he had written to a girlfriend.

"In the letter you stated that you had a few aces up your sleeve. And at least one of these aces was the testimony you were going to give against these three people?" Balliro said, pointing at Patriarca, Tameleo, and Cassesso. Barboza denied once again that his testimony was driven by profit but freely admitted that he had, as he put it, "deals in the fireplace" for a book and possible movie about his life.

"Did you intend to kill Willie Marfeo when you went down to Providence?"

"Did I intend to? Yes," Barboza replied.

○ ○ ○ ○ ○ ○ ○ ○ ○ ○ ○ ○ ○ ○ ○ ○ ○ ○

After concluding his testimony, Joe walked over to the defense table, looked into Patriarca's eyes, and simply smiled. He knew that his words had inflicted pain. In a period of only two months, Barboza had become a much more polished witness. He had nothing more to hide, nothing for the lawyers to use against him. He was a matter-of-fact killer who did the deadly bidding of more powerful men like Henry Tameleo and Raymond Patriarca. Still, the defense attorneys held onto their belief that the jury would not convict their clients based primarily on the testimony of a man like Barboza. In light of this, they decided to rest their case without calling any witnesses.

"His story is just a fiction that is made up in cold calculation, in cold blood of which he himself said he was capable,"[149] Balliro told the jury during his closing argument. "The case boils down to whether or not you believe Baron [Barboza]. You have ample reason not to believe him."

U.S. Attorney Paul Markham agreed with Balliro that Barboza was no angel.

"The world would be a better place without the Joe Barons," Markham admitted to the jury before pointing over to the defendants.[150] "If you didn't have Raymond Patriarca, you wouldn't have the Joe Barons. Who is worse, the fellow who opens the door for the killers or the man who kills?"

Markham then implored the jury to discount the argument that Barboza's testimony was a work of fiction. "His story is too implausible not to be true!"

The jury was handed the case on the fourth day of the trial. To prevent jurors from getting lost in the mire of gray areas, Judge Francis J. W. Ford instructed them to deliver a guilty verdict if Barboza's testimony was to be believed. But if the panel had any reason to doubt the Animal's veracity, it would have to allow Raymond Patriarca and the others to walk.

Joe was sent back to the basement storage room to await the verdict. Since the Angiulo verdict had been decided quickly, Barboza prayed for a lengthy deliberation, as it would increase the likelihood of a guilty verdict. Four long hours went by before John Partington was called up to the twelfth-floor courtroom.

"This is it," he told Barboza, who was too nervous to respond. He paced around the storage room like the caged animal he was. If he couldn't send Patriarca to prison, Barboza had no doubt that the FBI would throw him to the wolves. Minutes later, the door of the storage room opened and in walked John Partington. The lanky marshal could not conceal the smile that matched perfectly with his soft, blue eyes. "Guilty on all counts!" he shouted.[151]

Barboza waved his beefy arms over his head as though he'd just won the heavyweight title. He launched himself into the air and screamed, "We did it! We did it!"

The immediate jubilation eventually subsided, and Joe allowed himself a moment to reflect on what he had done. His eyes began to well with tears. He thought of the friends that had died or been maimed for him. He thought of the trials he had put his wife and daughter through. He thought of the man he had once respected and now reviled. The Portuguese kid from New Bedford had beaten the Mafia at its own crooked game. But he still had a few more scores to settle.

Partington handed him a marshal's uniform and told him to put it on. He had to keep Joe alive for trial number three, and deception was still the key. Barboza changed into the clothes and was given an M-I rifle— unloaded, of course.

"You'll pretend to guard one of the real guards, who'll pretend to be you," Partington told him.[152] Another marshal fitting Barboza's build and hair color put on Joe's suit jacket and kept his head low.

"All right, Barboza you asshole, keep moving," Joe said as he nudged his decoy forward.

On the day of his sentencing, Raymond Patriarca asked to speak before the court. He was not happy with his defense strategy and wanted everyone to know it. "Your honor, I got something to say. It may be out of line. I had my witnesses here but counsel said it wasn't necessary to use them. If we had used my witnesses it might be different."[153]

Both the Mafia boss and his legal counsel had underestimated Barboza, and now Patriarca was going to pay a hefty price. The judge sentenced all three men to five years in prison and a $10,000 fine. Tameleo was shipped back to the Charles Street Jail to await the Deegan murder trial, and Ronnie Cassesso was sent back to Norfolk Prison Colony, where he would first have to serve out the remainder of a sentence for armed robbery.

Raymond Patriarca would begin his prison term a year later, after his appeal was denied. John Partington escorted the Mafia boss on a plane from Rhode Island to a federal penitentiary in Atlanta, Georgia. Partington the "boy scout" had gotten the last laugh.

Everybody lies a little sometimes

○ B.B. KING

The Lying Game

The Patriarca verdict was a watershed moment in the federal government's war on organized crime. For the first time in history, a major Mafia figure had been taken down solely by the testimony of one of his men. It proved the FBI's theory that the only way to defeat *La Cosa Nostra* was to destroy it from within. The significance of the verdict and the Animal's contribution was not lost on those in the thick of the battle. "The case in the main depended on his [Barboza] credibility," U.S. Attorney Paul Markham told reporters. "The jury obviously believed him, believed him 100 percent. It was a significant victory. To put it in a negative way, if we didn't win it, it would be all over."[154] Much of the credit went to Paul Rico and Dennis Condon. U.S. Attorney General Ramsey Clark wrote a personal letter to J. Edgar Hoover, stating, "The recent conviction of New England Cosa Nostra leader Raymond Patriarca and two of his cohorts is one of the major accomplishments in the Organized Crime Drive Program. Without the outstanding work performed by Special Agents Dennis Condon and H. Paul Rico these convictions could not have been obtained."[155] Rico was recommended for a quality salary increase, while Condon was given a $150 incentive award for "skillfully handling an important government witness whose cooperation was vital to the conviction of Patriarca and his two associates." While praise was being heaped on Condon and Rico, Joe Barboza was stuck at Freshwater Cove feeling angry and underappreciated. He was upset that Markham and other members of the prosecution team did not personally thank him for his role in the trial. Barboza once again threatened to shop on the other side of the street. "While these people don't want to show their appreciation, I'm sure that Joe Balliro would show his appreciation to me," he told Condon and Rico.

Donald Barboza visited his brother at Freshwater Cove after the Patriarca verdict. Donald had brought their father along. Joe Barboza, Sr., and his namesake had been waging a cold war against each other for decades. The son was angry that the father had virtually abandoned the family during his youth, while the father was upset that the son had changed both his religion and his name.

"Why'd you have to do that?" Donald asked Joe.

"I did it for my Stacy," Joe replied. "She'll never get a fair shot in life with the last name Barboza. There's too much history there. If she's raised Jewish and if she has a different name, she just may be given a fair chance."[156]

· ·

With Barboza on edge and on the fence about testifying in the upcoming Deegan trial, Condon and Rico paid a hospital visit to attorney John Fitzgerald, who was still recovering from massive injuries sustained in the car bombing a few months prior. The lawyer would spend a full year in the hospital, and it would take several more years before he felt safe enough to get into a car that had not already been started by someone else. On the day of the FBI visit, Fitzgerald was angry and ready to exact some revenge of his own. He told Condon and Rico that he would testify in the Deegan trial if it reached a critical point where his words might mean the difference between a conviction and letting the suspects walk free. He also pledged to write a letter to his client Barboza, urging him to continue the war on the mob and send as many gangsters to prison as possible.

The Animal had already bitten off the serpent's head in the conviction of Patriarca, and he now felt that the FBI owed him a debt of gratitude. Claire was now pregnant with the couple's second child and feeling ill. Joe pressed the marshals to have her and Stacy brought to a military base, where doctors would be readily available. The request was denied, so Joe penned a letter to Bobby Kennedy himself to complain about his treatment since being taken into federal custody. There is no telling if Kennedy ever received the letter, as he was now in the full throes of a presidential campaign. RFK had entered the race on March 16, 1968, just eight days after the government's victory against Patriarca, Kennedy's "pig on the hill." RFK's real launching point came after U.S. senator Hubert Humphrey's strong showing in the New Hampshire primary. Seeing that Johnson was vulnerable, Kennedy entered the race. The president then stunned the nation by announcing that he would not seek re-election, leaving RFK and Humphrey locked in a heated battle for delegates. Bobby Kennedy's political philosophy had evolved greatly since his days as a hard-charging, mob-baiting, union-busting government lawyer. The times had changed, and Kennedy had changed with them.

RFK made no public statements following the conviction of Raymond Patriarca. His focus now was on ending the war in Vietnam and closing the economic and racial gaps that existed in the United States. Still, the guilty verdict must have been music to Kennedy's ears. Only a year before, RFK had discussed the Mafia boss with John Partington as the two drove to a funeral Mass for Rhode Island congressman John E. Fogarty in Providence. "How do we get that bum on the hill?" Kennedy asked Partington, who had been given the assignment of chauffeuring the senator from the airport to the Cathedral of Saints Peter and Paul.[157] Kennedy talked about Joe Valachi and how his testimony before congress had forced the Mafia out of the shadows. Still, more must be done, Kennedy told the young marshal. Partington agreed wholeheartedly but was surprised to learn shortly after their conversation that he had been named to lead the newly formed Witness Protection Program. Partington never asked but certainly believed that Kennedy had been influential in landing him the new position.

∘ ∘ ∘ ∘ ∘ ∘ ∘ ∘ ∘ ∘ ∘ ∘ ∘ ∘ ∘ ∘

"So thanks to all of you, and now it's on to Chicago and let's win there," RFK told an adoring crowd of supporters who had packed themselves inside the Embassy Room ballroom of the Ambassador Hotel in Los Angeles to hear his victory speech after winning the California and South Dakota primary elections. Just after midnight on June 5, 1968, Kennedy and his security detail followed the hotel maitre d' toward a back exit through the kitchen, where employees lined both sides of the passageway for a chance to shake the candidate's hand. Kennedy smiled and waved to his well wishers and then stopped and turned around to look for his wife, Ethel, whom he feared had gotten separated in the crush of people chanting, "We want Bobby! We want Bobby!" At that moment, a Jordanian citizen and long-time California resident named Sirhan Sirhan stepped forward from the crowd and raised a snub-nosed pistol to the back of

Kennedy's head. The assassin fired several shots; the most damaging entered Kennedy's brain through the back of his right ear. The candidate fell backward onto the floor.

Kennedy remained conscious for a few moments while emergency responders placed him on a stretcher. Ethel ran her fingers gently over her husband's face and chest as he closed his eyes for the last time. He was rushed to Central Receiving Hospital just a short distance from the Ambassador Hotel. Once doctors there obtained a good heartbeat, he was transferred to the Hospital of the Good Samaritan for surgery. The Kennedy family held vigil at the hospital through the night and the next day. RFK had been shot three times: once in the head and twice behind his right armpit. He never regained consciousness and his condition deteriorated as the hours ticked away. Kennedy was pronounced dead at 1:44 a.m. on June 6, 1968.

Some 3,018 miles away from Los Angeles, in Gloucester, Massachusetts, Joe Barboza and John Partington were stunned by the news. Unlike most mobsters, who saw Bobby Kennedy as their Public Enemy Number One, Barboza had great admiration for the young Democrat. Partington, however, felt as if he had lost a friend, which he had. A few weeks earlier, Kennedy had asked the U.S. Marshal Service to allow Partington to provide security for him at the 1968 Democratic National Convention in Chicago should he win the nomination. The marshal wished that Kennedy had made the request sooner, as he might have been in position to protect the candidate at the Ambassador Hotel. Instead, he vowed to continue RFK's legacy by protecting those dangerous men who were willing to turn their backs on *La Cosa Nostra*.

What Partington did not know was that this part of Kennedy's legacy was also his dirty little secret. As attorney general, RFK had been a champion of the CIA's Operation Mongoose, which was designed to assassinate Cuban leader Fidel Castro. Through this support, Kennedy had shown that he was willing to eliminate foreign enemies of the state by any means necessary. One is left to question whether he would have approved of the tactics now being employed by the FBI to destroy a domestic enemy such as the Mafia. Special agents Rico and Condon had spent years circumventing the laws of the United States in an effort to gain an edge against a foe they believed was more of a threat to the American way of life than

Fidel Castro could ever be. If this was indeed a war against organized crime, the agents were prepared to fight in the trenches using the same methods as their adversaries. Rico had already proved that he was willing to commit murder by helping to set up rivals of the Winter Hill Gang for Buddy McLean. Now he was ready to send men to their deaths for a crime they did not commit, and Joe Barboza would be his weapon.

· · · · · · · · · · · · · · · · · ·

Jury selection for the Deegan murder trial had begun in late May 1968. The names of the jurors were printed in the newspaper, a practice outlawed today for fear of reprisal from either side of the case. Robert L. Vacha from Dorchester was the first member chosen. Some 750 prospective jurors were interviewed over twenty-four days before both sides settled on a panel of fourteen men and two women. During his opening statement, Assistant Suffolk County district attorney Jack Zalkind told the jury that $7,500 was the price tag for the murder of Teddy Deegan, with another $2,500 thrown in to kill Deegan's friend Anthony "Tony Stats" Stathopoulos, who would provide them with bone-chilling testimony about the night of the murder. More testimony would be provided by Joe Barboza, the star witness in the case, who had recently pleaded guilty to conspiracy in the murder of Deegan and conspiracy to commit murder with regard to Stathopoulos. Like Barboza, Tony Stats had been isolated in protective custody in the weeks leading up to the trial. He had been transported to the Berkshires in Western Massachusetts, where he was kept under the watchful eye of two detectives from the district attorney's office. Unlike Barboza, who had told him to "fuck those Guinea bastards," Tony Stats was not sure he was capable of sending innocent men to the electric chair. One of the detectives tried to ease his conscience. "Sometimes defendants can be convicted of a crime they didn't do," the detective said. "These are bad people anyway and are probably guilty of a lot worse crimes."[158]

Tony Stats knew full well what the Mafia was capable of. Mobsters had tried to poison his food in prison and had set him up for a hit on a lonely road in Old Orchard Beach, Maine. It was for this reason that he had himself placed in protective custody. Like Barboza, he knew the feds would cast him aside and let him fend for himself if he didn't testify.

Shortly before the trial, Tony Stats was taken to a Boston hotel for a clandestine meeting with prosecutor Jack Zalkind. The assistant district attorney, dressed in a baseball cap, shorts, and sunglasses, told Stathopoulos he wanted him to testify that Louis Grieco was the man who came out of the alley with the gun, not Barboza. Also at issue was whether the gun was in his right or left hand when he came out of the alley. Tony Stats had made previous statements that the gunman who emerged from the alley had carried the pistol in his right hand. That could be potentially dangerous at trial, as Grieco was left-handed. Zalkind ordered Stats to change his testimony and tell the jury that the gunman carried his weapon in his left hand. Zalkind also told him to testify that the gunman walked with a pronounced limp, as Grieco did from an injury he had sustained in World War II. Stathopoulos was unsure. "These motherfuckers are trying to kill you," the D.A. reminded him. "And if you do anything to fuck up this case, the name Zalkind will stick in your throat like cancer."[159]

Stathopoulos testified for the prosecution, but his words were overshadowed by those of Joe Barboza, who took the stand in early July 1968 as a stifling heat wave swept through Boston. The Red Sox had just begun an eight-game winning streak, but the city's attention was focused on the Suffolk Superior Courthouse. As with the Patriarca trial, John Partington made sure that the proper security measures were in place. He had all the shades on the courthouse windows drawn so a sniper could not line up Barboza in his crosshairs from a nearby building. Partington also foiled the attempt of a contract killer who posed as a drunk to get himself arrested and brought inside the courthouse, hoping that he might have the chance to cross paths with the Animal. Barboza testified that he met with Jerry Angiulo's bodyguard, Peter Limone, during the winter of 1965 in the North End, and that Limone told him that Deegan was being targeted for murder because he had robbed the wrong man and had killed another; Anthony Sacramone, who had close ties to the Office.

"Limone told me there's $7,500 in it if I could kill Deegan or have him killed," Barboza told the jury. "I said I'd look into it, but I wanted to speak to Henry [Tameleo] first."[160]

On the okay of Tameleo, Barboza told the jury he then assembled a hit squad that included Roy French, Louis Grieco, and Joe Salvati as the getaway driver. He also said that the gang was loaded for bear when they lured Deegan to the Chelsea finance company on the night of the murder. Barboza rattled off a laundry list of high-powered weapons that included two .357 Magnum handguns, three .38 revolvers, and a .45 pistol. The men also carried an M1 carbine in case they were forced to shoot it out with police.[161] Barboza told the jury that he did not witness the murder because he, Chico Amico, and Ronnie Cassesso had been forced to flee when Chelsea police captain Joe Kozlowski spotted their vehicle near the scene. Barboza said that the trio returned to the Ebb Tide Lounge, where Roy French turned up later with blood stains on his clothes and shoes.

The trial got heated during cross-examination when a member of the defense counsel, attorney Ronald Chisolm, questioned Barboza as to whether he had a personal vendetta against Teddy Deegan.

"Didn't Mr. Deegan pull a gun on you at the Ebb Tide three weeks before and make you back down?"[162]

"Definitely not," Barboza answered. "Mr. Chisolm, no one pulled a gun on me."

The Animal continued his testimony over nine grueling days as defense attorneys poked and prodded the combative witness. When asked by one of the lawyers to provide a location for a pin to be placed on a chart that described logistics of the murder scene, Barboza answered, "You want me to show you what you can do with that pin?"[163]

The Animal had told the jury that Peter Limone had given him a slap on the back for a job well done on the day after the murder. This claim was called into question during cross-examination.

According to Barboza, Deegan was supposed to be shot inside the hallway of the finance company instead of out in the alley where the killing had actually taken place.

"So it wasn't a good job, was it?" a defense attorney asked.

Barboza simply shrugged his shoulders. "He's dead though."[164]

When testimony centered on Joe Salvati, the innocent man who had replaced real killer Jimmy Flemmi on the hit squad, Barboza stayed true to his script.

"I told him [Salvati] to go outside and put Romeo's [Martin's] car down the far end of the parking lot. Then I told Salvati that when he saw me and the others come out the back door of the Ebb Tide to blink your lights once to let us know where you are and in what direction in the back of the parking lot you are." When asked about the fake glasses, mustache, and wig he claimed Salvati wore as a disguise, Barboza testified that he could "see Joe [Salvati] putting on this wig and the snapping of the elastic."[165]

FBI agent Dennis Condon also testified in the trial that he did not show Barboza any reports or other documents pertaining to Deegan's murder, and that both he and Rico were "very careful not to impart any information about the case to Barboza."[166]

Four of the accused men, Roy French, Louis Grieco, Peter Limone, and Joe Salvati took the stand in their own defense.

"Were you wearing a phony wig on the night of March 12, 1965, in Chelsea?" Defense attorney Chester Paris asked Salvati.[167]

"I was not."

"Were you bald in any way in 1965?"

"No sir."

"Was your hair in essentially the same condition it is today?"

Salvati allowed himself a hint of a smile. "It's just a little grayer."

"You didn't have a bald spot?" Paris pressed.

"No sir."

Paris then asked Salvati if he distributed the arsenal of weapons to the hit squad on the night of the murder, to which he replied no. Salvati went on to say that he had never held a firearm in his life.

Joe Salvati was the defendant prosecutors had feared most. He wasn't a made member of the Mafia, and there was nothing in his past that would indicate that he was capable of participating in an act of such violence. In the press coverage surrounding the trial, most articles included the fact that both Henry Tameleo and Peter Limone had been named by the U.S. Senate as members of the *La Cosa Nostra* hierarchy in New England. French and Grieco were also known thugs, but Joe Salvati seemed to be the one defendant completely out of place. The one mistake Salvati made on the stand was telling the jury that he did not remember whether he had gone to work on the day of the Deegan murder.

"But yet you say you have a specific memory of not being in that apartment?" prosecutor Zalkind asked. The apartment he referred to was the Fleet Street meeting place where the Deegan murder was allegedly finalized.

Zalkind also pounded on Salvati for his lack of a full-time job at the time and the fact that he had been arrested ten years before.

"Are you the same Joseph Salvati who . . . had in his possession certain tools and implements designed for cutting through fencing and breaking into buildings, rooms, vaults and safes in order to steal?"

"It was only a pair of pliers," Salvati responded.[168]

Zalkind told the jury that Joe "the Horse" had been given a suspended sentence of one year in the house of correction. A shaky memory, financial motivation, and a slightly blemished past were certainly enough to damage Salvati's credibility. He stepped down from the witness stand no doubt wondering if he would ever return to his wife, Marie, and their children. He remembered a recent jailhouse visit from his young daughter Sharon who had asked, "Daddy, what is the electric chair?" Tears formed in Joe's eyes upon hearing those words. "Where'd you hear that?" he asked the child. "The kids at school say they're gonna give you the electric chair. Are they giving you a present?"[169] Would his daughter's classmates correctly predict the outcome of the trial? Salvati was left to ponder this thought as he watched his fellow defendants tell their own stories to the jury.

Peter Limone had actually been the first accused man to testify, providing yes and no answers to his attorney's questions. Yes, he admitted that he knew Barboza. No, he said he did not contract the Animal to murder Teddy Deegan. Limone claimed that he was just an ordinary businessman who had operated a cigarette vending company before becoming the manager of a bar owned by the Angiulo brothers in downtown Boston. "Jerry Angiulo is a very good friend of mine," Limone admitted on the stand.[170]

Louis Grieco told the jury that he was guilty of only two things, lying about the purchase of a refrigerator and trouble with his wife. "I'm fighting for my life," he shouted angrily from the witness stand as Zalkind peppered him with questions. Grieco's wife took the stand in defense of her husband, claiming that he was with her in Florida on the night of the Deegan murder. Although her claim was true, it was discounted by another FBI agent, William Boland, who testified effectively that Grieco was in Massachusetts when Deegan was murdered.

Prosecutors had two more cards to play before resting the state's case in late July. One surprise witness, a convict named Robert Glavin, testified that he had been offered $50,000 to confess to the Deegan murder. The money would be put in escrow until Glavin's release from prison, which the Office would work to secure. Assistant Attorney General Zalkind then called John Fitzgerald to the stand. It was the lawyer's first public appearance since the car bombing. Spectators gasped as the once strapping Fitzgerald was wheeled into the courtroom, half the man he once was. Jurors who had seen black-and-white photos of the Deegan murder were given a full-color image of the true darkness of *La Cosa Nostra*. Fitzgerald's words were less important than the symbol he now represented, but still he managed to provide evidence to bolster the state's case. The wheelchair-bound attorney told the panel that he had contacted the FBI after learning that his partner, Al Farese, was working with the Office to offer Joe Barboza $25,000 not to testify in the Deegan trial. Lawyers for the defendants spent very little time questioning Fitzgerald during cross-examination, because they did not want to look like they were beating up on a man whose physical wounds had not yet healed, and whose emotional wounds would never heal.

During their closing arguments, Grieco's lawyer, Lawrence O'Donnell, called Barboza nothing more than a loanshark "devoid of any human or moral emotions."

"Show me just one man aside from Barboza who said Louis Grieco is a murderer," O'Donnell demanded of the jury.[171] The attorney for Roy French also stepped up and accused Barboza of "attempting to use this courtroom as his executioner." Limone's attorney, Robert Stanziasi, recited a passage from a letter that Barboza had written a girlfriend. "He [Barboza] wrote: I don't care whether they're innocent or not. They go."[172]

Chester Paris, who defended Joe Salvati, maintained that "the only evidence against my client came from the lips of Joseph Barboza, uncorroborated in every respect."

Jack Zalkind urged the jury to focus its attention not on Joe Barboza but on the defendants themselves.

"The judge and jury of Teddy Deegan were Mr. Tameleo and Mr. Limone," Zalkind argued. "The executioners were Mr. French and Mr. Grieco. The other two, Mr. Salvati and Mr. Cassesso, are just as guilty. Can you believe Joseph Baron [Barboza]? I suggest to you ladies and gentlemen that in order for a person to tell a story such as Joseph Baron has told in this case, he would have to have the cooperation of the FBI, the Chelsea Police Department, the district attorney's office, and the United States Attorney's Office."[173]

Both Condon and Rico must have swallowed hard during this part of Zalkind's monologue. But the prosecutor had a good point. The year was 1968, before Watergate and before the American public began questioning en masse the character and trustworthiness of its leaders and of law enforcement. There was little chance the jury would believe that the vaunted FBI would partner up with a degenerate killer like Joe Barboza.

During his instructions to the jury, Judge Felix Forte also made statements to bolster the state's case. The trial had been especially long— forty-six days and increasingly hostile. Forte found himself constantly locked in a verbal battle with each of the five defense attorneys who had accused him of operating his court in a double standard to favor the prosecution, and who all at one point had demanded a mistrial after the state had entered the term *La Cosa Nostra* into the record during its cross-examination of Peter Limone. Before sending the jurors off to deliberate the charges, Forte wanted to clarify the issue of corroborating evidence.

"His [Barboza's] word does not need to be corroborated," Forte explained. "The uncorroborated evidence of an accomplice is complete and sufficient evidence if you, as jurors, give it that support. It's all up to you."[174]

The jury was handed the case on the afternoon of July 30, 1968, and deliberated until 10:45 p.m. before retiring for the night. The panel resumed deliberations the following morning and came to a decision on the charges before noon. An exhausted Judge Forte, who had been resting at Deaconess Hospital, rushed back to the courthouse to pronounce the verdict. After seven hours of deliberations, the jury found the defendants guilty on all charges.

"You gave notice that the community will not stand for gangland murders," Judge Forte told the jury. "You had the courage of your convictions, and it did take courage."[175]

The crowded courtroom remained quiet but for the silent sobs of the defendants' family members while the judge imposed his sentences. For Henry Tameleo, Peter Limone, and Ronald Cassesso, all members of *La Cosa Nostra*, the sentence was death. Louis Grieco was also condemned to die in the electric chair. The jury had recommended leniency for Roy French and Joe Salvati, who were each given life sentences without the possibility of parole.

"Oh no," Grieco's wife screamed as she learned of her husband's fate. Roy French's wife had to be assisted out of the courtroom after her knees buckled.

The Boston office of the FBI fired off a memo to Director Hoover, stating:

ALL SUBJECTS IN DEEGAN GANGLAND MURDER FOUND GUILTY THIS DATE, SUFFOLK COUNTY SUPERIOR COURT, BOSTON, MASS. . . . TAMELEO. LIMONE AND CASSESSO ALL PROMINENT MEMBERS OF LCN IN PATRIARCA FAMILY. TAMELEO WAS CAPOREGIME OF PATRI-ARCA IN PROVIDENCE, R.I. AREA. . . . GARRETT H. BYRNE, DISTRICT ATTORNEY, SUFFOLK COUNTY, STATED PROSECUTION WAS DIRECT RESULT OF FBI INVESTIGATION AND PARTICULARLY NOTED DEVEL-OPMENT OF PRINCIPAL GOVERNMENT WITNESSES JOSEPH BARON, AKA BARBOZA, AND ROBERT GLAVIN. SAS H. PAUL RICO AND DENNIS CONDON WERE INSTRUMENTAL IN DEVELOPMENT OF BARON AND GLAVIN.[176]

Director Hoover responded to the news with personal letters to both Condon and Rico praising them for their work. U.S. Marshal John Partington was also elated by the verdict. He had kept his prisoner alive long enough to send seven men to prison, four of those men to death row. He had also unwittingly contributed to one of the most egregious miscarriages of justice in American history.

> *So I run to the river. It was boilin',*
> *I run to the sea. It was boilin'*
>
> ◦ NINA SIMONE

WIT'SEC

Joe Barboza returned to Suffolk Superior Court in November 1968 to be sentenced for his role in the murder of Teddy Deegan. Thanks to his co-operation with the FBI, the carnage he had caused would cost him only a year and a day in prison. He was also indicted on charges of being a habitual criminal. However, the indictments would not be carried out as long as the Animal never returned to Massachusetts. Barboza was to spend the rest of his sentence locked up at a U.S. Army post at Fort Knox, Kentucky. The idea of housing the Animal within spitting distance of America's gold reserve must have given some law enforcement officials pause. U.S. Marshal John Partington could not wait to see Barboza off and get back to some sense of normalcy in his own life. He had spent the past sixteen months away from his wife and living with an unapologetic mob killer and his family. Yet there was separation anxiety on both sides. Partington had actually grown to like Joe, and especially his wife and their daughter. They had become a family of sorts, and Partington could not help but feel a tinge of sadness to watch them leave. Barboza had enjoyed the marshal's companionship also, but what he would miss most was the attention he had received over the past year. Joe Barboza had become the biggest story in Boston. His name had appeared in news articles from coast to coast. He had been treated more like a dignitary than a prisoner and criminal. The man who once had abhorred media coverage was now addicted to it. The lights that had shined brightly on center stage had begun to dim. The government and now the public had no more use for Barboza. But the Animal would not go away quietly. When Partington informed Joe that he was to be transferred to Kentucky the next day by plane, he took the news much as a scorned lover would.

"You're gonna see the real Joe Barboza tomorrow, not the rat fink," he said angrily. "Bring your shiny badge. Bring your shiny gun, because you're gonna need them."[177]

Partington feared that his unpredictable prisoner would not get on the plane without a fight. He had deputies guard Barboza's hotel room so that he would not escape. The next morning, Partington went to retrieve the Animal for the ride to the airport. Before entering the hotel room, he told one of his deputies that if he clicked twice on his walkie-talkie, it meant that he should run to the room and shoot Barboza if he had to. The deputy was coiled to attack, but there would be no need. Partington preached to the better angels of Barboza's beastly nature.

"We've gone through too much together. I'll tell you what we're going to do. We're going out the way we came in, just you and me."[178]

Barboza was taken aback. "No handcuffs? No leg irons? Just you and me?"

Partington nodded, and the two walked out of the hotel like old friends. When they arrived at the airport, Barboza pulled a pack of cigarettes out of his pocket and lit one as he climbed into the Coast Guard seaplane. He smiled back at Partington. It was a nod to their first meeting at the airport on Cape Cod, when the marshal had ordered him to put out his cigarette before boarding the plane. Barboza took a deep drag from the smoke and blew it back in the marshal's direction. It was a small act of defiance as the curtain closed on their relationship. As the plane lifted off, Partington remembered that he had one more duty to perform on behalf of Joe Barboza. His wife, Claire, was now contemplating her next move. Should she join her husband in Kentucky? Or should she run and never look back? She had been on a roller-coaster ride as Mrs. Joe Barboza, which at first had been dangerous and exciting. The danger remained, but the excitement had been replaced long ago by humiliation and despair. She had stayed with him during the trials because she had convinced herself that Joe was doing something both courageous and noble. However, letters written by her husband to his girlfriends and presented at trial had extinguished her love for the man. She had stood by him only to learn that he had returned her faith with deceit. Claire had plenty of reasons to leave her husband, but none more important than their daughter and their infant son, Richard, who had been born in late summer. The children would never have a chance at a normal life with a father as deadly and erratic as Joe. John Partington drove to the small Boston hotel where Claire was staying and found her sobbing in her room. She had been running through her options in her mind, and she could not make a decision. Claire once again leaned on her protector and confidant, John Partington, for advice. The marshal's guidance on the matter was not what she had expected. Instead of backing Claire's decision to run, Partington urged her to remain with Joe.

"Do it for Stacy's sake," he pleaded. "She needs her father."[179]

The marshal could sense the trouble ahead if Claire decided to walk out now. Barboza would revert to the wild animal he was, and that would pose a serious danger for those who had been ordered to guard him during the remainder of his sentence. After a long and emotional conversation, Partington finally persuaded Claire to reunite with her husband in Kentucky. He visited the couple a few months later at Fort Knox and found them relatively happy, despite the fact that Joe was still under guard. Barboza found security at the Fort Knox facility extremely lax and accused some marshals of being drunk on the job and stealing from his room. With no more Mafia trials on the horizon, the federal government decided that it was too costly to guard Barboza with a myriad of U.S. marshals any longer. They could not place him in a regular prison, because he would surely become a target for other inmates looking to score points with the La Cosa Nostra. The feds had no other choice but to grant him an early release in late March 1969.

The question that remained—where could Barboza go without the Mafia finding him? The U.S. government had been developing a new program that called for the lifetime protection of high-level witnesses and was now in the process of trying to relocate a Buffalo, New York, gangster named Pascal "Paddy" Calabrese, who like Barboza had recently testified against LCN. The federal Witness Security Program (WITSEC) would provide new identities and new lives for men like Barboza and Calabrese and their families. Calabrese was given a new last name, Angelo, and was packed off to Jackson, Michigan, where he was granted work at a manufacturing plant. For Barboza, remaining in the United States was seen as too much of a risk. At first authorities petitioned FBI director J. Edgar Hoover to allow Barboza to relocate to Australia. Hoover approved the plan, but the idea was later nixed in favor of northern California. No doubt, Claire Barboza expressed her concerns that Australia was simply too far away. Joe also shot down the plan when he was told that the Australian government would not allow his two dogs into the country. Santa Rosa, California, was as good an alternative as any. The city, just fifty-five miles north of San Francisco, serves as a gateway to California's wine country. Santa Rosa was considered a quiet place to live, despite blemishes in the city's past that included the murder of its police chief in 1935. It was also the city made famous by director Alfred Hitchcock in his 1943 thriller *Shadow of a Doubt*. In the classic film, a killer had come to town unbeknownst to members of the community.

With a new name, Joe Bentley, the Animal was given a small place to live and worked with the FBI to choose a new occupation. Agents sat down with Joe and thumbed through the yellow pages of the local phone directory looking for a business that might trigger his interest. He had always prided himself on his cooking ability and had served up a number of tasty Portuguese dishes for his security detail over the past year. Barboza enrolled in cooking school, and the feds found him a job in the galley of the ss *President Wilson*, a merchant ship that made frequent voyages to China. The meager pay was a fraction of what he had made during his days as a gangster, and Joe complained about money constantly. Claire was also having a difficult time transitioning to her new life as Mrs. Joe Bentley. Neighbors had asked her questions about her thick Boston accent, and she and little Stacy had to be tutored regularly about their personal legends, which had been created by the Justice Department. Claire Cohen did not exist any longer. She had vanished into thin air. The Justice Department had told newspaper reporters that Barboza and his family had been flown to Europe courtesy of the U.S. government. The Animal thought he was safe, at least for now.

The FBI received a scare shortly after the relocation when agents received an anonymous tip that the mob knew where Barboza was hiding. Agents kept a close eye on Santa Rosa, but no threat materialized. Soon Joe shipped out on his first and last voyage on the ss *President Wilson*. He did not take well to following orders and found assembly-line cooking tedious. Always looking at all available angles, Joe staged a slip and fall job onboard the ship and was awarded $18,500 as compensation for the work-related injury. He returned to California and his old ways. Through an intermediary, Barboza got word to the Office that he would be willing to recant his testimony in the cases of both Deegan and Patriarca for $500,000. The Mafia expressed interest, so Barboza began traveling back and forth to Massachusetts in an effort to secure a deal. What the FBI had failed to realize was that the allegiance of men like Joe Barboza could be rented but never bought. The Animal had asked the government to give his family more money but had been turned away by the feds. He now decided once again to offer his story to the highest bidder. Barboza kept H. Paul Rico and Dennis Condon in the dark about his bid for a double deal.

The agents' arrogance had grown since the Deegan verdict, and they were now casting a wide net for any disgruntled mobster looking to secure the "Barboza Treatment" in exchange for damaging information and testimony against LCN. Rico and Condon paid a visit to Stevie Flemmi shortly after the convictions of Peter Limone, Joe Salvati, and company. It was Flemmi who had convinced Barboza to flip and who later tried to kill attorney John Fitzgerald, presumably at Rico's urging. They met at a Roxbury auto shop owned by Flemmi's partner, Frank Salemme. "Cadillac Frank" was an old-school gangster who did not mind meeting with cops when it suited his interest. However, he could not fathom the possibility of forging a partnership with the FBI. Flemmi had kept his friend in the dark about his dealings with Rico and Condon, and Salemme had no idea that his partner had become a Top Echelon informant. Salemme attended the little get-together and offered the agents donuts and coffee as they recounted the Deegan case.

"I wonder how Louis [Grieco] likes it on death row," Condon said gleefully. "He went from Florida to death row and he wasn't even there."[180]

Salemme did not know Grieco personally but took offense at the comment.

"How can you talk about that?" he asked Condon. "You know they weren't there."

Salemme's father was a member of the Knights of Columbus, and he knew that Condon was also a member of the Catholic fraternal organization.

"You're a fourth-degree knight," he reminded Condon. "One of the commandments is Thou Shall Not Bear False Witness. How do you expect to get through the pearly gates with Saint Peter, putting that slob [Barboza] up there to put four guys away on death row?"

Condon, who was normally cool, exploded when Salemme had the gall to bring up his religion.

"You're so smart, why don't you take the stand?" Condon shouted.

"I will, let's go up, you and I. We'll take the stand and we'll testify. Who's gonna believe me?"

As the cop and crook continued their argument, Rico shared a concerned look with Stevie Flemmi.

A few months later, both Flemmi and Salemme were indicted for the bombing that almost killed attorney John Fitzgerald. H. Paul Rico tipped off Flemmi, who was already on the run in California for murdering Wimpy Bennett's brother William, to the charges. Flemmi remained in hiding for nearly five years, first making his way to Manhattan and then to Montreal. "Cadillac Frank" went underground in New York City and stayed there until he was arrested in 1972 by a young FBI agent from South Boston named John Connolly. Connolly, a protege of Condon and Rico, had acted on information supplied by Salemme's partner and friend, Stevie Flemmi.

While Rico and Condon had their time tied up with Flemmi and Salemme, there was little supervision or interest in Joe Barboza. The Animal made several trips to Boston and Providence and always in disguise. If the feds got a whiff that he was back in town, they would lock him up for the seventy-plus years he had remaining on his suspended sentence for being a habitual criminal.

If the Mafia found him, he was as good as dead. Barboza created elaborate disguises for himself, including a hippie disguise complete with long-haired wig, fake beard, and love beads. He would also pass himself off as a longshoreman in petticoat and cap. Barboza called for a private meeting with Frank Davis, a Patriarca emissary, in a wooded area in Freetown, just outside of New Bedford. Joe tapped a few childhood friends to provide security for the meeting and also asked newspaper reporter James Southwood to attend. Southwood had remained close to Barboza since the two had worked on a story for the *Boston Herald* together, outlining his reasons for testifying against the mob. Southwood was contemplating a book project with Joe to chronicle his life story. Barboza felt the reporter should get as close as he could to the action. Southwood grabbed an old army gas mask out of a trunk to shield his identity and accompanied Barboza to the meeting. Joe told the Patriarca emissary that he would refute his testimony against the imprisoned Mafia boss and others for half a million dollars plus $1,000 per month while the deal was getting finalized. Barboza said he could also get his hands on $300,000 in stolen securities that he would sell the Office for a commission. Patriarca's man countered with a deal of $100,000 plus all the money still owed to Joe by his shylock customers. No decision was made that day in the woods. Instead, Joe returned to Santa Rosa in pursuit of the stolen stocks and bonds.

He began frequenting the Mirror Man Lounge, a seedy bar in Santa Rosa where he befriended a small-time drug dealer and junkie named Ricky Clay Wilson, who was the current owner of the stolen securities. One night after a meeting with Wilson and others, Barboza mistakenly left his address book behind at the bar. The book was filled with contact numbers for the FBI, U.S. marshals, and the Justice Department. The address book was picked up by a friend of Wilson's who demanded to know why their new associate from the East Coast was friendly with "the pigs." Barboza concocted an elaborate story when he retrieved the address book the next day and hoped the discussion would end there. A few days later, Wilson asked Barboza if he would help retrieve some guns that he had buried outside of town. Joe agreed, as he was looking for a new weapon. Wilson's wife and another female hippie accompanied them as they drove to a wooded area near Glen Ellen, California, just fifteen miles outside Santa Rosa. They pulled down a wagon path about fifty feet into the woods and got out of the car. The men walked ahead of the girls, and, at one point, Wilson turned around to confront Barboza.

"Listen, you're a fucking snitch," Wilson said. "I heard about those guys you put on death row back East. You can get me for conspiracy because of those stocks."[181]

The Animal remained calm despite the fact that his cover had now been blown. "If you believe that, you deserve anything that happens to you."

Wilson reached for a gun in his waistband. Barboza wrestled him to the ground as the gun went off, the shot echoing through the quiet California night. The Animal snatched the weapon out of Wilson's hand and jammed it against his skull. Wilson then made another move for a smaller gun he had hidden in his boot. Seeing this, Barboza fired twice — one bullet tore through Wilson's eye, the other traveled through his temple. Joe ran to the girls and told them to flee the scene. He dragged Wilson's body deep into the bushes and left it there. He wiped the murder weapon clean and threw it as far as he could. When he rendezvoused later with Wilson's wife and the other girl, they were high on drugs and nonchalantly offered to help bury Wilson's body. The trio spent the rest of the evening moving the body from the murder scene to another wooded area where they had dug a shallow grave. Barboza dumped the body in and tried to forget about it. His killer instincts had served him well during his bloody confrontation with Wilson, but they had failed him now. It may have been a simple oversight, or it may have been the fact that he had never hurt a woman. Either way, Joe let the hippie girls live to tell their tale.

A Murder in the Woods

Joe Barboza left town shortly after the murder of Ricky Clay Wilson and traveled back East to continue his negotiations with the Mafia. He was broke now and was looking to make a quick score with the stolen securities, which were now in his sole position, and by recanting his testimony. He had given the government fair warning. Months before leaving California for Massachusetts, Barboza shared his financial frustration with Edward Harrington, a government prosecutor and member of the Justice Department's Boston Strike Force. Harrington, who had become a confidant and friend of Barboza's, drafted a memo to the U.S. Attorney General's office in which he wrote:

> I think it is fair to state that it was agreed by all in the Department of Justice that at the time [Joe Barboza] was released from government protection, every effort would be made to provide him with a job and an unspecified sum of money. . . . [A] year has passed and we've been unable to provide Barboza with a job. At the time he was released from protective custody he was given only $1,000 in government funds. However he is now nearly penniless and has been given a fair chance to begin a new life. Barboza is now desperate. He states he is without any money and feels that the government has reneged on its promise to provide him with sufficient money. He has indicated that he will publicly retract his testimony given in the aforementioned cases and will make known to the press that the government did not give him a fair chance to go "straight." In the opinion of the writers if either of the above should occur, the federal government will receive a severe setback as the [Raymond] Patriarca and [Henry] Tameleo cases might be overturned and plunge the Government into protracted and acrimonious litigation.[182]

The attorney general's office did not heed Harrington's warning. The Animal was considered old news in the eyes of the government. Meanwhile, the FBI continued to reward Special Agent H. Paul Rico, who had recently procured the testimony of killer and Plymouth mail truck robber John J. "Red" Kelley in a second Raymond Patriarca trial for the murder of Willie Marfeo's brother Rudolph, in which the New England mob boss was sentenced to an additional ten years in prison.

For his development of Kelley as a Top Echelon informant and prosecution witness, Rico received a $300 bonus and congratulatory letter from J. Edgar Hoover.

Barboza had seen and heard enough. If it had not been for him, gangsters like Red Kelley would not be so willing to turn against the Mafia. Feeling angry and manipulated, Barboza reached out to attorney F. Lee Bailey, and the two scheduled a meeting in Joe's hometown of New Bedford. According to Barboza, Bailey slipped him an envelope stuffed with $800 and said, "Somebody left it in my office. I don't know who left it for you." Barboza then told Bailey that his testimony against Raymond Patriarca had been highly fabricated with the help of the FBI, and that most of the men convicted in the Deegan case were innocent. Bailey asked the Animal to take a polygraph test, and he agreed. The Animal's volatile nature stopped negotiations from going any further, however. Just days after his meeting with Bailey, Barboza got into an argument with a group of black men near the Fairhaven Bridge. Racial tensions had been high in New Bedford after three white youths had been charged with murdering a black teenager. The incident had triggered rioting in the city and a call for peace by some prominent clergymen. Barboza pulled a .45 automatic on the group of black men and later tried to force their car off the road. A member of the group provided police with a description of Barboza's car, and he was quickly arrested. Police were shocked to learn that the Animal, who had been ordered by the court never to return to Massachusetts, had violated the decree and had been cruising around his hometown. Barboza tried to talk his way out of the arrest, telling cops that he had returned to New Bedford as a federal emissary to help restore law and order following the riots. Police did not buy the explanation, and Barboza was booked on weapons charges and for possession of marijuana. The charges were later dropped because Barboza had not been represented by a defense attorney during his arraignment. The judge ordered his parole revoked, however, for not sticking to the agreement to stay out of Massachusetts. During his arraignment, Barboza pleaded for low bail. "I can't say I'm going to wind up dead on the streets, but I promise I'll come back," he told the judge.[183]

"If you're going to be running around loose, you won't be running around long," Judge Frank E. Smith replied, before setting Barboza's bail at a steep $100,000.

In late July 1970, he was transferred from the Barnstable House of Corrections to the state prison in Walpole, where the men he had helped convict in the Deegan case were either on death row or serving life behind bars. Barboza was housed in 10 Block, a segregated unit in the prison, for fear that the men he had wronged would exact some level of revenge. The Animal quickly tried to mitigate the situation by signing an affidavit for attorney Joe Balliro stating that he would recant his testimony against Henry Tameleo, Louis Grieco, Peter Limone, and Joe Salvati. Balliro immediately filed a motion for a new trial. Lawyers representing Raymond Patriarca and others also filed motions for a new trial based on the new information Barboza now appeared willing and able to offer about how he was coerced by the FBI to testify falsely against the New England power structure of LCN. Upon hearing the news, Edward Harrington and his colleague Walter Barnes rushed to Walpole to confer with Barboza, who told them that he was still on the side of the government and just wanted the Office to think he was working for them.

"My testimony in the Deegan trial was the truth and a lie detector test will prove this," Barboza told Harrington.[184]

The secret meeting with Harrington did not sit well with F. Lee Bailey, who immediately withdrew as Barboza's counsel. Bailey had also been troubled by the fact that Barboza had now refused to take a polygraph after initially agreeing to the test. The Animal was once again playing both sides against the middle, but this time his allies were few and far between. He wrote a letter to Harrington, stating:

Ted, when you and [Walter Barnes] came down to see me, you [and] Walter asked me not to do something [and] I didn't. How long can the little money I bled out of those creeps last, what'll happen to my wife [and] babies then? Bailey said I'll come running to him in the end, I never will!! . . . That's all I want is that job, to be moved to a new location [and] new I.D. [and] I'll be out of your hair [and] Walter's completely! I'll never complain again.[185]

Barboza also shared his feelings with Billy Geraway, a convicted killer, counterfeiter, and thief who occupied the next cell and whom Barboza had known since his days at the Concord Reformatory. The two men would spend as much as fifteen hours a day talking to each other between their cells. Geraway taught Barboza how to play chess, a game he had learned from self-confessed Boston Strangler Albert DeSalvo, who admitted to Geraway that he used chess as a means to gain sexual contact with other inmates. DeSalvo also hinted to Geraway on several occasions that he was not responsible for the eleven Boston Strangler murders. DeSalvo trusted that Geraway would keep his secret, and so did Barboza. Joe regaled Geraway with grisly details about the murders he had committed, including the recent slaying of Ricky Clay Wilson in California. Their relationship began to sour after a heated argument over chess. Geraway had insisted that he had checkmated Barboza, who claimed that Geraway's queen was not where he said it was. Since both men were playing virtual matches against each other in separate cells, neither could see the other man's board. The Animal began to threaten Geraway with information he had gathered about his family. One night, Barboza slipped Geraway a piece of paper in his cell.

"What's this?" Geraway asked.

"That's your sister Louise's telephone number," the Animal replied coldly.[186]

Barboza had put Geraway on notice that he was keeping tabs on his family and would harm them once he got out of jail. Geraway could not let that happen. The following day, he conferred with Ronnie Cassesso who was also in Walpole on the Deegan rap.

"This guy's gone," Geraway told Cassesso. "He's never getting out of prison. He's not hitting the street."

"He might get off and go his own way," suggested Cassesso, who would feel much safer with Barboza outside prison walls.

"No, he's not going his own way because he's not getting out. I'm nailing him today. I'm sending for the fucking D.A. today!"[187]

Geraway got word to the Norfolk County district attorney that Barboza had killed a man in California. He also followed up with a letter to the chief of police in Santa Rosa, California that read in part:

A former Boston loanshark and "hit" man from the Mafia was living in your city recently. He is now in custody here but will return to your city upon release from here. While in Santa Rosa, he murdered a man and buried the body with the help of a female. Two witnesses were within 50 feet when the man, Joseph Barboza Baron, killed the victim. I know from Baron what the victim was wearing, how many times he was shot and why, and who the witnesses were. I know this because he wanted me to move the body if my appeal should come through soon since he is afraid the female will eventually divulge the whereabouts of the body.[188]

Barboza had also discussed the murder with Lawrence Wood, another inmate in 10 Block, who was now willing to testify against him. Dennis Condon was notified about the Geraway letter almost immediately, thanks to a counterpart in the San Francisco FBI office, who said they were closely following the Wilson matter with local authorities. J. Edgar Hoover was also notified. Hoover responded by advising both offices to keep him informed about any prosecutions pending against Barboza. The news about Barboza's recent criminal activity had caught the bureau by surprise, and its first order of business was to find out exactly what evidence the Sonoma County Sheriff's Department had on its former star witness. Two local investigators, Santa Rosa police chief Melvin Flohr and Sonoma County assistant district attorney Ed Cameron, flew to Massachusetts to interview Geraway and Lawrence Wood at Walpole. Before speaking with the inmates the pair met with Dennis Condon, who would only provide them with information about Barboza that was publicly available. Cameron placed several phone calls to Condon over the next several weeks requesting records and information about Barboza, but his calls were never returned.

Cameron, a veteran investigator with fifteen years' experience in the D.A's office and on the police force, could hardly believe the level of resistance applied by Condon and the FBI. He could not tell the good guys from the bad guys. Cameron became convinced that someone had broken into his hotel room and searched his briefcase while he was in Boston. When he finally met with Billy Geraway and Lawrence Wood, they provided him with the names of the two women Barboza had allowed to live on the night they buried Ricky Clay Wilson, their addresses, a description of the vehicle they had been driving that night, and even the names of their children and pets. When Sonoma County detectives paid a visit to Ricky Clay Wilson's wife, Dee, and her hippie friend Paulette Ramos, they were accompanied by Doug Ahlstrom, an FBI agent from the Santa Rosa office who falsely told them that he was not interested in the Wilson murder but in an unrelated matter regarding the women. The women told authorities they had witnessed Barboza—or Joe Bentley, as they knew him—shoot and kill Wilson. Upon hearing their story, Agent Ahlstrom knew immediately that these women posed a dangerous threat to Barboza and the bureau.

With a detailed description of the grave site provided by Dee Wilson and Paulette Ramos—which included how much earth Ricky Clay Wilson had been buried under, and the fact that Barboza had moved a tree trunk over the shallow grave—police discovered Wilson's rotting corpse in the woods near Glen Ellen, California. It took three men from the Sonoma County Sheriff's Department to lift the tree trunk off the grave. The body was badly decomposed, and positive identification took several days. Once the victim was confirmed to be Ricky Clay Wilson, authorities searched Barboza's Santa Rosa home and interviewed Claire, who had been left alone to care for their two young children. The following day, the Sonoma County Sheriff's Department filed a murder charge against Barboza, who was still behind bars in Massachusetts. The FBI quickly mobilized its surrogates. The chief public defender for Massachusetts penned a letter to his counterpart in Sacramento County calling Billy Geraway a chronic liar and urging him to investigate the allegations further before extraditing Barboza back to California. The federal government reversed its course a few months later, when a Justice Department official informed the Sonoma County D.A. that he had no plans to interfere with Barboza's prosecution but wanted assurances that he was not being framed and that he was represented by competent counsel.

A murder charge was filed against Barboza in mid-October 1970. After receiving the news, Barboza called the district attorney directly and pleaded with him to leave Claire and the children alone while they negotiated his return to Sonoma County. Joe's public defender had initially tried to block extradition, claiming that Barboza had not been in California at the time of Wilson's murder. The request was denied, and he was escorted by armed guards onto a flight bound for the West Coast in February 1971. He was visited a month later by his friend Edward Harrington, who explained the purpose of the meeting in a memo to the Justice Department prior to the trip:

> In keeping with the government's obligation to [Barboza], I have assured [Barboza] that this office would take all proper steps to insure that he receives a fair and impartial trial on his pending murder charge. This obligation must be kept in view of the fact that many law enforcement officials in the Boston area consider that the pending murder charge has been concocted by the underworld as a means of retaliating against [Barboza].[189]

Harrington promised that he would not interfere with the prosecution's case against the Animal but would alert them to the possibility that Wilson had been murdered by the Mafia in an attempt to frame Barboza. The Animal tossed cold water on Harrington's conspiracy theory by admitting that he had killed Clay Wilson, and that it had nothing to do with a Mafia vendetta from back East. Barboza claimed that Wilson had attacked him and that he had been placed in a kill or be killed situation. The Sonoma County district attorney was outraged when he learned about the meeting. The D.A. called Harrington into his office and chastised him for visiting Barboza without first getting his approval. Harrington said that he just happened to be in California and that the visit was merely a courtesy call. The district attorney did not buy the explanation and warned Harrington that he would prevent any future clandestine meetings between Barboza and federal officials. Barboza claimed that he had acted in self-defense after Wilson attacked him. Although Harrington would later admit that he did not believe Barboza's story, he still went above and beyond the call of duty to protect him. Harrington told Joe's public defender, Marteen Miller, that he was prepared to testify in Barboza's behalf and that H. Paul Rico and Dennis Condon would do the same.

At around the same time, agents Rico and Condon were scouring the streets of Boston searching for the next Joe Barboza. They set their sights on James "Whitey" Bulger, who had been in prison during the entirety of the Boston mob war but was now trying to make a name for himself in the local underworld. Bulger had promised to furnish the feds with intelligence about his enemies and rivals and was opened as an informant by Dennis Condon on May 13, 1971. Unfortunately, Bulger at that point was willing to pay only lip service to the relationship and was closed as an informant because of unproductivity five months later.

Marteen Miller also got advice from one of Joe's lawyers in Boston, who claimed that he had been within an eyelash of establishing that the Animal was in Massachusetts at the time of the murder and that inmates Geraway and Wood had concocted their story for the purpose of getting a free vacation to California.

Billy Geraway had not limited his testimony against Barboza solely to the Wilson murder. He also swore that Joe had confided to him that Joe "the Horse" Salvati had nothing to do with the hit on Teddy Deegan and that he had placed Salvati at the scene of the crime because of a personal feud. The media soon began to pick up on the story of a possible frame-up in the Deegan case. In an article that appeared in Louis Grieco's hometown newspaper, the *Peabody Times*, reporter Alan Jehlen suggested that there were "strong indications" in the underworld that Barboza might have lied. Joseph Wipfler, a prison guard at Walpole, later went public with his claim that he had witnessed Barboza apologize to Henry Tameleo and vow to make amends for his deceit. "I brought Tameleo to see Baron [Barboza]," Wipfler told a reporter for the *Boston Globe*. "Baron told him that he was sorry he had lied about Tameleo after Tameleo had been like a father to him. He said it grieved him, that he couldn't sleep at night."

Billy Geraway continued his pressure on Joe Barboza and the feds from his prison cell. In a letter to Suffolk County district attorney Garrett Byrne, he wrote:

> If you had submitted Baron to a polygraph, a number of men would not be on death row and/or in prison today, but of course you couldn't do that because your subordinates, with your knowledge, were rehearsing with him his perjured testimony. The cases smell so badly that their odor is beginning to reach even the most secluded public nostrils.[190]

Geraway wanted to put Barboza in the gas chamber for the Clay Wilson murder, so he tried to poke and prod the Animal any way he could. Later he would wear all black at the Wilson murder trial, as if he were attending Barboza's funeral. In the weeks leading up to the court date, Geraway scribbled notes to the prosecution accusing Barboza of being a prison homosexual who had never been a good husband or father to his children. The information had no bearing on the trial, but Geraway knew the notes would get back to the Animal because of the California legal system's liberal discovery rules. Opening statements in the Ricky Clay Wilson murder trial were heard in mid-October 1971. Public Defender Marteen Miller told the jury that he would be calling Harrington, the attorney in charge of the U.S. Justice Department's crime task force, and two FBI agents to testify in support of Barboza's claim that he had acted in self-defense. The jury panel, as well as reporters covering the case, were shocked to learn that the federal government was attempting to protect a self-confessed killer.

Sonoma County district attorney Keirnan Hyland also smoldered at the news. In a letter to FBI director J. Edgar Hoover, Hyland wrote:

> This is disconcerting for the prosecution because it presents a picture of a house divided against itself. The murder for which we are prosecuting the Baron has nothing to do with his Mafia connections. When and if FBI agents testify as defense witnesses, it would be appreciated that they do me the courtesy of contacting me first and allowing me to interview them concerning their possible testimony.[191]

Hyland did have a few cards of his own to play. A New Bedford gangster named Lawrence Hughes (aka Lawrence Brown) came forward and testified that he had received some of the stolen bonds from Barboza. Hughes also presented the bonds to the jury, which helped strengthen the prosecution's argument that Barboza had killed Wilson not in self-defense but in a calculated move to steal the bonds. Hughes also claimed that Barboza had told him he had sex with Wilson's widow an hour after burying him.

Harrington, Condon, and Rico testified for the defense as to the seriousness of previous threats against Barboza resulting from his cooperation with their war on organized crime. They did not offer any information about the murder of Clay Wilson. Instead, they told the jury how important a role Barboza had played in dismantling the New England mob. Edward Harrington explained that Barboza had been the chief witness for the successful prosecution of six notorious Mafia members in the Deegan trial and had helped take down the boss of bosses—Raymond Patriarca.

Marteen Miller was less concerned with their testimony than he was with the symbol that Harrington, Condon, and Rico represented to the jury. "The FBI was held in such esteem," Miller explained later, "that if I could call them as a witness and have them say substantially anything, relevant or not, that would be a point in my favor."[192]

Prosecutors could see that the testimony from three federal authority figures was having an impact on the jury. "We had a pretty good capital murder case," Assistant District Attorney Ed Cameron later told the Congressional Committee on Government Reform. "And we got to the end and we're having FBI agents suddenly appear as almost character witnesses. . . . [T]hey had damaged our case to the point we didn't think the jury was going to convict on a first-degree murder case."[193] Cameron and Hyland quickly began working on a plan-B, and just two days after the testimony of Condon, Harrington, and Rico had concluded, they approached Barboza's lawyer about a compromise. On December 13, 1971, the Animal entered a guilty plea to a charge of second-degree murder. The plea would mean that Barboza would have to serve five years in prison, but thanks to help from the FBI he was spared a first-degree murder conviction and the death penalty.

The government's assistance did not end there. Following Barboza's sentencing, Edward Harrington sent a letter to one of California's top correctional counselors urging her to place the Animal in a "constructive correctional program designed for his ultimate release as a constructive member of society."[194]

In me you see a man alone,
held by the habit of being on his own

◦ FRANK SINATRA

California Dreaming

Joe Barboza's return to prison was the final straw for his wife, Claire, who packed up the couple's two young children and their belongings and quietly returned to Massachusetts. The Animal was truly on his own now. Fortunately for him, his friendship with Edward Harrington continued to grow, and the government lawyer pressed the Justice Department to help Barboza find a job once he was paroled. "It would be in the best interest of the United States to maintain a continued concern for the personal problems of an individual who has contributed greatly to the government's campaign against organized crime," Harrington wrote to his superiors.[195] He had even promised Joe that he would cooperate with a book project about Barboza's life and assist the author by identifying "other individuals who would have background information relating to your career." Barboza had signed a deal with author Bob Patterson to collaborate on a book they would title *In and Outside the Family*. Joe was to be assisted on the project by James Chalmas, an ex-con who moved to California in 1962 after he was charged with hijacking a truckload of shoes in Manchester, New Hampshire. He had also served a sentence for armed robbery that was lengthened by the fact that he had broken out of prison and had held two guards hostage.

Chalmas did not want to go back to Massachusetts because he was fearful of going back to jail, and also fearful of facing any remnants of the once powerful McLaughlin Brothers Gang. Chalmas had taken up with the former girlfriend of Georgie McLaughlin, and there was now bad blood between the two men. Chalmas would serve as Barboza's gofer on the project: gathering photographs, memos, and other documents for the author. Joe understood that he had to remain in the public eye if he was to broker a lucrative book contract with a major publisher. Shortly after beginning his sentence for the murder of Ricky Clay Wilson, the

Animal offered to testify for the government once again, this time for Congressman Claude Pepper's Select Committee on Crime. The Florida Democrat led an eleven-member panel looking to explore and expose the mob's involvement in sports. Dressed in a track suit, his signature wrap-around sunglasses, and with a cigarette dangling from his lips, Barboza told the committee that his former boss, Raymond Patriarca, had invested $215,000 as a silent partner in Berkshire Downs, a bankrupt race-track in Hancock, Massachusetts, in the 1960s. Patriarca's alleged partner was iconic crooner Frank Sinatra, who had sunk $55,000 into the project for 5 percent of the voting stock. Sinatra and fellow Rat Packer Dean Martin were named officers of the Hancock Raceway Association, with Sinatra listed as vice president. Sinatra later resigned from the track and demanded that his investment be returned.

Joe Barboza told the committee that the so-called Chairman of the Board had routinely done business with several Mafia chieftains. The Animal was relying solely on stories he had heard over the years, as he had never met Sinatra and knew nothing of the entertainer's business dealings. Frank Sinatra did not take the accusations lightly and was willing to testify himself, in hopes of clearing his name. Wearing a light brown sport coat, checkered tie, and shiny patent leather boots with elevated lifts, the fifty-four-year-old entertainer strode confidently past the glittering flashbulbs of twenty-five cameramen and a gathering of fans screaming his name into the Cannon House Office Building's caucus room. Sinatra took control of the hearing immediately as he waved a newspaper over his head with the blazing headline: "Witness Links Sinatra to Mafia Figure."

"That's charming, isn't it? Really charming," Sinatra said angrily. "I'm asking someone to be fair about it. How do you repair the damage done to me? This bum [Barboza] went off at the mouth, and I resent it, and I won't have it. I'm not a second-class citizen. Let's get that straight."[196]

John Phillips, chief counsel of the committee, tried to calm the crooner down by suggesting that his testimony could refute Barboza's accusations. Sinatra took what was meant to be an olive branch and snapped it in half. "Why didn't you refute it?" he challenged. "Mr. Counselor, I don't have to refute it because there's no truth to it. It's indecent. It's irresponsible to bandy my good name about. Why didn't someone protect my position? Why didn't you call in the press and tell them it was a character assassination?"[197]

Sinatra denied knowing Raymond Patriarca and told the committee that he had never visited the racetrack. One member of the committee informed the singer about wiretaps which had revealed that Patriarca had known the track planned to add Sinatra to its board of directors in an attempt to add a little class to the business. As the hearing came to a close, the legislators all but apologized to Sinatra. This unusual show of respect sparked *Washington Post* reporter Gerald Strine to write: "The House Select Committee on Crime appeared before Frank Sinatra yesterday." Strine also wrote that he had overheard one legislator wonder aloud, "Who does he think he is?" To which another congressman replied, "He must think he's Frank Sinatra."[198]

The day following Sinatra's testimony, the committee called on Raymond Patriarca, who was still serving time in a federal penitentiary in Atlanta. Patriarca told lawmakers that he had never met Sinatra and that he had seen him only "on television and in the moving pictures."[199] The jailed Mafia boss also denied any involvement in the failed racetrack.

"I read that I had $215,000 in Berkshire Downs," Patriarca said. "I wish I had. I've never had $215,000 in my life. I don't own no horses and nobody I know owns horses."[200]

For some members of the panel, their only exposure to the underworld had been through reading Mario Puzo's runaway bestseller *The Godfather*. When asked whether the fictional version of *La Cosa Nostra* resembled real life, Patriarca gave his thumbs up. "In my opinion, it's a good book," he said. "People like to read stuff about organized crime. If they came out with the Patriarca papers, it would make a million dollars."

He also continued the attack on Barboza, the hitman who had caused him so much trouble over the years. "He's a nutcake. To keep himself outta prison, he'd lie. He'd say anything. He'd even sell his own mother." Patriarca also volunteered to come back and testify about "what's really going on in the country. . . . I'm talking about the government, the administration, the FBI and the harassment that goes on in the United States. I got framed."

Patriarca would never testify against the government and the FBI, which was in a state of flux following the death of Director J. Edgar Hoover in

May 1972. Although the bureau's often illegal relationship with mob killers had not been brought to light, the FBI's reputation had taken a major public relations hit thanks to a series of articles written by *Washington Post* columnist Jack Anderson in which he accused Hoover and his agents of conducting investigations into the private lives of Dr. Martin Luther King, Jr., Marlon Brando, and Joe Namath, among others.

President Richard Nixon, a close friend of Hoover's, ordered that the legendary director receive a state funeral with full military honors.

"The good J. Edgar Hoover has done will not die," President Nixon told a gathering of a thousand friends and dignitaries at the National Presbyterian Church during his eulogy. "The profound principles associated with his name will not fade away. Rather I would predict that in the time ahead, those principles of respect for law, order and justice will come to govern our national life more completely than ever before."

After the funeral, President Nixon announced that the FBI's new headquarters, which was still under construction, would be named after its first director.

Shortly after Barboza's testimony in Washington, DC, Billy Geraway received a jailhouse visit from congressional investigator Roy Bedell, who represented Claude Pepper's Select Committee on Crime. Geraway understood this to be part of some quid pro quo deal between Barboza and the government to gain parole in exchange for his testimony against Sinatra, Patriarca, and others. Geraway later said that Bedell tried to extract corroboration that Barboza had killed Ricky Clay Wilson in self-defense, which Geraway found absurd. Bedell also pressed Geraway to say that Joe's testimony in the Deegan trial had not been perjury. Geraway refused to play ball and never heard from Bedell again. Meanwhile, Barboza sat in a jail cell thousands of miles away, at Folsom State Prison in California. He told friends that six attempts had already been made on his life, and that he would continue to work on his memoir to "add to the public awareness of the diabolical menacing foothold which the Mafia is embracing this country." Barboza continued to incentivize his mysterious friend James Chalmas to take a more active role in the production of the manuscript, for which he would be paid 25 percent of book profits, which Barboza naively estimated to be around $200,000.

Barboza was transferred from Folsom to Montana State Prison in Deer

Lodge, Montana, in late fall 1972. He spent the majority of his time re-counting his criminal exploits on a tape recorder and then sending the tapes to Edward Harrington, who passed them along to author Bob Patterson to transcribe. Barboza's prospect for literary riches began to fade as publishers became aware of the controversy surrounding the Deegan case. Too many people were grumbling now that Barboza might have lied on the witness stand.

"It looks like the book will be shelved until I get home," he wrote a friend. "I am not going to say anything more about it. A lot of plans have to be postponed until I get the book going. But time will work itself out. I'll be coming out broke so we'll have to plan and adjust to it until I get this book going on my own."[201]

Edward Harrington tried to keep Barboza's spirits up and offered to write remarks in the preface of the book, "extolling your [Barboza's] con-tribution to law enforcement in the organized crime field." Harrington also continued to lobby for Joe's parole, telling the director of Montana's parole board that Barboza's defection from the underworld and his deci-sion to become a government witness was "the single most important fac-tor in the success of the federal government's campaign against organized crime in New England."[202] Harrington also noted that more government witnesses, including Vinnie Teresa, were influenced by Barboza's com-mitment to break the Mafia's code of silence. The Animal was granted a parole hearing in Montana, but a decision regarding his freedom was slow in coming. The book deal was also coming apart at the seams. Bob Patterson had dropped out, leaving Joe with very few prospects if and when he won his release. Frustrated, Barboza lashed out at inmates and guards alike. He got into a fight with one guard and broke his jaw. The fracas got him transferred back to California, this time to San Quentin.

His long-gestating book project was finally completed with the help of another author named Hank Messick. The book was titled simply *Barboza*, and its publisher promised that it was "the most nakedly brutal book you have ever read. An infamous hitman tells his story kill by kill." The novel, which Barboza dedicated to his friend Ted Harrington — "with respect" — did not quite live up to its billing. The Animal did take readers through his criminal past but also made sure that he protected himself and his friends, such as Jimmy Flemmi. The result was a collection of anecdotal stories clumsily put together by his coauthor. *Barboza* was not the financial success he had hoped for, but he also hoped to turn that around by promoting it heavily after his release from prison.

Barboza elicited the help of a new girlfriend to begin a letter-writing campaign to his friends in the FBI in hopes they would pull some levers to grant him early parole. He told his girlfriend that Dennis Condon had the most class of any agent he had dealt with but warned her that he also had viper blood in him, and that she should watch her back.

Condon's partner, H. Paul Rico, retired from the FBI in May 1975 and shortly thereafter was named director of security for World Jai Alai. Before retiring from the bureau, Rico had groomed another young agent, John Connolly, to take his place on the front lines and back alleys of the war on organized crime. Connolly's first order of business was to reopen James "Whitey" Bulger as an FBI informant. For the bureau, Bulger represented the future, while Barboza was part of its past. Lessons learned from their experience with the Animal would no doubt help agents cultivate their relationship with the rising mob star from South Boston. One stark difference between Bulger and Barboza was that Whitey was content to remain in the shadows and not draw attention to himself, while the Animal was front and center and in your face. Barboza antagonized both the government and the Mafia incessantly. One California prison official warned the Justice Department's Organized Crime Strike Force that protecting Barboza was a lost cause. "I don't know what [Barboza] has indicated to you, but he is a most prolific letter writer. He can't keep his mouth shut. . . . [We] are fully aware that if something should happen to [Barboza] it might further affect your witness protection program in the New England area. However we aren't getting much help from [Barboza].[203]

Killing the Animal was still a top priority for the New England Mafia. *La Cosa Nostra* had placed a $100,000 price tag on Barboza's head and had no shortage of trained assassins eager to collect the bounty. Boston underboss Jerry Angiulo reviled Barboza, but he also had much to thank him for. Angiulo had filled the power vacuum left by Raymond Patriarca after the boss was sent off to prison. The underboss had always felt underappreciated by Patriarca and privately harbored wishes for his demise. Barboza's testimony against the Man was in essence a bloodless coup d'etat that allowed Angiulo to ascend to the Mafia throne in New England. Angiulo had seen how dangerous Barboza could be with his mouth and with a gun. There were rumors circulating that once paroled, the Animal would head back East to attempt to wrestle control of Boston's underworld from Angiulo and his gang. Certainly, Barboza did not have the men to mobilize such an offensive, but Angiulo believed that he was just crazy enough to try.

In September 1975, Boston FBI agents sent word to their counterparts in San Francisco that Angiulo had dispatched two hitmen to the Bay Area to find out when and where Barboza would be paroled, and set him up for the kill. The FBI also warned that Angiulo's men were planning for a public execution. Joe Barboza was quietly paroled a month later from the Sierra Conservation Camp in California after serving four years of a five-year prison sentence for the murder of Ricky Clay Wilson. He was given a new name, Joseph Donati, and secured work as a cook at the Rathskeller Restaurant, a popular hangout for cops in San Francisco. He also moved in with James Chalmas. Barboza had grown suspicious of Chalmas, whom he knew by the alias Ted Sharliss. In a letter to a friend, Barboza expressed a deep concern that Chalmas, or "Teddy" as he called him, might be talking to gangsters on the East Coast, and Joe was determined to find out whom he was speaking with. Why he moved in with Chalmas remains a mystery. Barboza might have thought it best to stick close to Chalmas in order to find out if he was providing information to his enemies, or he might have simply let his guard down for the offer of a free place to stay.

Chalmas tried to appease Joe by giving him two to three hundred dollars per week as walking-around money and a .38 revolver to defend himself with. Yet the two men did not remain roommates for long, as Joe moved in with a girlfriend fifteen days after his parole. He continued to meet daily with Chalmas to discuss some possible scores they could set up in the San Francisco underworld, which Joe believed was ripe for a takeover. Chalmas listened to Barboza's grandiose plans and constantly fed the Animal's large ego. Joe vowed to get even with all those who had crossed him, and he also hoped that his book would earn him enough money to reunite with Claire, who had begun to correspond with him again using Dennis Condon as an intermediary. Chalmas made mental notes of each conversation and relayed the information to J. R. Russo, the East Boston

Mafiosi who had murdered Barboza's close friend Chico Amico several years before. Russo had recently met with Chalmas in the lobby of the Hilton Hotel in downtown San Francisco and asked the ex-con if he would like to make some big bucks by killing Barboza. Russo held up five fingers five times. "That's twenty-five big ones, and that's a lot of money," he told Chalmas.[204] Russo offered him $25,000 to kill Barboza but Chalmas refused, stating that he wanted to take a neutral position on the matter. The normally cool Russo, who was known for his dapper attire and his trigger proficiency, exploded at Chalmas, jabbing him in the chest with the finger that bore a ring with his initials, JR, surrounded by a peace symbol.

"You made friends with that lying bum who testified against George (LCN's name for Patriarca) and a number of other guys he put on death row," Russo pointed out.[205] The hitman later calmed down but warned Chalmas to keep his mouth shut. "Don't say anything to Barboza or anybody else," Russo advised. Chalmas, who was battling a serious drug addiction, finally decided that cold, hard cash was worth more than camaraderie. He told Russo that the restaurant where Barboza worked was "one good place to take care of business."[206]

The two men never met again but talked several times by phone. "Is that lying bum still out there?" Russo would ask. The Mafia hitman also offered to send Chalmas tasteless, colorless poison with which to kill Barboza.

"I can't handle it," Chalmas admitted. "I'm in no position to do that."

Knowing that applying pressure on Chalmas might mean a botched hit on Barboza, Russo ordered him to make no move against his so-called friend, even if an opportunity fell into his lap.

Chalmas was clearly no triggerman, but his relationship with the Animal was still very valuable to the Mafia. In early 1976, he met with another Angiulo surrogate, Larry Baione, at the Hilton Inn, San Francisco International Airport, where he allegedly received $5,000 to set a trap for the Animal. Still nervous, Chalmas asked Baione and Russo to wait until he went on a planned trip to Miami before moving on Barboza. Russo scratched the idea. He was concerned that Joe might flee the area in Chalmas's absence.

Meanwhile, other criminals were looking to get their hands on the

Barboza bounty. Two inmates at the Orange County Jail in Santa Ana had heard through the grapevine that the Animal dined regularly at two restaurants, Luigi's and La Pentera in San Francisco. They sent word to Boston and were told that two Mafia "torpedoes" would begin casing the cafes immediately.

Despite Barboza's determination to publicize his new book and launch a comeback in the underworld, he sensed that he was living on borrowed time. In late January 1976, Joe telephoned his daughter, Stacy, back in Massachusetts. It had been several years since he had spoken to her, and the young girl did not recognize her father's voice. Fighting back tears, Joe told his daughter to live a good and righteous life and stressed that education would be her pathway to success.

The words were certainly over the child's head, but Barboza had hoped that she would be able to absorb them over time.

On the morning of February 11, 1976, Barboza borrowed Chalmas's wife's car and took their dog for a long ride. He later dropped off the pet and picked up Chalmas and drove to a nearby deli, where the two men ate lunch. They returned to Chalmas's home and talked for several more minutes before Barboza left at 3:30 p.m. Chalmas walked Barboza back to his own car, which was parked at the intersection of Moraga Street and 25th Avenue. Joe took a can of Spam and other canned goods out of his pocket and placed them on the car. He was fishing for his car key and inserting it into the lock when he noticed Chalmas turn suddenly and walk nervously away. Barboza's attention was then drawn to a white van as it came barreling down the street. The sliding door of the van pulled open, and J. R. Russo, with a stocking covering his head, leaned out with a carbine pointed at the Animal's chest.

Another gunman stuck the barrel of a shotgun out the passenger side window. The assassins both opened fire. The first bullet missed Barboza and penetrated the side of his car. The next blast struck him squarely in the chest, lifting him off his feet as twenty-two shotgun pellets attacked his vital organs. The Animal fell to the ground next to his vehicle as the van sped away. Chalmas heard the gunshots and waited for the van to flee the scene before returning to Barboza's side. The Animal was covered in blood and his eyes were closed under his dark, wrap-around sunglasses. Chalmas noticed that Joe had not even had time to reach for his own pistol, a loaded

.38 that was tucked away in his jacket pocket. Joe Barboza, at forty-three years old, was dead in the street. The Mafia had promised a public execution for the vicious turncoat, and J. R. Russo made good on that pledge. The van was recovered the next day in a driveway five blocks from the murder scene. One of the murder weapons, a 12-gauge shotgun, was discovered inside. When news spread of Barboza's stunningly violent death, controversial attorney F. Lee Bailey, who happened to be in San Francisco defending Patricia Hearst, summed it up this way: "With all due respect to my former client, I don't think society has suffered a great loss."[207]

A great loss was felt, however, by Joe Barboza's family, who had all been holding their collective breath since his parole. Joe's brother, Donald, was enjoying a rare family vacation in Fort Lauderdale, Florida, when he received a phone call at the hotel from his sister Ann.

"Joe has died," she told him. "He was killed in California." Don Barboza did not have to ask her how their brother had been killed, as he already knew. Instead of taking his wife and their four children to Disney World that day as planned, Donald piled everyone into the family car for the long ride back to New Bedford, where he would have to take care of Joe's funeral arrangements.

The Animal's body was shipped back from San Francisco to Perry's Funeral Home in Barboza's hometown. Donald walked into the funeral parlor and peered into the open casket. He leaned down and whispered into his brother's ear. "You're one tough son of a bitch," he said softly. "You always told me this is how it would end. At least you're at peace now."[208] The funeral service for Joe Barboza was attended by Donald, their sisters Ann and Carol, and their brother Anthony, a U.S. marine who had served three tours in Vietnam. Joe's mother, Palmeda, had been long dead by that time, but his father, the man he had spent a lifetime rebelling against and emulating to a certain degree, did attend. Claire Barboza and their children, Stacy and Ricky, stayed away from the funeral, as did Joe's former friends in the FBI. As a small group of mourners gathered at the gravesite at St. Mary's Cemetery in North Dartmouth, Massachusetts, the presiding priest asked Donald whether the family wanted him to deliver his brother's eulogy in English.

"No father. Please deliver it in Portuguese," Donald requested. "My brother was Portuguese."

The Ghost of Joe Barboza

The investigation into Joe Barboza's assassination began with promise but stalled quickly. Three months after the murder, FBI special agent John Connolly fingered James Chalmas for helping to plan the gangland hit. Connolly claimed this helpful information was delivered to the feds by Top Echelon Informant BS 1544-CTE, the code word for James "Whitey" Bulger. In reality Bulger had not provided this information, but Connolly was under pressure to score a win for his friend, Whitey. According to Connolly's memo, the "outfit" was now discussing plans to move against Chalmas, whom they rightfully considered to be the direct link tying them to Barboza. The FBI interviewed Chalmas and warned him that he was going to be eliminated. Chalmas crumbled under questioning and admitted that he had helped mark Barboza for death. He pointed the finger of guilt at J. R. Russo, but prosecutors refused to indict the Mafiosi because Chalmas was their only witness and his credibility would be torn apart on the witness stand. Instead, Chalmas pleaded guilty to a federal charge of conspiring to violate—by means of murder—Barboza's right to testify against members of the New England Mafia. He was placed into the witness protection program with a standing agreement that he might be called back to testify against Barboza's killers should they ever be brought to trial.

The Animal's archenemy, Raymond L. S. Patriarca, would not die staring into the barrel of a loaded gun; instead the Man would die a gentleman's death. The New England Mafia boss suffered a fatal heart attack in the emergency room of Rhode Island Hospital in the summer of 1984. He had been rushed to the hospital after two women called emergency crews to an apartment on Douglas Avenue in North Providence, just a short distance from the Godfather's home. He had been suffering from diabetes and heart disease for several years. Most recently, a judge had found him too ill to stand trial for a new round of murder and racketeering charges.

A year after Patriarca's death, further evidence linking the Mafia to Joe Barboza's murder was presented during the 1985 federal racketeering trial of Jerry Angiulo. Investigators had arrested Angiulo while he was dining at a North End restaurant. "I'll be back before my pork chops get cold," he said defiantly. Despite his attempt to rule the New England underworld longer and smarter than Raymond Patriarca, Angiulo had not learned from his boss's mistakes. The FBI had been listening in on Angiulo's conversations since January of 1981, when agents successfully planted bugs in his headquarters at 98 Prince Street in Boston's North End. Informants Stevie Flemmi and James "Whitey" Bulger had drawn the agents a diagram of where to hide the bugs.

Given the operational name Bostar, agents overheard Angiulo's associates Larry Baione, Ralphie "Chong" Lamattina (who was now out of prison), and John C. Cincotti discussing how they had clipped Barboza.

"I was with him [J. R. Russo] every fucking day," Baione boasted. "Me and him discussed everything . . . he made snap decisions."[209]

Baione also called Russo a very brilliant guy. "He accomplished the whole fucking pot didn't he? Smart as a whip . . . stepped right out with a fucking carbine."

In a later conversation, Baione and Jerry Angiulo joked about facing the death penalty in California if ever convicted of Barboza's murder. "They've gone to double chairs," Baione laughed. "No shit. I won't go any other fucking way."

"We, we'll go separate," Angiulo promised. "We'll toss a fucking coin."[210]

After listening to the tapes in court, Angiulo's lawyer told the eighteen-member jury that the government had more to gain from Barboza's murder than his client did. The attorney may have been right. Barboza had wavered back and forth about recanting his testimony in the Deegan and Patriarca trials. Although a hit on the Animal would cause some short-term pain to the witness protection program, it would protect the FBI from lasting damage if the full truth of their relationship was ever revealed to the public. "I assure you that the evidence will show that people on death row wanted Barboza alive," challenged attorney Anthony Cardinale.[211] "They were waiting for Barboza to come forward and tell the truth again." The jury could not fathom the possibility that the federal government would partner with the Mafia to engage in selective assassination. Jerry Angiulo was found guilty on a slew of charges and handed forty-five years in prison, a virtual life sentence for the legendary Boston mob leader.

J. R. Russo, a fugitive at the time, was later caught on tape himself presiding over a Mafia induction ceremony in Medford, Massachusetts. It marked the first time in United States history that a sacred *La Cosa Nostra* ritual had been captured on audio tape. Russo, now sixty years old, was charged with racketeering in 1992 along with four other high-ranking members of the Boston mob. He was also presented with the additional charge of Joe Barboza's murder. Prosecutors reached plea agreements with each defendant, including Russo.

"I understand that there is enough evidence to prove me guilty of [Barboza's] murder," Russo said, acting as his own attorney despite holding only an eighth-grade education. "But I am not admitting to guilt."

U.S. District Judge Mark Wolf gushed over Russo's command of the courtroom. "You speak beautifully and I'm not sure any lawyer could have been more discriminating in picking what points to argue," Judge Wolf told Russo. "It took more courage for you to plead guilty than to go to trial, or than getting gunned down in an alley. There is evidence, although you won't admit it, to your leadership in the Patriarca family. You took that leadership seriously and you pleaded guilty."[212]

J. R. Russo was sentenced to sixteen years in prison for the murder of Joe "the Animal" Barboza and other crimes.

Barboza's family had received some level of closure for his death, yet the men he had put in prison for a murder they did not commit were still waiting for their own justice. Two of those men, Henry Tameleo and Louis Grieco, had died behind bars. Grieco had taken eight polygraph tests and had passed them all. He had also hired a new attorney, John Cavicchi, who spent an exhaustive amount of time beating bushes and gathering evidence to prove his client's innocence. For him, the pain of a wrongful conviction was compounded by the impact felt by his family. Grieco's wife, Roberta, began drinking heavily and eventually abandoned him and their two boys, fleeing to Las Vegas with the children's savings bonds and paper-route money.[213] Grieco's two sons later died of drug and alcohol overdoses.

Peter Limone and Joe Salvati each filed countless commutation petitions through various lawyers in hopes of reducing their life sentences. Over time, Salvati developed legions of supporters, including Jack Zalkind, the prosecutor in the Deegan trial, who would not go so far as to admit that he had made a mistake but instead wrote the parole board that Salvati's involvement in the Deegan murder was minimal. Salvati's pillar of strength had always been his wife, Marie. She had been serving a sentence of her own — on the outside. Instead of receiving support from her North End neighbors, she was ostracized by many of her so-called friends. Her children were constantly tormented at school. Marie Salvati had tried to give her children as normal a life as possible, and made sure that they visited their father regularly in prison. Joe would dispense his fatherly advice to his children during the visits but could not go home with them. Marie would have to play the role of mother and father when the family returned to the North End. She was a comfort to her children, but there was no comfort for her, and she spent most nights crying in the darkness of her lonely bedroom.

The Massachusetts Parole Board finally approved Salvati's clemency petition and sent it to Republican governor William Weld for his recommendation in 1991. Weld sat on the case for several months before rejecting the order, based on what he called "the seriousness of the crimes and the length of (Salvati's) criminal record." Unlike the other defendants in the case, Salvati had barely any criminal record to speak of before getting thrown into the Deegan case.

In 1993 Salvati's attorney, Vincent Garo, joined forces with Dan Rea, an investigative reporter at WBZ-TV in Boston, and together they worked on a series of explosive stories that spoke to Salvati's innocence. Governor Weld commuted Salvati's sentence in 1997 but claimed that public pressure applied by Rea, Garo, and Grieco's attorney, John Cavicchi, had nothing to do with his decision.

Peter Limone would be subjected to the same legal circus as Salvati. His clemency requests had been shot down several times, in part because he was still a high-ranking member of La Cosa Nostra. In January 2001, a judge ordered Limone's release from prison because so-called new evidence had cast doubt on Joe Barboza's credibility. Peter Limone did not receive a commutation, however.

Five months later, Congress began to shed light on decades of darkness surrounding the relationship between the FBI and the mob. The House Committee on Government Reform launched a sweeping investigation into the government's use of informants. When he learned about the probe, former FBI special agent Dennis Condon groused whether Congress had something better to do in light of the terrorist attacks of September 11, 2001. Committee chairman Dan Burton, a Republican from Indiana, began a series of high-profile hearings on Capitol Hill, where once again Joe Barboza, or the ghost of Joe Barboza, took center stage. His victim, Joe Salvati, choked back tears as he recounted his long ordeal.

"The government stole thirty years of my life. My life as a husband and father came to a tumbling halt," Salvati said. "In order to clear my name, it has been a long and frustrating battle. Yet, through all the heartbreak . . . my wife and I remained very much in love. Prison may have separated us physically, but our love has always kept us together mentally and emotionally. Our children have always been foremost in our minds. We tried our best to raise them in a loving and caring atmosphere even though we were separated by prison walls. More than once my heart was broken because I was unable to be with my family at very important times."[214]

Salvati's heartbreaking story echoed through the committee room. The congressional leaders were profoundly shocked at the treatment of Salvati and his family, and they were demanding answers to past secrets. One of the primary keepers of those secrets was H. Paul Rico. Rico, now seventy-six years old and ailing, had kept in close contact with the FBI over the years. In fact, after his retirement he was lured back to the bureau for a special assignment. The feds had asked Rico to play the role of a gangster in a bribery sting of federal judge and future Florida congressman Alcee Hastings. Rico was later commended for his performance, but it was a role he knew all too well. When it came time to testify before the committee, the once suave special agent had run out of convincing lines of dialogue. He looked haggard as he walked into the committee chamber with deep bags under each eye and a sea of liver spots masking his once handsome and confident face. The former agent still had a flair for fashion, however, as he walked past the media photographers in a smart gray suit, dark blue shirt, and yellow tie. Clearly taken by Salvati's testimony the previous day, Ohio representative Steve LaTourette asked Rico why the FBI was willing to sacrifice thirty-three years of Salvati's life to protect a man nicknamed the Animal.

"I don't think the FBI was interested in saving Joe Barboza from anything," Rico countered. "Joe Barboza was an instrument that you could use . . . we didn't think he was a knight in shining armor."[215]

Connecticut congressman Chris Shays took the microphone and peppered Rico about the fact that the FBI was privy to information in the Deegan murder that contradicted Barboza's testimony. The former special agent responded to the line of questioning by playing dumb. He told the committee that it had never occurred to him to interview Deegan's real killer, Jimmy Flemmi, or anyone else besides Barboza. The panel refused to buy Rico's story.

"Do you have any remorse?" asked Shays.

"Remorse for what?"

"For the fact that you played a role in this."

"I believe the role I played in this was the role I should have played," Rico responded. He then went on to describe the method by which the FBI agents supplied witnesses for local law enforcement, to handle and prosecute from there.

"So you don't really care much and you don't really have any remorse. Is that true?"

Rico rolled his eyes and muttered, "Would you like tears or something?"

"Pardon me?" Shays shouted into the microphone.

"What do you want, tears?" Rico responded loudly.

The committee room grew silent. All eyes remained on the retired agent. No further words needed. The true terror of the mad experiment developed by Bobby Kennedy and J. Edgar Hoover and conducted by Rico and others had been summed up in five simple words. Testimony did continue, as no one appeared willing to give Paul Rico the final say. Instead, committee members continued to extract their pound of flesh from Rico until there was little left on his brittle bones.

"It's a fascinating day for me, Mr. Rico. I think the thing I'm most surprised about is that it's clear to me that the FBI became as corrupt as the people they went after," said Congressman Shays. "It's clear to me that you have the same insensitivity that I would imagine in someone who is a hard and fast criminal. Cold as can be."

Paul Rico left the hearing bruised but not yet defeated. That would come later in 2004, when he was indicted for the 1981 murder of Roger Wheeler, his former boss at World Jai Alai. Rico would never stand trial for the crime. He died alone in a Tulsa, Oklahoma, hospital with armed police officers waiting outside his door. "It's not the closure desired or expected by law enforcement," said Tulsa County district attorney Timothy Harris. "But life holds different turns."[216]

Joe Salvati, Peter Limone, and relatives of the other falsely convicted men sued the U.S. Justice Department and were awarded a judgment of $101.7 million, the largest payout of its kind in American history. U.S. District Court Judge Nancy Gertner ruled that secret FBI documents had shown that the bureau was responsible for framing four innocent men of murder. The bulk of those documents consisted of memos which suggested that agents and officials, including J. Edgar Hoover, knew that their star witness, Joe "the Animal" Barboza, lied in his testimony. The government immediately appealed the verdict, but the decision was upheld in August 2009 by the U.S. First Circuit Court of Appeals. "The damage awards give us pause," wrote Senior Judge Bruce M. Selya. "The awards though high are not grossly disproportionate to the harm sustained as to either shock our collective conscience or raise a specter of a miscarriage of justice."

In 2010, the federal government decided to give up its fight for good and announced that it would not appeal the landmark verdict yet again. Salvati, Limone, and the relatives of Henry Tameleo and Louis Grieco received checks from the government for approximately $33 million, which included $2 million in interest accumulated while the case was on appeal.

Julianne Balliro was a sixth grader when her father, Joe Balliro, saw his client Henry Tameleo convicted of murder and sentenced to die in the electric chair. The younger Balliro is now an attorney representing members of the Deegan Four. "It's a good day for civil rights," she proclaimed after the ruling. "I hope that the FBI will be able to put this sordid chapter in their history behind them and redeem themselves to be the institution that they once were."[217]

WHERE ARE THEY NOW?

GENNARO "JERRY" ANGIULO

Died in 2009 at the age of ninety and given a full Mafia boss funeral, complete with nearly two hundred floral arrangements. Angiulo was also given a full U.S. Navy honor guard for his service in the Pacific during World War II. "He is probably the last very significant Mafia boss in Boston's history," said retired State Police colonel Thomas J. Foley. "In these times you don't have anybody who exerts the control, the force, or even maintains the discipline like he had with his organization during his day." *

LARRY BAIONE (AKA ILARIO ZANNINO)

Died in 1996 of natural causes while imprisoned for loansharking and illegal gambling.

JAMES "WHITEY" BULGER

Formerly one of America's Most Wanted fugitives, Bulger was captured in 2011 and is now imprisoned on charges that he committed at least nineteen murders.

DENNIS CONDON

Died in 1999 at age eighty-five after serving as Massachusetts state police commissioner and undersecretary of public safety for the Commonwealth of Massachusetts.

JOHN CONNOLLY

Currently serving a life sentence for second-degree murder in Florida for the death of Boston businessman John Callahan.

PATSY FABIANO

Murdered by the Mafia in 1976 shortly after the hit on Joe Barboza.

NICKY FEMIA

Shot and killed during attempted robbery of an auto body shop in 1983.

JOHN FITZGERALD

Relocated by federal government to South Dakota, where he became a circuit court judge. Died during heart surgery in 2001.

STEVIE "THE RIFLEMAN" FLEMMI

Currently serving a life sentence for murder at an undisclosed location.

---

* "Mob Boss Gennaro 'Jerry' Angiulo Dies at 90," by Shelley Murphy, *Boston Globe*, August 30, 2009.

VINCENT "JIMMY THE BEAR" FLEMMI

Alleged to have murdered self-confessed Boston Strangler Albert DeSalvo behind bars in 1973 to stop him from recanting his confession. Died in prison of drug overdose in 1979.

EDWARD "TEDDY" HARRINGTON

Currently serving as a federal judge in Massachusetts.

PETER LIMONE

Arrested in 2008 on charges of extortion, gambling, and loansharking and still believed to be a high-ranking member of La Cosa Nostra.

GEORGE MCLAUGHLIN

Imprisoned since 1964 and still serving a life sentence in Massachusetts.

JOHN PARTINGTON

After leaving the U.S. Marshals Service in 1980, Partington served as police chief in his hometown of Cumberland, Rhode Island, and later served fifteen years as commissioner of public safety in Providence, RI. He died in 2006 from a viral infection following surgery. He was seventy-seven years old.

JOSEPH J. R. RUSSO

Died in federal prison of throat cancer in 1998 at the age of sixty-seven.

"CADILLAC FRANK" SALEMME

Released from federal prison in 2009 and living in Massachusetts.

JOSEPH SALVATI

Currently living in Massachusetts enjoying both his freedom and his family.

AUTHOR'S NOTE

To complete this book, I had to stand on the shoulders of those great writers and journalists who covered the FBI's relationship with organized crime dating back to the midway point of the last century. I tip my cap to all of them.

I would also like to thank Donald Barboza, James Southwood, and John Cavicchi for their insight and guidance along the way. My goal was never to sensationalize or pay tribute to Joe "the Animal" Barboza; instead, I hoped to explain his crimes and the crimes of the federal government. The path taken by the FBI in the 1960s in the war on organized crime is eerily similar to the path some government agents took decades later in the war on terror, where their original noble efforts eventually created an enemy within.

I would like to thank my family, Laura, Mia, and Bella for putting up with lost weekends to the cause and some odd music emanating from time to time from my office. My personal playlist accompanies each chapter here.

I would also like to thank my mother, Diane, brother Todd, and Uncle Jim for their continued support. Thanks also to my good friend Toby Duane for first making me aware of Joe Barboza and his story more than two decades ago.

For further reading, I would suggest picking up Howie Carr's *The Brothers Bulger*; and *Hitman, The Underboss* by Dick Lehr and Gery O'Neill; *Paddywhacked* by T. J. English; *My Life in the Mafia* by Vincent Teresa; *Boston Organized Crime* by Emily Sweeney (thanks for the great photos); *The Mob and Me* by John Partington and Arlene Violet; *WITSEC* by Pete Earley and Gerald Shur; and, if you can find it, *Barboza* by Joe Barboza and Hank Messick. These books were an incredible help during my research.

Out of the shadows now
and off to chase the sun —
Regards,
CASEY SHERMAN, 2012

NOTES

1 Vincent Teresa (with Thomas C. Renner), *My Life in the Mafia* (Garden City, NY: Doubleday, 1973), 253.

2 See whalingcity.net: "Local New Bedford, Ma. History 1850 — 1858 in Chronological Order."

3 "Azoreans on Shore in New England," by Robert L. Santos, California State University, Stanislaus Librarian/Archivist.

4 "Mass Moments — Stock Exchange Crash Heralds Great Depression," Massachusetts Foundation for the Humanities 2011.

5 Author interview with Donald Barboza, June 2012.

6 Joseph Barboza (with Hank Messick), *Barboza* (New York: Dell, 1975), 29.

7 Ibid., 30.

8 Teresa, *My Life in the Mafia*, 57.

9 "Special Report: State of the Mob," *Providence Sunday Journal*, July 15, 1984.

10 "Worcester Mafia Boss Frank Iaconi's War with the Providence Mob," by Steven R. Maher, *InCity Times*, October 8, 2008.

11 Ibid.

12 Teresa, *My Life in the Mafia*, 54.

13 "Prisons: The Siege of Cherry Hill," *Time* magazine, January 31, 1955.

14 Barboza (with Messick), *Barboza*, 40.

15 Congressional Reports: H. Rpt. 108-414, "Everything Secret Degenerates: The FBI's Use of Murderers as Informants," vols. 1, 2.

16 John Partington (with Arlene Violet), *The Mob and Me: Wiseguys and the Witness Protection Program* (New York: Gallery Books, 2010), 3.

17 Ibid.

18 *Providence Journal Bulletin*, September 10, 1961.

19 Teresa, *My Life in the Mafia*, 52.

20 Gerard O'Neil and Dick Lehr, *The Underboss* (PublicAffairs Books, 1989), 51.

21 Howie Carr, *The Brothers Bulger* (Grand Central Publishing, 2006), 48.

22 *Joe the Rat Valachi*. A&E Home Video. 2004.

23 Ibid.

24 Evan Thomas, *Robert Kennedy: His Life* (New York: Simon and Schuster, 2000), 257.

25 "Investigations: The Smell of It," *Time* magazine, Friday, October 11, 1963.

26 Ibid.

27   Barboza (with Messick), *Barboza*, 42.

28   Ibid., 52.

29   Ibid., 21.

30   Ibid., 61.

31   Ibid.

32   Ibid., 62.

33   Congressional Reports, "Everything Secret Degenerates," vols. 1, 2.

34   Barboza (with Messick), *Barboza*, 65.

35   Howie Carr (with John Martorano), *Hitman* (New York: Forge Publishing Company, 2011), 87.

36   Barboza (with Messick), *Barboza*, 69.

37   Ibid., 70.

38   "Mob Warfare Is Replacing Stranglings," by James Calogero, Associated Press, January 13, 1965.

39   Ibid.

40   Teresa, *My Life in the Mafia*, 272.

41   FBI Field Memo, March 10, 1965.

42   Barboza (with Messick), *Barboza*, 103.

43   Ibid., 104.

44   Ibid., 103.

45   Ibid., 101.

46   FBI interview of Anthony Stathopoulos, August 22, 2001.

47   Ibid.

48   Ibid.

49   Deposition of Francis P. Salemme, *Limone vs. United States*, March 20, 2001.

50   Barboza (with Messick), *Barboza*, 112.

51   Ibid., 113.

52   Ibid., 114.

53   Ibid., 116.

54   Ibid., 117.

55   Ibid., 119.

56   Congressional Reports, "Everything Secret Degenerates," vols. 1, 2.

57   Ibid.

58   Ibid.

59   Teresa, *My Life in the Mafia*, 117.

60   Barboza (with Messick), *Barboza*, 126.

61   Ibid., 127.

62   Ibid., 128.

63   Congressional Reports, "Everything Secret Degenerates," vols. 1, 2.

64   Barboza (with Messick), *Barboza*, 130.

65   "2 Slain in Revere Bar," by Jeremiah Murphy, *Boston Globe*, November 16, 1965.

66 Ibid., 133.

67 "Was Just a Question of Time for the Hughes Brothers," by Richard Connolly, *Boston Globe*, September 24, 1966.

68 Barboza (with Messick), *Barboza*, 137.

69 Ibid., 136.

70 *State v. Patriarca*, 308 a.d 300 (1973), Supreme Court of Rhode Island, July 20, 1973.

71 Barboza (with Messick), *Barboza*, 145.

72 "It Was Just a Question of Time for the Hughes Brothers," by Richard J. Connolly, *Boston Globe*, September 24, 1966.

73 Barboza (with Messick), *Barboza*, 145.

74 Ibid., 155.

75 Ibid.

76 Ibid., 156.

77 Ibid., 158.

78 Ibid.

79 Ibid., 160.

80 Ibid., 162.

81 Ibid., 165.

82 Federal Bureau of Investigation Memo 166–629, March 8, 1967, pg. 1, submitted by SA's Dennis M. Condon and H. Paul Rico.

83 Ibid., 2.

84 Ibid., 3.

85 Barboza (with Messick), *Barboza*, 166.

86 Federal Bureau of Investigation Memo 166–629, March 21, 1967, 5.

87 Federal Bureau of Investigation Memo 166–629, March 8, 1967, 5.

88 Barboza (with Messick), *Barboza*, 167.

89 Federal Bureau of Investigation Memo 166–629, April 13, 1967, 18.

90 Federal Bureau of Investigation Memo 166–629, March 21, 1967, 12.

91 Federal Bureau of Investigation Memo 166–629, April 18, 1967, 17.

92 Congressional Reports, "Everything Secret Degenerates," vols. 1, 2.

93 Federal Bureau of Investigation Memo 166–629, April 13, 1967, 17.

94 Ibid.

95 Federal Bureau of Investigation Memo 166–629, March 8, 1967, 18.

96 Federal Bureau of Investigation Memo 166–629, April 13, 1967, 18.

97 Ibid., 19.

98 Ibid.

99 "The Patriarca Tapes: Crime Boss Dispenses Advice & Consent on All Family Matters," by Robert Kramer, *Providence Journal Bulletin*, November 17, 1985.

100 Partington (with Violet), *The Mob and Me*, 11.

101 Barboza (with Messick), *Barboza*, 172.

102   "A Letter from Barboza: Why I Decided to Tell All," by James Southwood, *Boston Herald*, July 9, 1967.

103   Teresa, *My Life in the Mafia*, 247.

104   Federal Bureau of Investigation Memo 166–629, May 22, 1967, 49.

105   Federal Bureau of Investigation Memo 166–629, May 1, 1967, 29.

106   Federal Bureau of Investigation Memo 166–629, June 8, 1967, 1.

107   Partington (with Violet), *The Mob and Me*, 20.

108   Federal Bureau of Investigation Memo 166–629, May 5, 1967, 32.

109   Congressional Reports, "Everything Secret Degenerates," vols. 1, 2.

110   Ibid.

111   Federal Bureau of Investigation Memo 166–629, June 21, 1967, 13.

112   Federal Bureau of Investigation Memo 166–629, July 31, 1967, 2.

113   Congressional Reports, "Everything Secret Degenerates," vols. 1, 2.

114   Ibid.

115   Ibid.

116   Joseph Salvati testimony in Deegan Trial transcript, 20.

117   Partington (with Violet), *The Mob and Me*, 21.

118   Ibid., 22.

119   Ibid., 23.

120   Ibid., 25.

121   Ibid., 29.

122   Ibid., 30.

123   Congressional Reports, "Everything Secret Degenerates," vols. 1, 2.

124   Ibid.

125   Ibid.

126   Ibid.

127   Barboza (with Messick), *Barboza*, 178.

128   Author interview with Donald Barboza, June 12, 2012.

129   Ibid.

130   Partington (with Violet), *The Mob and Me*, 40.

131   "Baron Faces Accused, Talks," by Robert J. Anglin, *Boston Globe*, January 11, 1968.

132   Ibid.

133   "Barboza Testifies on Double Cross," by Robert J. Anglin, *Boston Globe*, January 12, 1968.

134   Ibid.

135   "Defense Hints Baron Shot DiSeglio; Now up to Jury," by Robert J. Anglin, *Boston Globe*, January 18, 1968.

136   Ibid.

137   Ibid.

138   Partington (with Violet), *The Mob and Me*, 35.

139 Ibid., 39.

140 Ibid.

141 "Car Ignition Wired: Barboza's Lawyer Loses Leg in Everett Dynamite Blast," by Robert J. Anglin, *Boston Globe*, January 31, 1968.

142 Ibid.

143 Ibid.

144 Partington (with Violet), *The Mob and Me*, 47.

145 Barboza (with Messick), *Barboza*, 181.

146 "US Blames Murder on Patriarca," by Robert J. Anglin, *Boston Globe*, March 5, 1968.

147 "Baron Tells of Patriarca Kill Order," by Robert J. Anglin, *Boston Globe*, March 6, 1968.

148 "Patriarca Case to the Jury Today," by Robert J. Anglin, *Boston Globe*, March 8, 1968.

149 Ibid.

150 Ibid.

151 Partington (with Violet), *The Mob and Me*, 51.

152 Ibid.

153 "Patriarca Gets 5 Years in Plot," *Boston Globe*, March 26, 1968.

154 Congressional Reports, "Everything Secret Degenerates," vols. 1, 2.

155 Ibid.

156 Author interview with Donald Barboza, June 12, 2012.

157 Partington (with Violet), *The Mob and Me*, 5.

158 Federal Bureau of Investigation transcript of Anthony Stathopoulos interview on August 23, 2001.

159 Ibid.

160 "Baron Tells Why Deegan Died," by Robert J. Anglin, *Boston Globe*, July 2, 1968.

161 "Baron Describes Arsenal Used to Rub Out Deegan," by Robert J. Anglin, July 3, 1968.

162 "Defense Hints Personal Motive in Deegan Killing," by Robert J. Anglin, July 4, 1968.

163 Partington (with Violet), *The Mob and Me*, 59.

164 Ibid., 60.

165 Congressional Reports, "Everything Secret Degenerates," vols. 1, 2.

166 Ibid.

167 Joseph Salvati testimony in Deegan Murder Trial, July 1968.

168 Ibid.

169 Congressional Reports, "Everything Secret Degenerates," vols. 1, 2.

170 "Defendant Testifies in Deegan Trial," by Jeremiah Murphy, *Boston Globe*, July 23, 1968.

171 "Deegan Trial Lawyers Call Baron 'Liar,'" by David Taylor, *Boston Globe*, July 30, 1968.

172 Ibid.

173 "Jury Gets Deegan Case, Resumes Deliberations Today," by David Taylor, *Boston Globe*, July 31, 1968.

174 Ibid.

175 "Deegan Trial: Four Get Chair, Two Get Life, Judge Hails Jury," *Boston Globe*, August 1, 1968.

176 FBI Memo 94-536-3267, July 31, 1968, from Boston Special Agent in Charge to Director J. Edgar Hoover.

177 Partington (with Violet), *The Mob and Me*, 64.

178 Ibid., 65.

179 Ibid., 67.

180 Deposition of Francis P. Salemme, March 20, 2003. *Peter J. Limone vs. United States of America.*

181 Ibid.

182 Congressional Reports, "Everything Secret Degenerates," vols. 1, 2.

183 "Judge Sets Bail at $100,000," Associated Press, September 24, 1970.

184 Congressional Reports, "Everything Secret Degenerates," vols. 1, 2.

185 Ibid.

186 "Confessions with a Stool Pigeon," by Anson Smith, *Boston Globe*, May 12, 1974.

187 Ibid.

188 Congressional Reports, "Everything Secret Degenerates," vols. 1, 2.

189 Ibid.

190 Ibid.

191 Ibid.

192 Ibid.

193 Ibid.

194 Ibid.

195 Ibid.

196 "Legislators Hear Sinatra in High Fie," by Gerald Strine, *Washington Post*, July 19, 1972.

197 Ibid.

198 Ibid.

199 "Patriarca Denies Link to Sinatra, Track," by Charles E. Claffey, *Boston Globe*, July 20, 1972.

200 Ibid.

201 Congressional Reports, "Everything Secret Degenerates," vols. 1, 2.

202 Ibid.

203 Ibid.

204 Ibid.

205 Ibid.

206 "Jury Told of Plan to Kill for Angiulo," by William F. Doherty and Richard Connolly, *Boston Globe*, October 31, 1985.

207 "Barboza Death Tied to Dispute on West Coast," by Robert J. Anglin, *Boston Globe*, February 13, 1976.

208 Author Interview with Donald Barboza, June 12, 2012.

209 "Boasting of a Murder: Angiulo Jury Hears Description of Baron Killing," by William F. Doherty, *Boston Globe*, August 29, 1985.

210 "FBI Tapes Reportedly Contain Discussion of Baron Murder," *Boston Globe*, July 9, 1985.

211 "Angiulo Attorney Raps US on Baron," by William F. Doherty, *Boston Globe*, July 16, 1985.

212 "Mobsters Get Tough Sentences, Soft Words," by Matthew Brelis, *Boston Globe*, April 30, 1992.

213 "The Murder Case That Never Ends, The Crime That Keeps on Giving," by David Boeri, WBUR Radio, July 30, 2010.

214 Hearing before the Comm. On Govt. Reform, 107th Congress, May 3, 2001.

215 Ibid., May 4, 2001.

216 "At 78 Rico Dies under Guard," by J. M. Lawrence, *Boston Herald*, January 18, 2004.

217 "Appeals Court OKs Wrongful Convictions," by Rodrique Ngowi, Associated Press, August 27, 2009.